VOICES 4 LIBYA

Anthology of 17 February Revolution Stories

Voices4Libya

Copyright © 2012 by Voices4Libya Project

Cover by: Abubaker Almasdour, Osama "Weeshi" Al Shaikhy and Ilya Gorodisher

ISBN-978-0945385-83-7

Book Website
www.Voices4Libya.com
Email: editors@Voices4Libya.com

Give feedback on the book at:
feedback@Voices4Libya.com

Printed in U.S.A

Contents

Supplementary Materials

All of the photographs in *Voices4Libya* can be viewed in full color on our website:

http://voices4libya.com

INTRODUCTION

This is a book about the Libyan Revolution of 17 February 2011. It is not a day-by-day account of the fighting, nor an analysis of military or diplomatic strategy. It is a collection of voices of ordinary people who became involved in that conflict in many different ways. These are the stories they chose to tell about how the Libyan conflict touched all their lives.

Gaddafi had a collection of gilded guns.

Gaddafi had huge stockpiles of Soviet armor and the elite British-trained Khamis Brigade.

The other side were civilians with no military training and no weapons. But what they did possess was such ingenuity, passion and fearlessness that it captured the admiration and support of the entire world.

From the top of their impregnable barracks, Gaddafi's ruthless murderers used anti-aircraft weapons to gun down unarmed kids. On the other side, it was an ordinary man, a supplies manager named Mahdi Zew, who spent three days burying kids' bodies, then could stand it no longer. He brought down the wall of this fortress by driving a car packed with a couple of cylinders of cooking gas into a thunder-storm of Gaddafi machine-gun fire. He lost his life and his two daughters lost a father, but the Revolution was saved.

The "Freedom Fighters" the Libyan Revolutionaries, were a collection of civilians, clerks, lawyers, engineers, pharmacists, students and salespeople who learned to weld captured rocket launchers guns to wheelbarrows and beds of their Toyota pickups. Clad in flip-flops and t-shirts, they crafted weapons out of sewage pipes and, lacking an air force, hoisted artillery to rooftops with cranes. The fight for justice which they undertook is a history of endless sacrifice, constant improvisation and incredible bravery.

A pen is mightier than a sword, or so the oft-repeated quotation goes.

As well as his Libyan forces and an army of thousands of mercenary fighters, Gaddafi had a state-run propaganda machine with 42 years of experience and massive financial resources.

But the Freedom Fighter side had Mo Nabbous, a mathematician and founder of Libya Al Hurra TV in Benghazi to bring the world's attention to the dire plight of Libya. The Freedom Fighter side had Bernard-Henri Lévy who persuaded French President Sarkozy to act, and this brought the United Nations and NATO into co-operation with those seeking to protect the innocent.

And they had a small army of supporters posting on Facebook, on Twitter and on Internet blogs. These "Freedom Writers" did everything they could to publicize the plight of the Libyan Revolutionaries, helping with their pens (or keyboards) those unlikely freedom fighters who had followed Mahdi Zew in taking up the sword against Gaddafi.

The stories told here are penned by those who never wielded anything more menacing than a fork or struck anything more intimidating than a computer key. These are the voices of those who could no longer remain silent and passive in the face of totalitarian injustice. Some are told by Freedom Fighters. Some are told by those who loved them, fed them, cared for them and wrote about them, making sure their flame burnt brightly enough to be seen all across the world. Intertwined with the stories of Libyan people are those of strangers from all over the globe. They came together to care and write about people they had never met and a country most had never visited.

The Libyan struggle for freedom resonated throughout the world. And the place we felt that resonance first and foremost was, of all places, on the internet live blog pages of Al Jazeera English! AJE is the lens through which we've all come to see and appreciate the depths of pain and the heights of triumph of these incredibly brave people in Libya.

How is it of all the media outlets, that Al Jazeera English became such a focus for foreign supporters of the Libyan Freedom Fighters.

It is because AJE reported from the very start of the Libyan Revolution, and, when the attention of other news gatherers drifted away, remained so faithful in its continued coverage of the Arab Spring that millions around the world supplemented their news diet with Al Jazeera English. That's really where this story begins for all of us in this book: AJE and its interactive Libyan blogs.

AJE: vini, vidi, scripsi

The AJE blogs have attracted the most amazing, educated, diverse and caring audience mass media ever gathered. After all, who would read Al Jazeera in English? The English speakers who cannot get their Middle Eastern news from other sources are a pretty sophisticated bunch of primarily American, Canadian, British, Australian and New Zealander readers. There are even more refined groups from among the non-English native speakers: French, Swiss, German, Spanish, Portuguese, Dutch, and yes, Arabic. The list goes on to South America, Africa – pretty much everywhere else. The only continent not yet represented is Antarctica. But that's only a matter of time.

At its peak, the AJE Libya blog was getting over 10,000 comments per day. If you follow Groundswell statistics, that easily represents hundreds of thousands of readers. That is a remarkable accomplishment for Al Jazeera, and one that has gone largely untrumpeted.

Radwan Ziadeh, a member of Syrian National Council, said the best source for accurate news on any Arab Spring revolution is Al Jezeera English and their live blogs. He remarked that this world wide connection and support for democracy is the greatest improvement in human rights the world has ever seen, and it is unstoppable. This connection has and will pull down any dictatorship that opposes it. Ziadeh pleaded with the audience to join it and to do for Syria what was done for Libya.

The Al Jazeera blogs, having established themselves as a forum for the dissemination of unbiased up-to-the-minute information about Libya, inevitably attracted Gaddafi's propaganda machine. The vehemently anti-Muslim, the defiantly anti-NATO, the reflexively anti-West, it seemed at times as though they wore the Wizard of Oz's green tinted spectacles as they sought to shout down the Freedom Fighters' side of the argument and to dominate the information agenda in favour of Colonel Gaddafi's regime. These entertaining folks still believe that the liberation of Tripoli was staged and filmed in Qatar and that Gaddafi forces captured Misurata in late August. For them Gaddafi never died, and the truth never lived.

But first and foremost, it is here, on the pages of the AJE that the caring world community gathered for over half a year to share the news, repost and make sense of often contradictory tweets, to discuss the future of Libya, to try to figure out various ways to help. It is some of these people that gathered and organized on the improbable koussa.info site who bring you this book. Why koussa.info? Well, that too is in the book. Read on!

As you read the stories in our book, you will see that many of the Libyan contributors live in Benghazi. Benghazi was the first area of Libya able to liberate itself from the yoke of Gaddafi's stifling of news and control of most means of communication. Thus, Benghazi residents were able to participate on AJE blogs and the koussa.info site earlier than most Libyans so they were the people who became best known to those of us living in other parts of the world.

When contributing to this book, many Libyan writers shared their photos and videos so that we were able to understand more than can be shared through words alone. Many of the photos are included in the book, but more photos and some videos are available at www.voices4libya.com where we will update readers with any further information or stories that become available to us.

We thank everyone who has been involved in sharing, editing and collating these first-hand accounts of an important, sacrificial but wonderful period in the fight for freedom in the world. We hope all readers feel as we do: that the stories told bring many insights and understandings to our knowledge of all that happened in Libya in 2011. Again, read on!

The "I' LEVE LEBYA" sign at the entry to the Hawari Village in Benghazi embodies the spirit of our project. This book was conceived and created by volunteers online. The volunteers who translated and edited the stories and produced the book layout are professionals in other walks of life. The cover graphic art was another online collaboration between Libyan, American and UAE artists. None of us are pros; the book is a group effort by virtual friends, stretching both their time and skill to the limit to help Libyan kids. No doubt, despite our best efforts, errors persist in this volume. Should you find them, please remember: "WE LEVE LEBYA".

> *"Think not of those who are slain in Allah's way as dead.*
> *Indeed they are living in the presence of their Lord and are provided for."*
> *The Holy Qur'an*

Mahdi Mohamed Zew
born in 1962 and martyred on February 20, 2011

The daughter of martyr Mahdi Zew born in 1993, Benghazi, Libya

My father was born in 1962 in Benghazi. He lived with his parents, brothers and sisters in the family house. They were a middle class family. He had three brothers, named Nasser, Salem and Abubaker, and four sisters, named Oureida, Suad, Zafeer and Hamida.

When he finished secondary school, he started work with the Arabian Gulf Oil Company, as a member of the supply department. In 1990 he married my mother, Samira Awad Nabous, and two daughters were born to them. I, Zuhur, was born in 1993 and my sister, Sajeeda, was born in 1996.

My father was a simple person who was honest, straight, and religious. He liked his work and was dedicated to it. He was very gentle towards his family. He liked his friends and his way of talking was quiet and polite. He was good at heart. He was known as a social person and he was loved by relatives and neighbors. He never had an enemy. He did not care about politics and he was not a religious extremist. He liked life and had great hope for a good life. He loved to travel and to read historical books about

Libya and poetry, and he liked to draw.

He did not like Gaddafi's despotic regime as he could see from working in the oil company that the oil revenue from the oil fields was going to Muammar and his thugs. He was very affected by the revolutions in Tunisia and Egypt. He was excited by them and followed the events from minute to minute. A few weeks before the Revolution of 17 February, he travelled with my mother to Lebanon and Syria for medical treatment for diabetes. They came back to Libya on Wednesday evening, 16 February.

On 17 February he joined protesters in front of the Court House and was very excited by this revolution, too. I saw the happiness in his eyes. He said, "I have never expected to see that our people could make a revolution". He did not come back to our home except for lunch or he came very late at night, and then only to sleep. He used to phone us, telling us what was happening and how brave and determined the young men were. He prayed for the martyrs and went to the funerals.

As our house is next to the military camp (katiba) we could see what was happening outside. My father was such a sensitive person that he could not stand to see somebody crying in front of him. So, when he saw so many young men dying, he was very affected because he was a patriot who was dedicated to his beloved country, Libya. He made a final decision because of his love towards his country.

On the night of 19 February, he took us to my grandfather's house because of the fierce shooting. On Sunday morning, 20 February, he came to us, drank coffee and talked about what had happened the night before. When he left, I had no idea what was in his mind. On the same day, at 2pm, we heard an explosion and saw black smoke far away, but it never crossed my mind that this explosion was made by my father.

He entered the katiba from which snipers were killing and wounding the young men. He put two cylinders of cooking gas and bottles filled with petrol in his car and lay down in the driver's seat so as not to be killed by snipers. He entered at high speed through the first door of the katiba, they shot at him with anti-aircraft guns and the car exploded in front of the second door.

Nobody knew what he was going to do. That night we did not know that my father was martyred. We were looking for him everywhere, asking his friends and relatives about him. We did not find him at any place. We called him by mobile and his phone was off. On the second day, early in the morning, we went back to our house hoping to find him there. But we did not find him in the house. My uncle came and we went with him to my grandfather's house and then we knew that my father was martyred. My mother, me and my sister were shocked because he was very gentle and loved us very much. He could never leave us. He was always by our side, even supporting us in our study. At the beginning of the Revolution we had never imagined what our father could do because he was a very sensitive person who was gentle and caring with people.

Gradually we became aware of the value of his deed. He did not open only the door of the katiba, he also opened the hearts of Libyan people because they realized that the man left behind two daughters when he rushed his car to open the katiba's door. Now, we know that he woke up the patriotic feelings of all Libyans and entered into history through the widest door with this brave act. We know that he is a hero and a real man because he did not want to watch young men dying and yet do nothing to stop it.

I am proud of his act but at the same time he left a big emptiness in our lives. I had never imagined that my father had valued anything more than he valued us, but he valued his motherland.

My father was to me friend, brother and mate. He went away and we stayed without him, but I see him in Libyan faces every day.

The departure of my father makes me cry but the present he gave to me removes the sadness from my heart. He gave to us two very big things. He taught us moral responsibility and love for our motherland.

God inspire me to pass over the separation from my father.

Libya in a Grandmother's Garden

Simbad, France

In a small French village, there is a much-neglected garden. Where roses used to delight passers-by with their hues of pink, red and yellow, there is now a withered mess. The path is overgrown with weeds and the frogs have long left the dried-out pond. The elderly couple living on the premises had had health problems, and the rumour of them being unwell soon spread around the village.

One day, a neighbour dropped in to say that they were sorry about this renewed bout of illness.

"Sick!" I exclaimed. "I am feeling fine, why?!"

Then my eyes followed my neighbour's glance to the tall weeds on the terrace. Ah, yes, the garden. This would need some explaining….

….how it came to be that I, a respectable granny, was staying glued to my laptop into the early morning hours, watching the dramatic events in Libya unfold. After her visit, I took some time off Libya to tend to my garden. Too late in the year as we were well into autumn, but at least the frogs came back.

Sitting near the pond one evening I asked them:

"Why does one do things?" They did not deign to answer.

"To keep oneself busy," said my husband who had overheard my question.

Agreed, but what makes us do this rather than that? Why support Libya of all places, a country I had never been to?

My love story with the North African peoples had begun in a small Tunisian town whose name I cannot remember, when a twelve year old Amazigh girl had taken me by my hand to lead me, a perfect stranger, to her family home. I will never forget her nor the face of her old mother, the most beautiful woman I have ever seen. Out of a sun tanned and wrinkled face covered by an artwork of filigree tattoos, her luminous, green eyes were looking at us with all the kindness of the world.

When over four decades later their children and grandchildren rose up against Ben Ali's regime, my gladness for them was immense.

After Tunisia it was Egypt's turn and then Libya's – where my joy soon turned into dismay. Al Jazeera English channel followed the bloody events closely, and it was on its blogs that I learnt with growing horror of all the years of deceit, torture and murder the Gaddafi regime had kept hidden from the world.

A newcomer to blogging, I was immediately overwhelmed by the swell of voices surging in from around the world, asking for justice for the Libyan people. Libyan women and men told of their years of suffering, their anguish, their grief, their hope that someday their nightmare would end. And they told of their pride in the freedom fighters and their despair at the senseless bloodshed.

Other voices denounced Gaddafi's lies spread by his intelligence network, the same network he used to spy on his people. To my utter amazement, I found that these lies were believed by many unwitting, western journalists. While the Freedom Fighters were steadily advancing over many hundreds of kilometres to liberate village after village, most media kept repeating the "stalemate" and "weak rebels" of the

Gaddafi propaganda up to the very fall of Tripoli.

The bulk of voices, though, spoke of love. Each post was a gesture of love. There were hundreds, perhaps more, like this Texan truck driver. No matter how hard his day had been, he would not put his tired body to rest without sending a thought across the wide Atlantic to Libya, to that country so far away from his own home.

There has been much talk about the role of social media in the Arab Spring. Although it would be nice to think that I was able to contribute a tiny bit to getting rid of the Libyan dictator, I doubt my usefulness. "Actions speak louder than words," goes the saying, and my only perceptible activity had been my bottom growing fatter from all these hours sitting on a chair while the Libyans were facing death and destruction. Yet, there had been voices asking us not to give up:

"Tell the world what is happening," they had begged, "do not leave us alone."

Did my words make a difference for the Libyan people after all? I do not know. The only thing I know for certain is that I will be tending my garden next year while the now-free Libyans will be grappling with the gigantic task of building their country from scratch. My thoughts will often travel to these deserts where golden and orange hues meet with the deep blues of the sea, and I will hope that their inhabitants will find the peace they had been longing for. In my own little world, the roses will be more beautiful than ever, because some of the love of those voices will have flown into them. One summer evening, my puzzled neighbours will be chatting on their bench in the shade:

"Now, that old lady up the road is definitely losing her mind. Yesterday she said something about voices inside roses."

"Did she? I had better take her an egg or two then, that might do her some good."

Nalut – Old Town

A man holding an Amazigh flag in one hand and a Libyan flag in the other during the celebration of the One-Year Anniversary of the 17 February Revolution, Benghazi, February 17, 2012

How I Became Moussa Koussa

Ilya aka Moussa Koussa, Minnesota, Unites States of America

> *Moussa - dresser very snazzy!*
> *To prepare for Benghazi!*
> *Moussa go atelier!*
> *To spruce up his derriere!*
>
> *Moussa jump at hand of tailor!*
> *Is hand more like horny sailor!*
> *Moussa pinched by nasty pinch*
> *Moussa buttock painful clinch!*
>
> *Very awkward situation!*
> *In the midst of alteration!*
> *No Moussa fancy suit!*
> *Because pervert man pursuit!*
>
> *Moussa got Benghazi blues!*
> *These are Mousa Koussa news!*

I wrote that. I posted it on AJE Libyan blog as Moussa Koussa in April, 2011.

> *Who the heck is Moussa Koussa?*
> *He sounds quite like a nuisance.*

Moussa Koussa was Gaddafi's Foreign Minister whose notorious defection hours before April Fools' Day made his the most tweeted name for the next 48 hours. If a man is implicated not only with the Lockerbie bombing but also with the deaths of tens of thousands of Libyans in the decades since the '60s, he is a scumbag of the highest order. MK is probably the most identified and hated name in the Libyan world outside of a Gaddafi.

> *So why would anyone chose that moniker?*
> *'Cause it's funnier than "2nd Harmonica"* who is also a member of our group.

But there's more to it than that. His name sounds downright Seussean. It begs to be rhymed and alliterated. Maybe his name trended so long on Twitter for the same reason. There are deeper reasons, sure. But first and foremost, the handle Moussa Koussa held comedic literary value. I chose to "become" MK as a joke, to ridicule the man.

> *And who are you?*
> *A Russian Jew!*

I'm a Russian Jew, one of a million my former motherland traded for sacks of wheat back in the '70s. I came to America as a 13-year old, went to high school, college and graduate school here. I'm a scientist and a bleeding heart liberal. You might think involvement in social justice causes like supporting a struggle for human rights in Libya a natural fit. But if you think about it, being liberal could've just as easily made me anti-war, period. So, how did a Russian Jew become so involved in Libya? Well, that's what this story is about.

> *OK, but what's this blog on Al Jazeera?*
> *Read! And answer will be clear!*

That's the easy part. Where does one get his news fix? American mass media blonds down its news. Fox started it, and CNN all too eagerly grabbed the baton. BBC coverage of the Arab Spring was great, up until the natural tragedy in Japan went nuclear. Then, the only place I could get my news fix became Al Jazeera.

So, since late February I've been reading AJE and, being a Russian Jew, I very hesitantly at first posted innocuous comments there under an innocent penname. That changed when the notorious scumbag Moussa Koussa defected. On the threshold of April Fools' Day at that! As soon as I grabbed that moniker and started posting my Seussean "News O'Moussa Koussa", for reasons still unclear AJE dramatically curtailed its coverage of Libya. Live interactive blogs stopped being updated on a daily basis, the news became sparse, my virtual friends started feeling uneasy.

In mid-April I launched our koussa.info site almost on a whim. Late one night, one my friends from across the globe jokingly pitched the idea of reserving an MK site. Again, for the shear humor value, I did a quick search to find out that all the good moussa's were taken, all the good moussakoussa's were gone, but inexplicably koussa.info was still up for grabs. For under two bucks a year! That was a no-brainer.

> *Reader know what she in for*
> *When she visit koussa.info*

With an initial half a dozen virtual friends we set up an authentication procedure and began dropping hints for AJE posters we liked to join. We turned away as many as we authenticated, and in a matter of 4 months, we had grown to 100 "certified" members and nearly 100,000 visits.

> *So, how and why did a Russian Jew get so involved?*
> *Russian Jews tend to get involved in the most unexpected undertakings.*

In short, I got involved to keep the friends I made on AJE, but more importantly, because others wanted to as well. The long answer is complicated, and involves spending my formative years as refugee, which resonates within my heart with the similar, yet more difficult, universal struggle of the Libyan people.

35 years ago my family was traded for a sack of wheat.

We may never find out how big a sack, but the exchange rate doesn't really matter. Back then, how much grain per Jew the Soviets got fluctuated with the annual magnitude of the collective farming fiasco.

Fast forward three dozen years. Hop over the Iron Curtain and into the Sahara. Look at Tunisia, Libya, Egypt. Hug the Mediterranean Coast NE, and take a right into Syria.

Look around. Until this year, human life still had no value at your local dictatorship. This is why I feel so connected with the Arab Spring.

Their struggle for basic dignity and universal freedoms resonates in me. It simmers in all our hearts. When that simmer comes to boil, look out dictators! In the end, our shared passions and fears connect us simply and personally in this increasingly sophisticated and impersonal world.

An Englishwoman: A Witness
To Half a Century of Libyan History

Annalisbeth, Benghazi, Libya

I first arrived in Libya with my family as a 12-year-old child in 1962. We lived in a small village (literally two main streets) called Khoms which is east of Tripoli, near the Roman ruins of Leptis Magna.

Libya was very cosmopolitan then with a lot of Americans, British and Italians living here. Life was easy-going and simple for everybody, including the Libyans. These were the days of King Idris when the oil industry was in its infancy.

We moved to Tobruk, which is close to the Egyptian border. Again, life was simple – we even used to see the camel trains taking people to perform the Hajj, which is certainly something you wouldn't see today. After nine months we moved to Benghazi which was quite a few steps up from sandy, sleepy Tobruk. There were nightclubs, bars, beach clubs – even bingo! These weren't exclusively for foreigners – plenty of Libyans frequented them too.

I met my husband, who is Libyan, in 1965 and we got married on September 28, 1967 (the British Army did the catering). We had the marriage blessed in a church, and then we were married in the Moslem way.

On September 1, 1969 (by this time I had one child and was pregnant with my second), I woke up – my husband left to go to work, but came straight back and told me that there had been a revolution.

There were tanks and soldiers with guns everywhere, but it was a bloodless, peaceful revolution unlike what was to happen 41 years later. The people welcomed this revolution, and people don't seem to realise that this was not Gaddafi's revolution; it was a joint revolution made up of five people leading it. At first, people were overjoyed, and this optimism lasted for about five years. But then things began to slowly and distinctly change. This seemed to coincide with the petrol going out and the money coming in.

Up until 1978 there was still freedom to trade and open businesses and everything was available. Even meat was only 25p per kilo. However, an undercurrent of fear began about this time because there had been two attempted coups and the perpetrators were publicly hanged. Also people began to disappear if anyone spoke out against Gaddafi or his regime, so freedom of speech was starting to disappear. About this time he began to nationalise private businesses which people had built up, banks and joint foreign companies.

At the end of 1978 "ayna lacka hatha" began which means "where did you get it from" and Gaddafi started to investigate everyone to see where they got their money from. He made rich men poor overnight. He took people's land and buildings on the premise that you only need one place to live. They were compensated or not, depending who you knew or didn't know. And people were still disappearing.

In the 1980s food became very scarce because everything had been nationalised and Gaddafi had closed all the private shops. He opened cooperatives, which were controlled by his government, but there was always a lack of food, so people spent their time queuing for anything – if you saw a queue you joined it and hoped for the best. This took people's minds off the problems in their lives (lack of food and money) and in the country.

Then Gaddafi started causing problems outside of the country, and was blamed for the German night-club bombing, so, in retaliation, the Americans bombed us. What fun! From then on things in Libya deteriorated badly (as if they weren't bad enough) and even more people disappeared. People couldn't trust each other and were looking over their shoulders all the time.

In 1989, the Lockerbie bombing occurred, so sanctions were imposed on the Libyan people, and life became even harder. However, in the 1990s, shops slowly opened, but prices were astronomical and people didn't have the money to pay these prices because salaries hadn't increased since the 1970s. The only people who gained anything were the Peoples Committees who Gaddafi bought with corruption. And people were very afraid of them – they spied on people everywhere, even outside the country. People had to watch what they said, they didn't know who to trust, telephone conversations were listened in on – freedom had certainly gone right out the window.

People had, unsurprisingly, changed a lot by now; they were bitter and disillusioned and unable to fight a ruthless regime. Some people tried and most of them were never seen again. Children were brainwashed at school – history and geography no longer existed, only Gaddafi's interpretation of them. From year four upwards a new subject was introduced – Gaddafi's Green Book – which the children had to learn, and if they did not pass this subject they would have to repeat the year.

Things began to improve when Gaddafi wanted to get back on the world stage. Everyone knows how that happened, but, importantly for us, sanctions were lifted. Things were still expensive, but nothing like under the sanctions, but still people's salaries stayed the same as they were in the 1970s (that is if they had a job and a salary).

In all this time no one had seen 1p of the petrol money. Hopefully, now, Libyans will benefit from this (me too)! Although things got better with shops opening, Internet access and mobile phones etc., a lot of people still lived in poverty and fear. We knew the Gaddafi family lived a luxurious lifestyle, but we didn't know how luxurious until this revolution. You can imagine how angry people are. The average wage for a Libyan was 250 dinars per month and meat was 14 dinars per kilo – work out how you feed a family on that.

So, on February 17, 2011 the people of Benghazi had had enough! After the fall of Ben Ali and Mubarak, people decided that they too would have a voice at last for freedom and for Gaddafi to leave. I think the world knows his reaction to this.

Personally, it was terrifying when fighter planes began bombing Benghazi. When we heard that his plans were to send a convoy to virtually wipe out Benghazi (which I have no doubt he would have done if he hadn't been stopped) we decided to make a hasty retreat to Tobruk.

I will never forget that journey east towards the Egyptian border. A journey that would normally take five hours took eight because people from various towns and villages along the way were stopping us to offer us shelter, money and food – anything they had. It showed in those early days how united the Libyan people were in their bid for freedom from a tyrant. We stayed in Tobruk for eight days and then returned to Benghazi to be close to my friends and my husband's family. We felt safer now because we knew NATO was in the skies protecting civilians and we were being protected by our own brave "rag tag" army who were also fighting to keep us safe.

This was eight months ago and the rest is history. God willing we will live in a free democratic Libya. We know there will be hard, difficult times ahead, but we know it can't be worse than before.

I've been married for forty-four years, and I've seen two revolutions in this country; one "Gaddafi in" and one "Gaddafi out", and what led from one to the other. I have many more stories, but I think I would have to write a book which I may one day.

"Think not of those who are slain in Allah's way as dead.
Indeed they are living in the presence of their Lord and are provided for."
The Holy Qur'an

Salem Ali Zayed Momen
born in 1940 and martyred on December 5, 2011

Salem Ali Zayed Momen
One of the eminent members of the Local Transitional Committee, City of Derna
Sheikh of Al-Barahma tribe, Derna

The beginning of the conflict with the Gaddafi regime for the family of Momen Zayed was not in 2011 but in 1976. This was the year that students in the Al-Fateh University of Tripoli, now known as The University of Tripoli, refused military training against the orders of the regime. My niece, Fathia Masoud Momen, a student in the Faculty of Engineering, rejected this military service along with 20 other female students and 200 male students. A military court was set up to try these students by the Al Azizia military officers and was attended by Muammar Gaddafi personally. Gaddafi personally accused these students of being traitors to the nation and threatened that they must be executed. He set the date of the 6th of April to announce the names of those students to be expelled and executed. Among those named was my niece.

Abdulsalam Jalloud arrived and declared that the Engineering College Square will be the venue for the trial and it will be flooded by blood of the traitors, the accused students.

All the University's students, especially those from the eastern regions of Libya, supported those accused students. My nephew, Fawzi Abdelhamid Zayed, who later became a professor of engineering at the University of Derna, and another niece, Najia Masoud Momen, a food engineer, were among these supporters.

On the day of the trial, there were conflicts and protests by students who were arrested and later expelled from the university. My niece, Fathia, a member of the group of students on trial, was suspended temporarily from the University, but luckily was not expelled. This was due to the enormous social and academic activities she had done in the University. Consequently, the faculty members stood against expelling Fathia. She was allowed to complete her final year of studies, where she graduated as the first in her class, but was not allowed to continue with graduate studies.

At a later time – but with the events of the 7th of April, 1976, when students were hung in universities and families were accused of extremism and of being reactionaries, still in the minds and hearts of our family – my brother, Yusuf Mohamed Zayed, was arrested and imprisoned in Abu Salim prison. He was executed in that same prison in 1996 at the age 30. Because of this history of events, the entire Momen family supported the 17th of February Revolution.

On the 15th of February, the liberation of Derna started during the day time and continued till the night when it and Al-Abraq airport were liberated.

I, Al Haj, Salem Ali Zayed Momen, personally joined freedom fighters in July on the eastern front line. I provided financial support and transportation for freedom fighters. This lasted through the Holy month of Ramadan. Then, I joined the liberation of Brega, the battle for the first, second, and third sectors. I participated in the battle for the liberation of Sirte.

I was involved in many battles, where I saw the young men, like lions, raise high the honor of their country, Libya, in many places. Among them from my family were Col. Shukri Masoud Zayed Momen; Atiya Abulhamed Zayed Momen; the martyr Al Motasim Saleh Zayed Momen who was martyred at the battle for the third sector of Brega; the martyr Mohamed Ramadan Mohamed Zayed Momen who was martyred in the battle for Zella in the desert; Waled Atiya Abdelhamid Zayed Momen; Mohamed Atiya Abdelhamid Zayed Momen; and Ramadan Mohamed Zayed Momen, the father of the martyr Mohamed Ramadan Mohamed Zayed Momen.

We had direct clashes with Gaddafi loyalists in the battle for Wadi Al Ahmar and destroyed a grad-rocket launcher truck with a Milan rocket.

The last battle I was involved in was the battle for Sirte. This was a great honor for me. On the 3rd of October, I led the fighters into the neighborhood behind the hotel near the seaport. I told them that we would suffer great losses and casualties during this battle, but they insisted on proceeding. We entered into the neighborhood, fought hard, like lions, and made Gaddafi's soldiers retreat. Then, we found that they had even left their uniforms by the side of the road and fled like rats. They changed into civilian clothes not to be recognized.

Then we attacked the snipers to prevent them killing other freedom fighters and to reduce casualties. We didn't give them time to relax and aim at freedom fighters precisely. But, that day the loss was great: 10 martyrs and 18 injured. I was one of those among the injured.

I was in command of a group of freedom fighters which planned to attack Gaddafi's soldiers from the back. I was wounded because there was a freedom fighter shooting a general purpose gun, and I wanted him to join us. I was calling him, but he couldn't hear because of the noise of shooting. So, I tried to go to him, but my right leg was hit, broken by a sniper. It was a proof that the sniper was shooting randomly. He had no time to aim at freedom fighters to kill them. If it had been the case, I'd be dead.

Also in this battle there were members of the Momen family, young men and women. Among them were: Abdulla Mahmoud AlMangosh, Omar Ramadan Yarej, Sohaib Shokri AlHesadi and many more.

Now, I am being sent for treatment abroad.

Al Haj Salem Ali in a Hospital in Jordan, October, 2011

Al Haj Salem Ali on the Front Line 2011

In this photograph of 71 year old Al Haj Salem Ali Zayed Momen, taken for this book during his time in Hawari Hospital, he holds one hand high to give the victory sign with pride and certainty. In his other hand, he holds the greetings of AJE bloggers prepared as a booklet by doctors at the hospital for distribution to wounded FF.

Postscript

Al Haj Salem Ali Zayed Momen was 71 years old when he was wounded in the battle for Sirte in October. He wrote his story while in Hawari hospital. After the completion of his subsequent treatment abroad, he returned to Derna, his home city.

On the 5th of December, after fasting on the 4th and 5th in preparation for the Day of Ashura, Al Haj Salem Ali Zayed Momen went out from his house at 5.30 a.m. to go to the mosque to pray. On his way to the mosque he was killed by a Kalashnikov fired from a lurking car by a person thought to be a pro-Gaddafi thug full of a desire for revenge either for the defeat of the Gaddafi regime or for earlier times when Al Haj Salem Ali Zayed Momen had been prominent amongst those in Derna who stood firmly against the force of the regime.

Those of us from all over the world who put this book together were shocked to hear that Al Haj Salem, who had survived so much, was killed in peace time. We had come to know him as a man loved, admired and respected by his family, by those who fought with him for Libya's freedom, and by those who met him by chance. Our prayers and condolences go to his family and to the people of Derna. We see even within his telling of his own story, the picture of a man who lived righteously and was loyal to ideals concerned with faith, family, community, freedom and justice.

Coming Home to Libya

Salwinder, United Kingdom

30 years ago my father fled Libya and went into exile at a time when Gaddafi was hanging opponents in the streets at home and had a policy of assassination abroad. During these past 30 years he lost his hope of returning home — close family members died and he couldn't attend their funerals, relatives and friends became increasingly difficult to contact and his very identity as a Libyan seemed to be eroding with the passage of time and the seeming indestructibility of the Gaddafi regime.

Then the Arab Spring happened. At first we dared not hope that it would reach Libya. Even with the fall of Mubarak in Egypt it seemed impossible. But then the brave souls of Libya rose up and with it started a chain of events that saw many martyrs but ultimately led to the liberation of our homeland. The past eight months have been soul-destroying, ecstatic, tragic and wonderful all at once — evoking feelings that are simply impossible to put into words.

And so the day came that we never dreamed would come to pass. Last Thursday my father returned to Libya — a journey he had lost all hope of ever making. Unbelievably when he reached the Ras Ajdir border post he called me:

"Gaddafi has been captured!"

I couldn't process this at first — my father was about to enter his homeland after 30 years and that very morning the brutal psychopathic dictator who exiled him had been caught! My father then crossed into Libya and in Sabratah joined a throng of jubilant Freedom Fighters and joined them on their journey into Tripoli.

The next day my father entered the coffee shop in Tripoli's Old City where he had worked as a boy — upon entering he was greeted by a group of Freedom Fighters sipping coffee, guns in hand. When they learnt of my father's long exile and return home, they threw rose water on him, and headed out into the street firing their guns into the air:

"This is why we did it! This is why we freed Libya — so that our brothers can return home!"

My apologies for not contributing more to the blog over the past week since Gaddafi's demise — it has all been so overwhelming and several times I have tried to convey what I have been feeling — but nothing I wrote seemed adequate! Maybe my account of the end of my father's exile might give some kind of sense of what this revolution means to so many in Libya — it is an emotional, spiritual and psychological revolution as much as a political one.

As for me — as the son of such a long-time exile I have never been able to visit Libya until now. I have never seen my extended family, never smelt the desert air, never visited the graves of my dead grandparents. I desperately wanted to — but Gaddafi's existence meant that I never dared dream it would ever be possible. I now plan to go before the end of the year and make up for the thirty years in Libya that Gaddafi robbed from me...

Thank you all for your contribution on this blog — I know it has made a real difference to Libyans around the world. I know it kept me sane at times when I thought all hope was lost. There are too many bloggers to name individually, but I do want to mention Gerhard Heinz in particular. Back in the dark days of March, April and May it was to a large extent Gerhard who kept hope alive for me and helped me to understand that Libya was on an inexorable path towards liberation even if the mainstream media could not see it. So thank you Gerhard and the rest of the regular contributors on here for keeping me sane and helping me get through the darkness into the light of a free Libya and my father's return home!

I Lost One of My Legs but Not My Hope

Date of Birth: 1988
Occupation: Administrative Affairs - asphalt plant - Benghazi
Name: Emad Saleh Alagouri
Qualification: Degree in Management

My story of the February 17 Revolution started when youths began to write on the Internet and chose the date of February 17 for peaceful demonstrations against the tyrant's regime. I wondered if the Libyan people would actually stand up against this tyrannical rule of 42 years.

What happened was that on February 15 internal security detained defense attorney Fathi Turbul who was representing the families of the men executed in Abu Salim prison. The families of the executed prisoners held a peaceful demonstration asking for Fathi Turbul to be freed. Because the place where he was detained was so close to my house, the demonstrators came into my neighborhood. They kept saying: "The people want to bring the regime down," and here my journey with the revolution began.

I went out that day and added my voice to the other demonstrators' asking for the regime to fall. From that night on I joined in all the protests. The protests lasted for two days and I took part from morning to evening. I was surprised on February 17, the official day of protest. We saw huge numbers of people in the streets protesting. I saw many more people than I expected to see. Forty people were killed that day and from that day on, we were resolved that Gaddafi and his soldiers and mercenaries must go and the bloodbath had to stop.

Because my house is close to the Security Headquarters, I was one of the people who tried to break into it. We were continuously trying to take over the place for two days. During this period, almost 70 martyrs fell and over 100 were injured including my brother who was shot in his right hand. With the protesters' resolve we were able to achieve victory here over the regime police officers.

Then the revolutionaries headed toward the Al Fadeel Katiba, where all the weapons which had been used against us were stored. I decided to become part of these protests. In addition to all the people who died during these days, which had reached 200, the garrison was broken into by the revolutionaries and the rest of Gaddafi's troops and mercenaries were expelled from the garrison. Finally, the city was fully liberated!

We then headed off to the airport and liberated it from the regime's troops. There was news that the regime was planning to send its forces, supported by mercenaries, to Benghazi, so we chose to take the weapons and got ready to defend ourselves, our city and our honor. A group of us went to the munitions storage in the Rajma area and took weapons which were located there.

The next day there came news that Gaddafi's battalion had gone into the oil production town of Brega, so I went with a group of revolutionaries from Benghazi and other eastern cities to Brega. We clashed with Gaddafi's battalion there and finally repulsed them from the area and pursued them to Ras Lanuf, where there had been clashes with the battalions at the army camp. The clashes lasted from the evening until about 1:00am, until we were able to get into the army camp where we found 12 people who had been bound with their hands behind their backs and executed by a bullet to the head.

The next day I headed out with the revolutionaries to the town of Bin Jawad where there was no resistance, so I chose to return to Ras Lanuf to spend the night because I had relatives there. On my way to the town of Bin Jawad the next day, I was surprised to see large numbers of the tyrant's brigades. We knew that the revolutionaries who had spent the night in Bin Jawad had died.

Clashes began with the brigades and lasted from morning until evening and the brigades were mostly victorious, because of their superior numbers, weapons and military training, which we did not have at the time. We went back to Ras Lanuf, then back to Brega and finally back to Ajdabiyeh. That was March 15.

Then we went back to Benghazi because the regime had sent military reinforcement to its brigades. The regime had provided them with all weaponry available at that time. On March 19, the tyrant's brigades reached Benghazi – the day that United Nations Resolution 1973 was ratified to protect civilians in Libya – finally action was taken but not until 100 people had been martyred and 1,000 injured. The brigades retreated to Ajdabiyeh and then to Ras Lanuf for reinforcements and then returned to attack Benghazi. In Brega the regime troops laid 25,000 anti-personal land mines.

After that I went to Misurata by fishing boat. The trip lasted for two days and it was very dangerous at sea. When I got to the port of Misurata, I found Misurata's revolutionaries waiting. I joined Al Habbous Brigade. At the time Misurata was not yet fully liberated from Gaddafi's battalions; there were daily clashes and every day we lost a number of martyrs. These clashes went on every day. We were in the active field of battle with the Gaddafi brigades. Grad rockets were everywhere and cluster bombs were falling in neighborhood streets.

With the revolutionaries resolve we were able to liberate Misurata, area by area, starting from Tripoli Street where the fiercest clashes occurred with snipers positioned on the tops of high buildings. We then liberated other locations throughout the city which was surrounded. Shelling the city was the only option Gaddafi's troops had. The seaport was the only place to get needed supplies into the city and reinforcement weapons for the revolutionaries. I was there from April 2 until the end of May.

I got back to Benghazi on June 3 where I joined a training course on de-mining areas of land mines. After Brega was liberated, we removed almost 25,000 land mines. Next, I joined the forces in Sirte because foot soldiers in Sirte needed technicians who could deal with land mines. I was with them until September 20. Then there was a fight with Gaddafi's brigades from dawn until evening of September 20. Gaddafi's forces had been defeated and we took control of the gate of "Al Khamseen" (the fifty). It was such an important strategic and emotional thing for the revolutionaries to gain control of this area.

The battle was over. While we were securing the area, some of the last vehicles of the retreating forces, armed with anti-craft 23 caliber weapon, continued firing and I was wounded by a bullet in my right leg. I had to be taken to the local hospital where I received first aid because I lost a lot of blood. As I needed more complex treatment, I was sent to Benghazi and then to Jordan. In the end, I lost my right leg.

On top of all of this, after the announcement of the death of the tyrant, I felt very satisfied about everything that I had done and everything that happened to me. I feel so happy to be one of the February 17 revolutionaries. It is true that I lost one of my legs, but I have not lost hope for the liberation of all the soil of Libya. I am hoping to hear the announcement of the new constitution of Libya and our democratic county where everyone has the right to express their opinion on concerns of their nation. Finally I am able to say that a tyrant can take away our lives, but not our freedom.

In Misurata, May, 2011

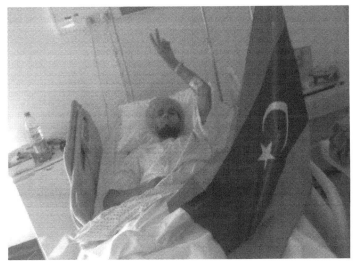

In Istishari hospital in Jordan, September 2011

Home in Benghazi, October 26, 2011

The Arts Blossomed

From the Editors

When Benghazi freed itself from the yoke of Gaddafi's oppression, its arts scene exploded. Music, painting, literature and new media blossomed in the freedom achieved in eastern Libya. The arts had been oppressed and subjugated for 40 years because unfettered creative expression had not been seen to be in the interests of the cult of the dictator's personality.

The arts were liberated and inspired by the 17 February Revolution and in return Libya's artists, musicians, writers and new media experts brought inspiration, life and courage to the movement. The power of their media to capture the imagination of ordinary people multiplied the effectiveness of their contribution to the course of the revolution.

In our collection we are very lucky, indeed, to have the stories of several luminaries of the Free Libya arts scene: Mohammed Nabbous; a poet who writes under the pseudonym "Pido"; Masood Bwisir; and Kais Alhilali. They are people widely known and revered in Libya and abroad.

Kais Alhilali was a young painter and sculptor of amazing talent. He paid with his life for his revolutionary art. His death shocked his followers; and its report by the news media inspired a poem by a far-away Australian. That poem is presented in our book following Kais' mother's story of his life, art and martyrdom. Kais' anti-Gaddafi street art can still be seen throughout Benghazi, and we are happy to offer a glimpse of his work in our collection of stories.

A picture of fantastic courage was captured in numerous photographs (AFP, Al Jazeera, etc.) of a man, with his Kalashnikov flung over a shoulder, drowning out a gun battle by bellowing songs and playing an acoustic guitar. Bullets whizz past him, but he keeps strumming the chords: "My country shall be free". Masood Bwisir – singer, songwriter and Freedom Fighter – has become known throughout Libya and the world as "Epic Guitar Hero". Thank you, Masood, for sharing your view of the revolution with us.

Our third artist penned poetry under the pseudonym "Pido" and set the words in the midst of photographs, thus giving incomparable reality to his insights and imagery. In this book, we present but two of his works, but additional poems can be found on our website at www.voices4libya.com where readers can also enjoy the vivid color photographs that accompany Pido's poetry.

Mohammed Nabbous became one of the best known heroes of the 17 February Revolution. It is largely thanks to his selfless efforts that the world became aware of the Libyan struggle for freedom. On 19 February, 2011, he founded Libya Alhurra TV, the first independent news broadcasting outlet established in Libya since Gaddafi grabbed power in 1969. Those of us who participated in AJE's Libya blogs often used Libya Alhurra TV as a source of information about events in Libya. Mo, as he became known to the world, was a creative genius of new media. We share his cousin's story of his life and martyrdom with readers.

"Think not of those who are slain in Allah's way as dead.
Indeed they are living in the presence of their Lord and are provided for."
The Holy Qur'an

Mohammad Mustafa Hassan Nabbous
born in 1983 and martyred on March 19, 2011
The First Global Voice of the Libyan Revolution
Citizen journalist

The story is told by the martyr's cousin, Hassan Ahmed Nabbous, Benghazi, Libya

Mohammad Nabbous a hero and a martyr was born on February 27, 1983 in the city of Benghazi. He had one brother who was sixteen years older than him and also four sisters.

Our martyr graduated from the University of Garyounis, Department of Mathematics and Computer Science. He was a very hardworking young man and wanted to study abroad but later on he decided to return to his country. He returned because he wanted to contribute to the progress of his country by establishing the first and only artificial ice skating centre in Libya for children. He kept upgrading his project by organizing a world class car race as well as stone walls for climbing. Before the revolution of February 17, he planned to launch yet another project which was supposed to be a shooting range and school which would help children build up their character and self-confidence.

After this project succeeded he decided to get married and start a family. The wedding took place in 2010 approximately one year before the blessed revolution. Shortly after his death, God had blessed him with a beautiful daughter and it was God's will that he didn't live long enough to see or hold her.

When the first spark ignited the revolution, he left everything and the main concern for him became being able to contribute and help the young people of Libya. He did that by sending the voices of Libyan youths, who were shouting for freedom, throughout the world. He quickly began gathering equipment required to establish video and audio communications (he used local satellites). The place where he established the equipment was close to the people who demanded and cried out for justice and the downfall of the tyrant.

Our martyr placed several cameras that broadcast live feed at Freedom Square (beside Benghazi's court) in addition to his nonstop correspondence with three foreign news agencies who spread the truth about the killing and massacres which were taking place in Benghazi, the birthplace of the February 17 revolution.

Mohammad's ambition was to deliver both audio and video proof of Gaddafi's crimes, and that was the reason he was targeted and killed by Gaddafi's security forces when they entered Benghazi, with the help of several local traitors and accomplices who were informing them of his location and movement.

He founded the first news channel in the cities that were controlled by the National Transitional Council on February 19. The channel began broadcasting via Internet live stream and was broadcasting 24 hours a day via nine cameras. After communications improved, our martyr Mohammad managed to use his camera and upgraded and widened his coverage of the revolution by filming and providing live coverage of everything important that was happening back then.

Our beloved martyr managed to send video and audio information to media from five continents of the world regularly and thus broke the barrier of fear that had imprisoned the Libyan people and helped them push even harder for their freedom. His unshakeable belief in the cause of this revolution rose from four decades of deprivation of rights and freedom, and the misery that the Libyan people had been put through by this tyrant. He had no personal gain or interest in this revolution; on the contrary, he thought that this was the right of all Libyans, because this tyrant did not have the right to inherit this land to build institutions and not maintain the vital infrastructure.

On March 19, 2011, our beloved martyr hero, Mohammad Nabbous was killed by one of Gaddafi's snipers, while he was trying to film and take pictures of the devastation and destruction brought upon the city of Benghazi by Gaddafi and his forces. At that time he was filming the aftermath of Gaddafi's bombing in the district of Dollar and when he heard that Gaddafi's forces had entered the outskirts of Benghazi he immediately contacted the American news channel CNN and told them that the people of Benghazi were very close to being completely annihilated. So he took his camera and, along with his friend, headed towards the Tripoli Bridge where Gaddafi's tanks and mortars were randomly firing on residential areas. In order to film as clearly as possible he had to stand on the back of a pickup truck. After a while his friend suddenly heard a bump which was Mohammad falling from the back of the truck. His friend emerged from the truck and found Mohammad lying on the ground with blood covering his face. It turned out that he had been shot in the eye and that the bullet came out through the back of his head. They tried to resuscitate Mohammad on the way to hospital, but unfortunately he died in the emergency room. Oh how he desired to see the fall of this tyrant and to share the joy of freedom with his fellow countrymen!

The murder of Mohammad Nabbous enraged many members of various press organizations as well as many people who were touched by his courage and fearless spirit. He will be sorely missed, especially by his wife and his little girl.

Some bloggers tried to propose him as a candidate for "CNN Heroes" because he was the image of the February 17 revolution and was the first person to welcome foreign journalists after the liberation of Benghazi by the freedom fighters as claimed by the British newspaper The Guardian. According to The Guardian he was the face of "citizen journalism" in Libya.

Our beloved martyr Mohammad Nabbous once said "I DO NOT FEAR DEATH, BUT I FEAR FOR THE SUCCESS OF THIS REVOLUTION."

A Buried Tank

Radwan, 22 years old, Ajaylat, Libya
A petroleum engineering student before the Revolution

Acting on information received, my unit is asked to check some houses in my home town of Ajaylat for weapons. Ajayat sits on the shore of Mediterranean, 80 km west of Tripoli, just between Az Zawiya and Zuwarah. We are nine men on a mission. To be specific it was a rotten mission that nearly turned into a nightmare.

The last house is deep in the very southern part of the town, practically in the desert. It takes us a while to get there. Much of the day is burnt. We surround the house: two guys go to the back with me; the other six secure the front. I hop the two-meter fence and wait in position as my comrades scale the wall and lock down the perimeter. My buddies covering me, I burst through the back, but by the time I get there, the front team has already captured the three residents inside.

The earthen floor house proves quite the armory, stuffed with every portable weapon and ammo Gaddafi had. We fine 35 AK-47 machine guns, 27 FN-FAL automatic rifles, 3 rocket propelled grenades and 17 Russian PKT machine gun. We also find a storage house full of ammo .It takes us an hour to load the cache up on the trucks. I call the headquarters: mission successful. But, turns out, we weren't quite done yet!

My cousin, our troop commander, says to me: "Rad, look down at your feet." I stare, see nothing. "Anything wrong?" I ask. "The dirt's not right", he says. "What do you mean by that?" I want to know. "Looks like something's been buried there. Recently. The dirt looks too fresh. Go get a shovel."

I look, but there isn't one handy, so I tell one of the prisoners: "I need a shovel". He comes back with "What are you gonna do with it?" "Shut up, I said, "and get me a shovel". "It's in the garage," he finally says, so I go to the garage to find not one shovel, but six. Six? Six is kind of a lot for just one house, seems like more than one house would need. But, whatever. I shrug, take three back to where I was standing, and we start digging. I carry three and go to the place I was standing and we start digging and digging. We find nothing. Just dirt. Just before I lose hope, I hear a sound of metal. What the hell is in here?

My cousin is right. The dirt is stomped, but kinda soft, not like the old hard packed stuff would be. So, we dig and dig and we dig, and nothing. Ten minutes later, I am ready to quit, my shovel hits something metallic. "What the hell is it?" I ask. We keep digging for another five minutes, start making out the outline, and my cousin says: "I think it's a tank!" The excitement of the discovery makes us dig faster. We rotate the shovels between the guys; the digging is good; the tank is beautiful. Naturally, we want to drive it out.

By the time we finish digging a ramp to drive the tank out of its hole, the day is ending. We call for back-up, and it takes them half an hour to come and take the prisoners away. We spend the night in the house. First thing in the morning, we drive the thing out of its hole. Do we keep driving ? We know it's dangerous. What if NATO spots us and mistakes us for the bad guys?! But what the hell; life is short, and you only live once. So, I climb on top, mount our Free Libyan flag on the tank, and

I get to drive it to our headquarters. And that's how I got to drive my first tank!

Pilot Brigadier Al Mahdi Rasheed Mohammad Al Sameen
born in 1959 and martyred on March 19, 2011

The story is told by the martyr's daughter
Ruwand Al Mahdi Al Sameen
Student of secondary school of engineering

Martyr Pilot Brigadier Al Mahdi Rasheed Mohammad Al Sameen, was born in Benghazi in 1959 and he was married with six girls.

He studied in elementary and middle school in Benghazi after which he joined the Air Force Academy in Tripoli and then he went to Russia to study aeronautics. He finished the aviation course because he was very interested in it and had a great desire to become a pilot. He also managed to learn and speak Russian and English fluently. After finishing his course in Russia, he returned home as a certified fighter pilot. He then took courses in flight tutoring in order to become flight instructor which he later succeeded in becoming. He also took courses in flight testing which was an extremely dangerous job because the planes he tested were either heavily damaged or required complicated repairs. He was assigned to test planes whose military age had expired. When the February 17 revolution began, he saw everything from the beginning due to the fact that he lived in the center of the events and what he saw hurt him very much , especially when he saw that the youths of Libya were being indiscriminately killed by the yellow helmeted Gaddafi mercenaries. He wanted to do something but a military order came ordering him to go to the city of Sirte so that he could help transport undamaged planes from Benghazi to Sirte. When he helped in the transportation, they ordered him to bomb the city of Benghazi and particularly Al Fadeel Bu Omar katiba. Before the rebels took over katiba, he thought of a plan that would compromise the order that he received by disabling and removing a small part of the plane which is essential for releasing bombs and he threw the part away, thus preventing the plane from releasing bombs on Benghazi. After that he managed to escape from Sirte along with other pilots, through the desert. Gaddafi's soldiers and brigades were everywhere so it was an extremely dangerous and risky expedition which, due to the mentioned difficulties, lasted three days. We searched for him everywhere, by car and on foot not knowing that he was in Sirte and when we finally contacted him in order to keep us from worrying, he told us that he was in a nearby eastern town and that he was completely safe. Eventually, when he returned from his expedition, he told us that a pilot who escaped with him had relatives in the city of Taurgha but they had to remain hidden so that nobody in the city knew they were there, because at the time Taurgha still had not denounced Gaddafi's government. Had the people from Taurgha known who they were, they would have killed them but fortunately they somehow managed to reach Benghazi safely. He then told us all about the events that took place in Sirte and admitted he was there instead of the eastern city as he had told us. After his return to Benghazi, he received threats and naturally he wasn't afraid for his life but for the life of his family and loved ones.

Upon his return he went to the headquarters of his brigade and there he joined the freedom fighters. He didn't come home but he called us regularly to let us know that he was safe. One day he came home and told us to leave the house and to go somewhere safe. We later heard from him that he bombarded several ships belonging to Gaddafi near the city of Ajdabiyeh and that he also destroyed Gaddafi's convoy coming from Sabha. He kept on informing us about his attacks and we could tell that he was very happy but he was also very worried about us. He was hoping that he would see the fall of Gaddafi soon and then came that black day which we named Black Saturday. On that dreadful day the tyrant and criminal Gaddafi, sent a very huge column of killing machines whose mission was to attack the city of Benghazi. All night long we were listening to awful and horrifying noises of bombs and destruction. My father waited for sunrise to get into the plane to eliminate them, a deed which he was extremely eager to do. After coming back from his scouting mission which helped him estimate Gaddafi's forces that were closing in on Benghazi, the information and findings that he shared with his colleague pilots was horrifying. He performed three aerial attacks on the killing column that was approaching Benghazi very quickly. In his third and final attack, he was with his co-pilot Fakhri Al Salabi. He attacked the column fiercely and managed to destroy a part of it and cripple it badly but unfortunately, he was hit by a missile coming from the anti-aircraft vehicle and even though he was able to save himself at the time, he didn't want the plane to crash into a residential area, so he steered the plane far from his beloved city of Benghazi and by the time he managed to do that it was too late for him to eject and to save himself.

May God take my father's gentle, merciful and pure soul because of what he did for his beloved country Libya and his fellow countrymen. And finally we got rid of the tyrant Gaddafi with God's help and the blood of the martyrs will never go in vain.

First Zawiya Prisoner of the 17 February Revolution

Emad al-Mashatt, Zawia, Libya

I was the first one to be arrested in my hometown, Zawia. A group of thuggish looking men in civilian clothes came to my house on February 14th. They blindfolded me, dragged me to their car, pressed my head down, and covered me with a jacket. Threatening me with guns, they drove away. They were part of the so-called "political police" force, which is largely unheard of in other countries. That day, my wife was actually sewing the tricolored Libyan flag. She was lucky that those people did not step a foot inside our apartment.

I was accused of conspiring to overthrow Gaddafi. When they presented me with a printout of my comments from opposition websites, I could not deny it. They ordered me to bring my computer and mobile phone in order to find other incriminating evidence against me. After that, they kept it all for themselves of course, together with my clothes, and even a mattress, pillow, blanket and thermos, which my friends brought for me. This was the last day for my family to know where I was and that I was in fact still alive. We would reunite only after 6 months and 10 days, during which we never had a chance to speak or see each other.

The next day, I was taken to Tripoli. There they told me that I would be sent home in about 2-3 days, to which I replied, "This does not happen in Libya, here you either get killed or imprisoned for the rest of your life."

I spent several days in Drebi Prison. First, I was put in a tiny cell, where nothing could fit except a mattress. Then I was transferred to another cell, which had a few other cells adjacent to it, making up a block. This gave me an opportunity to communicate with at least someone. Back then, we had still lingering hopes that they would let us go. What a stupid hope that was. That same night, Seif al-Islam came out with his speech on TV. We had a glimpse of it while being transferred to Abu Salim Prison. Our hands were tied with plastic bands used to attach wires. At that moment, we were still unaware what was happening in the country.

At the prison grounds, a whole bunch of soldiers were waiting for us in order to beat us up. We were also subjected to beating on the day of our trial. Our clothes and shoes were confiscated, leaving us with only underwear, t-shirts and light prison pants. It was cold during the night; it was February. The mattress was so old and thin, that it seemed as if I was sleeping right on the dirty floor tiles.

There were two of us in the cell. The ceiling was very high up and there was a small window five meters above the ground. We were able to talk to a few fellow inmates, 8 in total. Towards the end of April, the number of inmates increased dramatically; there were 3-4 prisoners in each cell. In the end, there were eight of us in a cell designed for two people. The guards never spoke to us; they only gave us our food through a small window. They kept the doors locked and certainly did not let us go for a walk outside.

What did we eat? They did not feed us much, but we got used to it. The meal was small, about four spoons or so. Whenever they asked us, "How many people are in the cell?" before bringing dinner, we used to respond, "five."

Breakfast consisted of typical Libyan food, but the portions were extremely small. In a typical week, they would feed us rice with tomato sauce two times a week, rice with bits of chicken (ruz bilau) once a week, pasta twice a week, couscous also twice a week, and juice. We got almost nothing for supper. At first, we were given 1.5 liters of water for 2-3 people every few days, then 1.5 liters water bottle per person daily.

How did we bathe? Inside the cell, there was a toilet and a shower covered by a small curtain. Water came straight from the sea and was cold. This caused a great deal of inconvenience; we were constantly getting sick. Yet, they deprived us of medications. There were no towels, no air conditioners during the summer and there was not enough air

Certainly, the life inside the prison was dull. We had a Mus'haf and conversations to keep us going. We managed to scribble letters on paper trays left from dinner and gathered phone numbers. We even made playing cards and chess out of juice and milk cartons, and beads out of olive pits.

We got our news from newcomers or whenever the guards opened up the gates to bring someone in. Each one of us had a nickname, so that we could communicate, because we could not see each other. Mine was Oya. We used to throw jokes at prison guards – calling each other "the one that spoke against Gaddafi…" – in order to somehow avenge the conditions we were in.

On the 18th of March the air raids had started. We had no idea how many people had already died. We had this naïve hope that the rebels from Benghazi had hijacked a military plane and had come to liberate Tripoli. Later we found out those were NATO planes. We were not afraid of them, but when they were beating me up inside the courtroom, they repeatedly asked, "When a NATO plane flies by, are you screaming 'Allahu akbar'?!"

During the month of Ramadan, I heard three explosions very close by. There were four of us in the cell, and then they brought another four. Those people were all covered in sand, some of them in their underwear only. They looked like madmen, and at that moment we had seriously contemplated an idea that this was yet another way of putting psychological pressure on us. As it turned out, these people had been transferred from another section that also housed all of the administrative offices. This was precisely the target of the bombs. These prisoners were able to run away, but were caught and brought to our section.

On the 20th of Ramadan we could hear the rockets flying above. We had prepared to die, constantly repeating the Shahadah. Gaddafi had placed rockets on the prison grounds so that NATO would bomb us as well. Those were the days when the war came really close to us. The food was scarce, we barely got anything to eat after 10pm, and this was during the fasting! After the 20th, many had managed to escape, but we were still inside. My family thought that I was dead.

On the 24th of August, the revolutionaries had entered the prison. We had realized that when we heard them screaming "Allahu akbar," Gaddafi's men were scared to pronounce such words! They had broken the doors open and let us out. They gave us money so that we could get home. Many of them offered their homes to spend the night.

Why were my "neighbours" arrested? One of them had crossed out Gaddafi's face on his portrait and wrote "repair Libya or leave." Another one had sprayed graffiti in Misrata that read: "Shut up, Gaddafi." Another one was taken from the airport simply because he was heading to Benghazi to visit his parents (they did not believe him because that day the demonstrations broke out on the streets of Benghazi).

They were planning to execute us on September 1st.

Beads made from olive pits

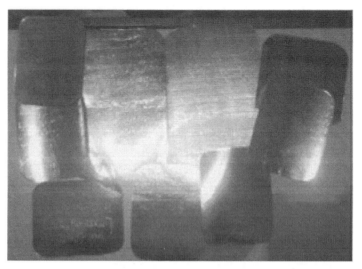

Dinner trays were employed instead of paper to write down Qur'an aya, phone numbers and mail addresses

The prison issued very thin pants, and during February-March these and a 2cm mat were all that separated the prisoners from the tile prison floor

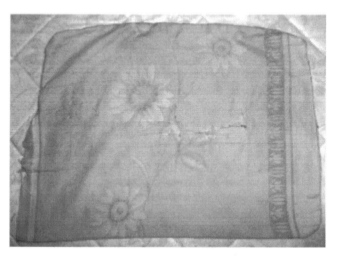

Pillowcase darned using whatever was available in prison

Victims of Gaddafi the Tyrant
Dr. Wanis Ali Al Shaari
Maraey Ahmed Al Shaari

Written by Ali Ahmed Al Shaari, father of Wanis and brother of Maraey Al Shaari, Benghazi, Libya

My son, after the dictator destroyer Gaddafi imprisoned you for 18 years, you left us forever. After you were released you had severe headaches and were unable to bear cold winters and the heat of hot summers and thus, after a while, you were taken away from us by death which left our hearts empty and sad.

In the USA, you acquired a PhD with honorary degrees and you were offered work as an engineer for the prestigious NASA. Of course, due to your enormous love for your country, you refused the job and returned to Libya in order to offer your knowledge and to help steer the country in the right direction. You were also offered a teaching position at the Faculty of Engineering, on a telecommunication subject that was completely new and only a few professors were qualified enough to teach it at the time. At the time of your funeral, Dr. AbdelAaty Belkhayr came to me to express his condolences and told me that you were one of a kind and one of the best in your field.

However, some people are created to bring harm to other people and one of those people was a member of the Revolutionary committee who worked at the university and who insisted on removing you from the university by claiming that you were against Gaddafi's revolution.

So that was the situation at the university and whenever I see your face my heart starts to bleed and tears stream down my face. And as it is and always was clear, the employment of quality professors depends on the people that are the cancer of the society and evil.

My son, whatever I write about you it will never be enough. And this is a confession of great loss and sadness. But crying and sadness are not going to bring you back, and that's life: happiness and sadness. All the people will die. Even if they live as long as Noah (950 years), death is the end. A life quickly slips away and only good memories and good things done will remain. Good memories of the man keep him alive.

Dr. Wanis Al Shaari

Victims of Abu Salim

28

As for my brother Maraey Al Shaari, who was a technician in the Ras Lanuf oil and gas company, the story is very similar to that of my son's, that is, a great injustice was laid upon both of them.

My brother was sent to the United Kingdom on a six months training course and upon completion of his training he was supposed to return to Libya. Before he returned a Libyan gave him a bag and asked him if he could take it to his family in Benghazi. At that time, Libyans studying or travelling abroad were watched by men employed by Gaddafi's intelligence service. These men provided regular reports on any student or traveller whom they regarded with suspicion or suspected of being opposed to Gaddafi. Unfortunately, an intelligence service man stated in a report that the bag that was carried by my brother was sent by one of the members of the Libyan opposition in the UK.

My brother had no knowledge whatsoever about the person who gave him the bag. The man asked him if he could take the bag to his mother who was missing him very much and he couldn't do it by himself because he was exiled. So my brother took the bag for humanitarian reasons and not to harm or oppose the system. As soon as the plane landed, my brother was followed by intelligence men in order to see to what address he would deliver the bag. My brother was arrested on the 20th of October, 1995, and was taken to the Hawari prison. The man in charge was Salem Bashun and we asked him if we could visit Maraey but of course he refused. It was not long before my brother was transferred to the Abu Salim prison in Tripoli, where he was killed by the Gaddafi criminals along with many other young people in the massacre of Abu Salim prison in 1996.

But don't be surprised, dear reader, because nothing coming from the tyrant Gaddafi is surprising or strange. I feel the need to mention two things. The only things that were packed in the bag that was with my brother were clothes and children's shoes. We heard of the Abu Salim massacre but did not hear of Maraey's death so for the next thirteen years we had hope. On the 13th of July, 2009, we received Maraey's death certificate and realised he had died less than one year after his arrest.

May Allah bless my brother Maraey and his fellow martyrs and may he be accepted by the Prophets and the Messengers; may peace be upon you all.

Maraey Al Shaari

No Way Did I See This Coming ...

Tom, commonly known as BlueHen95, USA

3,828 blog posts and 107 poems (and counting) on an Al Jazeera blog about a place that I scarcely thought about before February 17. Libya was a place on page 153 in an atlas, Egypt's less famous "little brother". It was interesting only because of a rather eccentric leader who had a propensity to dress in flowing brown robes and make bizarre speeches in front of the UN. And from a distance, well…he was kind of fun to watch. If you looked at him out of context, he was highly entertaining.

Tunisia happened, then Egypt, and I watched detached. Then came February 17. Suddenly there was an absolutely fascinating man that had to be taken IN context. It was no longer possible to separate the psychopath from the actual people who had to live under him. He became real to me, and as he became real, Libyans too entered my field of vision. From this new view, Libya was decidedly much less funny. Yes, it was the man who caught my attention, but it was the people who would keep it.

I'm sure that your basic Libyan would have happily skipped the next eight months to get right to the conclusion. I, on the other hand (having the benefit of not being shot at), would not fast forward past a single second of this revolution. I scoured the news for the latest updates, and I found myself glued to Al Jazeera English—the best source I could actually read. And when I opened my front door to grab the morning newspaper, the World rushed in, carrying the Libyans on its shoulders.

The extent to which the Libyan revolution captivated me is still hard to comprehend. I have no history that predisposes me to care about a dictator in some other country. I have no Libyan blood in me. In fact, before this, I didn't even know a Libyan. I actually thought that Corporal Klinger from MASH was Libyan, but he was Lebanese. Yet I have been touched in ways that are unreal. I have felt sorrow, excitement, grief, disgust, and elation as though I were in the middle of Tripoli the entire time.

There is a world out there that I never knew existed. It is a world marked by people with odd monikers and stories that would make no sense whatsoever to an on-looker, a world filled with blog trolls and Another Statements and, most of all, a world populated with real people who struggle every day to make things work for them. It is a world to which I have related through poetic license, a world whose face I tried to put a smile on every time I interacted, a world that wanted someone to make it laugh.

And Libya to me was a microcosm, a world within a world who just wanted to escape from the court jester who had more on his mind than being crazy. The more I got immersed, the more real it felt. I imagined every bullet, every land mine, every realization of sick, psychotic, maniacal behavior that a population had to endure. And I got both sick to my stomach and high on victory, and sobered by the fact that this hasn't ended. It has just begun, and it will happen with the world side-by-side.

We are lucky in a strange way that in the 21st century, we can follow a war almost literally alongside the people who are fighting it. The action seems in our living rooms, not halfway across the world. If we let ourselves, we have the opportunity to get to know the men, women, and children keeping their heads up while they dodge bullets in search of something better. It is a transformative experience. It's October now, and Libya has changed forever. And I am grateful that I have too.

No way did I see this coming ...

*"Think not of those who are slain in Allah's way as dead.
Indeed they are living in the presence of their Lord and are provided for."
The Holy Qur'an*

Dr. Abdullah Abdulfatah Al Mageerbe
born in 1981 and martyred on October 9, 2011

The story is told by the martyr's best friend
Dr. Mohamad Al Ammari, General Surgeon, Hawari Hospital, Benghazi

Condolences to myself and all Libya for our hero martyrs who gave their souls and blood for Libya.

God makes great people for us to benefit from during their lives and He increases the benefits for them many times over after their death. One of these great people is our martyr (God willing) the hero doctor, Abdullah Al Mageerbe who was born in Benghazi on December 5, 1981

He had a lot of great attributes: He was a brother you could look up to; a brother you could lean on; a brother you could greatly benefit from.

He had all kinds of beauty – beauty of the soul which eased his misfortunes in life as he lost his father; beauty of the spirit which eased his demands; beauty of the mind which gained him a lot.

He (May God bring mercy to his soul) treated us not the same as we treated him but he always was better than us. He was a man taught from the bitterness of life, and he taught others patience and how to face obstacles in life despite his young age. He lived this way until he died. As he often said: "Live happy above the ground or live under it as a martyr."

Since our hero graduated in 2007, until his death, he was known for his love and devotion to work

His work during the February 17 revolution was profuse; he used to stay many days in the hospital looking after the patients, doing his duty and being humble with them, and he did it till he decided to go to the front line. He was willing to be martyred. He stayed there for about a month-and-a-half, until he was captured on the 23rd of Ramadan (August 23) in Bin Jawad, even though he was a doctor and not carrying any weapon. But the sons of the devil didn't distinguish between the armed and those not armed – their concern was just to kill Libyans, so they executed him along with his other colleagues on the October 9 in Sirte. They thought they killed him but they are wrong: He is alive with God.

Someone said: "You can step on the flowers but you cannot delay the spring."

And the irony is that they couldn't find a place to accept the stinking body of his killer, Mutasem, son of the devil.

This was this dialogue between our martyr and the dammed Mutassim:

Dammed: *I am higher than you.*

Martyr: *I am steady.*

Dammed: *I am stronger.*

Martyr: *I am immortal.*

Dammed: *I have the power and the rich people with me.*

Martyr: Surah Al Anaam from the Holy Qur'an, Verse 123: "*And thus have We made in every city great ones of its wicked ones, that they should plot therein. They do but plot against themselves, though they perceive not.*"

Dammed: *Now I can kill you.*

Martyr: *But my brothers will kill you later. A home we don't protect we don't deserve to live in.*

We were told by some of the prisoners who had been with our martyr that whoever said the infidel's words, was released, but our hero refused to say those words, so God took him as a hero and set him above the oppressors.

Mercy on your soul my friend and you will be our pride always.

We are all of God and to God we all shall return

Martyr – Dr. Abdullah Abdulfatah Al Mageerbe

Martyr – Dr. Abdullah Abdulfatah Al Mageerbe

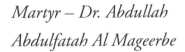

Benina Airport Project on the Outskirts of Benghazi, Libya, February 2011

John Macnab, Field Engineer, Benghazi, Libya

On 28 December, 2010, I travelled from Tunisia back to Benghazi, after a brief holiday, to continue work on the new Benina Airport Terminal. We had been constructing this project since 2009 and were on target to finish the job by year's end 2011. The uprising in Tunisia was just gaining momentum and the mood amongst the Tunisian workers was upbeat though I could sense an underlying concern for their families back home. On 14 January, Ben Ali fled Tunisia and the celebrating began amongst the Tunisians at Benina.

17 January: Libyan leader Muammar Gaddafi says he regrets the fall of Ben Ali, which has left the country in "chaos with no end in sight." When protests began in Egypt the Libyan air force started flying daily reconnaissance missions from Benina Airport to the border area. Till this point nobody had discussed the possibility of protests spreading to Libya as we were certain Gaddafi would crack down very hard on any dissention amongst the population especially in Eastern Libya. As the days passed and Egypt's revolution remained mostly peaceful we hoped that Mubarak would do the right thing and step down which he did on 11 February, 2011. It wasn't lost on us that Libya sat dead centre between these two revolutions but we just couldn't conceive the possibility of a Libyan uprising against the Gaddafi regime. How wrong we were! Internet service was disrupted so we were unable to receive any news as to what was happening on the streets of Benghazi.

18 February: Our Filipino office clerk received a message from his wife who worked in a Benghazi school that a doctor had been shot dead at the next door medical clinic and the Filipino nurses were too afraid to continue working. There was also word of mercenaries roaming the streets killing unarmed protestors.

19 February: We were aware that Benghazi was in chaos and mid afternoon I witnessed a Russian Hind gunship flying low to the west of the airport firing on targets. Later that afternoon, I was told by an SNC Lavalin employee who had been at the airport arrivals gate that a plane load of African mercenaries had landed. We set up a survey instrument to get a closer look at what was happening around the airport terminal. I could see a large contingent of soldiers (+/- 200) in a defensive pattern around the west side of the runway. We didn't know if these were mercenaries or Libyan government soldiers. Three aircraft landed at Benina in the afternoon including Turkish, Afrikiyah, plus a large unmarked Russian transport plane and they flew scores of passengers out. The four Mig fighter jets based at Benina had taken off as usual that morning but never returned. Two Russian Hind gunships were active patrolling Benghazi and adjacent military installations. We decided it was time to retreat back to camp for safety reasons as there was much smoke rising to the west of the airport where the gunship had been concentrating its attack. Just before dinner we witnessed a large aircraft with unlit running lights attempting to land. The soldiers at the airport opened fire with a massive barrage from machine guns and the plane veered away to the north and disappeared. After dinner a co-worker and I went to the main SNC Lavalin office to see if we could connect to the internet. The state authorities had disconnected Libyan internet, phone, and cell coverage for the past week so our only contact with the outside world was via a direct internet connection through our Tunis office. I was able to log on to the internet and sent out several messages and my co-worker was able to contact his son on Cyprus, who just happened to be a member of SAS, to give him our GPS coordinates. These would be our last messages sent via the office computers. We could hear continuous machine gun fire at the airport at a distance of approximately 1km. I noticed a tank coming up the highway towards the end of the airport perimeter. As we left the office there was a convoy of trucks coming towards us and as they passed by we noticed the machine guns and AK47s. We hurried

back to the compound where many of the Thai and Filipino employees had gathered. Suddenly there was a flurry of gunfire and everybody scattered. We told everyone to get back to their cabins and keep out of sight. The invaders then proceeded to ransack our offices taking everything including hundreds of computers, furniture, and all our pickup trucks, heavy duty equipment and buses. Our main office in Ganfounda was overrun and burned to the ground so those employees travelled by bus to Benina for shelter. Our food and drinking water cache was also ransacked leaving us with only limited supplies for the 2500+ people now in camp. We spent the night hunkered down in our cabins listening to a continuous barrage of machine guns and AK47s. With no security it made for a very long sleepless night.

20 February: The shooting stopped at 4 a.m. and we were able to confirm that nobody had been injured. We surveyed what remained of the food and started distributing rice and whatever meat was left to the Thais & Filipinos. They began cooking on open fires around camp and generously offered us pancakes and meat dishes. Gaddafi sent fight jets to bomb Benghazi on Sunday and our fear was he would bomb the runways. We were surrounded by military installations to the southeast, to the northwest and probably other sites that we weren't aware of. The ridge behind our camp was a massive network of bunkers and radar installation so we were in a very vulnerable situation with no cover other that our metal cabins. That afternoon a group of locals came to the camp and offered us protection. Many of the men had worked for Lavalin in the past, or knew somebody who had, and commented that they had been treated fairly and wanted to offer support. This development was a big relief for us as now the perimeter of the camp would be patrolled. It was another day of constant gunfire which kept us indoors and again the shooting continued throughout the night.

21 February: There was constant gun fire around the airport but we managed to get some rest. The Thais were very concerned about the situation and wanted assurance that SNC was working on an evacuation plan to get everybody out. All I could do was confirm that the Montreal office was working on a plan to have several planes flown from Europe that would evacuate everybody. The stumbling block to this plan was the airport runway being blocked by our heavy duty equipment to prevent more mercenaries from landing. SNC had somebody negotiating with the General who had defected to the rebels' side and was now directing the defence of the airport. We soon realized that the runway would not be opened any time soon and therefore flying out of Benina would not be an option.

22 February: The military set up anti aircraft guns at the airport and started firing over us towards the bunkers on the ridge above. As we were sitting in the kitchen we heard aircraft overhead and then bombs being dropped at a distance. We found out later the pilots had dropped the runway bombs to the north and south of the runway but had refused to follow orders to destroy the runways. We knew the importance of controlling the airport which added to our stress level. By now most of the food was gone and we were eating meals with the Thais & Filipinos who spent their days collecting firewood and cooking over open fires.

23 February: Security was busy with intruders and in the middle of the night somebody tried to enter our cabin. This night the first seven buses left Benina to attempt the 700km journey to the Egyptian border. Amongst the passengers were a Canadian and a Brit. Three of the buses broke down before even getting through Benghazi. The majority of us refused to travel by bus as it was a long, dangerous journey in poorly maintained vehicles. It must have been a horrific journey of two plus days with constant breakdowns and road blocks. I was told later that the buses had no glass in the windows and it was very cold throughout the night. They were stopped at roadblocks and armed men would board and intimidate the travellers. Eventually all the foreign workers would escape Libya via this long journey to the Egyptian

border where they were met by buses to be driven to Alexandria and then to Cairo for flights home.

24 February: Early in the day we received word that the British frigate HMS Cumberland would be arriving in Benghazi harbour and evacuating us to Malta. By this point the food was consisting of rice and whatever else could be scrapped together so we were eager to vacate. The bus ride to the port took us past the army barracks now occupied by the Freedom Fighters and what an amazing sight that was. The gates were open and dozens of people milled around the guard post. We noticed much graffiti on concrete walls and the tri-coloured flag had replaced the green Gaddafi flag. We encountered several road blocks but were waved through politely by the soldiers. The best sight in days was seeing HMS Cumberland docked at the port with the Union Jack fluttering in the breeze. We were quickly processed onto the ship and within the hour were on the 34 hour journey on rough seas to Malta. Many thanks to the crew of the Cumberland for such a warm welcome aboard.

It was such a relief to be out of Benghazi and in the coming days I would travel to Malta, Italy, France and eventually North America.

In early May I received a message from a friend in Jalu, Libya, saying they were being attacked by hundreds of Gaddafi soldiers. I had been following the Libya blog on Al Jazeera and out of desperation contacted a popular blogger to seek help for my friends in the desert. The guys would forward the GPS coordinates of the location of the Gaddafi soldiers and a description of the surrounding area, for example, "They are in Waha oil field in a grove of palm trees". I would confirm the coordinates on Google Earth then forward them to my contact. This worked very well and continued well into July when the final attacks were repelled and peace was restored to the desert oasis.

I wish I could have written this more as a story than words from my diary but this is okay. It is hard to put into words the fear we were feeling at this time in February; and it is just as hard to describe my resentment about the Gaddafi family for damaging so many lives and forcing us to leave, my reaction to the many threats I received and my sleeplessness on many nights as I thought of my friends being attacked. There is so much to say. I tell some people, "It was like watching a movie ... except we were in the movie".

We are all hoping for a peaceful transition to democracy for Libya and soon I hope to return to Benina to finish construction of the new airport that is so desperately needed. It would also be very nice to welcome to Benghazi some of the many bloggers who have offered so much support to Libya.

After the Hind gunships attack at the airport just before we were overrun

Note: This is a copy of an article written early in the summer of 2011 for The Libyan Post, one of many newspapers and magazines which quickly sprang up after the liberation of Benghazi. Creative works of all kinds such as cartoons and rap songs were in evidence everywhere in Benghazi as soon as the repressive regime was overthrown. It was as if the creativity of a people that had been held in check for over forty years just exploded all over the city.

The X-Y Generation

Tawfik Mansurey, Benghazi, Libya

The dark days of the regime are dimming and with every liberated city people's spirits grow. The "Arab Spring" that has blossomed across the Arab lands should lead to a bright summer of hope for the future.

Once Gaddafi literally becomes history our work as free Libyans will just begin.

Having lived through the revolution, I have cherished every moment during these historical times. Moments of fear and flight, yet ironically, at the same time, happiness and laughter. I know one day when I grow older, I'll think back to these days nostalgically and relive them by telling my grandchildren the tale.

Many people we personally know have lost their lives and many others were injured during this blessed revolution. The majority of these people were the youths of the city. Young men who met a rain of bullets, sniper and artillery fire head on – undeterred they stood. Their stance would lead to the crumbling of the regime in the east of the country in just a matter of four days. Four days of killing in the face of iron will.

The protests started in Tree Square on Omar Bin Al Aus Street and soon spread to other parts of the city. The authorities started using excessive force; live bullets were fired and the protesters were gunned down in cold blood. Snipers shot a funeral procession passing by Al Fadeel Army Base (Gaddafi's residence) on its way to the cemetery; the mourners fell to the ground. The headquarters became the enemy.

As more and more people were gunned down, more and more youth arrived from all neighborhoods across Benghazi. They came armed with their brothers.

I remember creeping into the old Turkish garrison in front of the base; armed with my camera using the walls as cover, I advanced further forward until I was behind an arch about 100 meters in front of the base. The next thing I knew, machinegun fire broke out in loud bursts. It didn't stop but just increased and got louder. I hid behind one of the columns of the arch. There were at least 30 of us hiding behind each column, each about two feet wide. I took out my camera and started snapping shots as the bullets got closer and closer.

One by one, the young men ran back for cover. The lucky ones dodged the bullets and made it safely to the other side of the fort; the less fortunate, however, fell to the ground in a pool of blood.

Gaddafi brigades and hired foreign mercenaries were shooting to kill as the majority of casualties were hit in the chest and head. The mercenaries danced cheerfully as they shot each victim which enraged the crowd even more. You'd think that the youths would be terrified but they weren't – the more young men fell, the more young men came to take their place.

Friends and passers-by picked up the injured and in some cases were targeted and shot as they tried to pick up their comrades. The soldiers would start shooting and advance forward into the streets following youths who hid behind corners and taunted them. The neighborhoods on all sides of the base were ripped with bullet holes and many residents were shot inside their own homes.

Things started to go the youths' way when they started using gelatina – a homemade bomb used in fishing – which they threw at the loyalist guards. You could tell that the soldiers were frightened by this new development.

The people were resolved to take over the base and became innovative in their approach to fighting the trained well-armed guards. Spear guns were brought in and gelatina was tied onto the spear and sent flying into the main checkpoint of the base.

The young men kept attacking and chanting – "The base will fall today; the base will fall today." Bulldozers were also used to charge at the reinforced concrete walls on all sides of the base to get the guards occupied on all fronts and also to allow the protesters to sneak into the compound.

Al Mahdi Zeiw, a father of two girls, sacrificed his life by piling his car with gas cylinders and gelatina and rammed the main gate of the base causing a massive explosion and a huge hole at the gate.

That was the fighting spirit on the streets of Benghazi. "We win or we die" was their motto, just as Omar Al Mukhtar had famously said during the many years he had struggled against the oppressive Italian occupation. The youths followed their hero's words to the letter.

Omar Al Mukhtar further advised the Libyans to seize the enemies' weapons to use against them; just as their forefathers had done before them, Libyans snatched weapons off Gaddafi's forces to arm and protect themselves.

Things escalated even further as the guards began using artillery to fire at the protesters. However, now the youths had access to small arms and ammunition and a growing will to succeed.

Once our brothers in the other eastern towns secured their borders, the youths of Al Beida, Shahat, Susah, Al Guba, Derna, Tobruk and other villages in the region came to stand and support their brothers in Benghazi with their newfound arsenal.

On the same day that our brethren arrived from the east, the 36th Special Forces Brigade based in Benghazi under the command of Four Star General Abdul Fatah Younis, revolted against Gaddafi and joined sides with the citizens of the east.

The base finally fell. Gaddafi loyalists deserted the base and ran off in civilian clothes, surrendered or were killed.

I remember an overwhelming feeling of joy as the crowd rushed through the gates in search of weapons to further advance towards Benina Airport. People wept openly as they entered the base; one man got on his knees and prayed to God in gratitude.

We were victorious but not without a price; thousands of young people had been wounded – many of them critically while hundreds of others had sacrificed their lives in the name of freedom.

Some of our young men who had been caught by Gaddafi's loyalists were found; some were dangling by an arm from the ceiling, others had been raped, others were missing. Even Gaddafi's soldiers who refused the orders to shoot civilians weren't spared as their bodies were found burned after they had been shot with a single bullet to the head.

Once the base fell, the Libyans gathered what weapons they found and moved on to secure Benina Airport. The airport fell to the hands of the people that same night and eastern Libya had been freed from the sinister shackles of a merciless regime.

Gaddafi's troops would try to re-enter Benghazi on March 19, but once again our brave youths stopped them in their tracks in Tabalino on the western road into Benghazi.

I grew up a lot during those days; the one thing I learned is to have respect for those unemployed young men who stood on street corners and watched life pass them by. It was some of these same kids and young men who faced the bullets and stood up as the bravest of men to rewrite the history of a nation.

We salute them and those that have passed away and promise never to forget their bravery and determination which should be an example for all Libyans of all ages as we move forward to guide our country to peace and stability.

Many of these courageous young men are still fighting on the front lines today, others have joined in as volunteers providing an essential workforce to help the cause in its many different requirements from humanitarian relief, rappers, cartoonists, local police to collecting garbage to keep our streets clean and tidy.

We must also mention the role that our young women and mothers played during the uprising. They sent their boys and their men to war, sprayed cool water on the men from the balconies and you could hear their Zoughrouta – a high-pitched shriek – reverberating above the skies of Benghazi as a sign to show their happiness and contentment. They also play a major role in the many voluntary positions needed to continue our struggles for freedom.

It is our obligation to make sure that our young men and women are offered scholarships and a better education system in which students are respected, vocational training given by experts from the United States and Europe in different fields from photography, media, art, music, engineering to carpentry; they should also be trained in foreign languages to further develop the bridges already built with the international community and to allow them to attend conferences and workshops abroad.

This will develop these young people intellectually, linguistically, culturally, socially, psychologically and in many other ways.

We thank the honorable men and women of the Libyan Interim National Council and all other public servants for their hard work so far in our blessed revolution.

Our government will have much to do in order to reconstruct our war-torn country and change the behavior patterns of 42 years of a corrupt system and regime.

A priority towards our children and the future of our beloved country should be the preparation of a thorough program to support and develop the youth movement as they are an important fountain of energy – utilizing this force will be the key to rebuilding the nation.

We suggest that our representatives consider having a younger generation of Libyans working directly with them and in positions of responsibility so that their fresh ideas and creative abilities are a part of the new system that will lead to a civil democratic society.

The vibrant force of youth directed in the right channel can become the flame of the torch of a new free dynamic Libya.

God bless Libya and the X-Y Generation.

"Think not of those who are slain in Allah's way as dead.
Indeed they are living in the presence of their Lord and are provided for."
The Holy Qur'an

Ahmed Mohamed Saleh Bago
born in 1971 and martyred on February 20, 2011

Written by Ahmed's brother Mustapha Mohamed Saleh Bago, Benghazi, Libya

Ahmed Mohamed Saleh Bago was born in Benghazi in 1971. Ever since he was a child, he was very diligent in his studies. In his adolescence and manhood, he was honest, generous, confident, courageous and helpful to his relatives and friends. His family and neighbors can confirm this.

During his second year of secondary school, English classes were cancelled. He was angry and wrote on the walls of the school: "Down with the regime". With the help of some neighbors they wrote leaflets and distributed them to students.

When he graduated, he entered the Professional Institute (Institute of Trade). But he was not left alone. Internal security forces were always observing him and continuously asked about his activities until he was arrested during the second year at the institute with his friends Nabil Al Silabi and Khaled Al Hajj. They were interrogated on who was behind them and their activities.

But they told the security services that there was no one behind them and that they worked alone. He was imprisoned for a year and they wanted to send him to Abu Salim prison, but he was below the legal age. He lost much time in prison when he could have been studying. As such, he was unable to have a profession or find work.

He was waiting for any chance to make a revolution against the dictator Gaddafi to eliminate him. When the February 17 revolution began he told to his mother: "I have waited for this day for 30 years." He personally participated in this revolution with his money and efforts.

At the beginning of the revolution, the day the internal security headquarters fell, he bought a weapon (a hunting rifle for 500LD) to defend Benghazi from the men with yellow hard hats. When he was asked by his family (his wife and his mother) as to where he was, he told them that he was in the city of Al Marj, but in reality, he was protesting with youngsters on Gamal Abdel Nasser Street in Benghazi.

Ahmed was newly married. It was the fifth month since his wedding which was on September 16, 2010, which was also the anniversary of the martyrdom of Sheikh Omar Al Mukhtar.

Ahmed was mature and full of self-confidence. He participated in the attack on the military camp in the Bou Atnai area. He was martyred on the day of the liberation of Benghazi (the day of the fall of the katiba) in front of the military hospital. He was hit by the bullets of Gaddafi's mercenaries and martyred on February 20, 2011.

> *"Think not of those who are slain in Allah's way as dead.*
> *Indeed they are living in the presence of their Lord and are provided for."*
> *The Holy Qur'an*

Saleh Mohamed Saleh Bago
born in 1974 and martyred on May 2, 2011

Written by the martyr's brother, Mustapha Mohamed Saleh Bago, Benghazi, Libya

The martyr was characterized as a kind and jovial person. He was loved by everyone, old and young. He liked to help his family and neighbors and was affectionate to his mother and helped her very much at home. Everybody witnessed his courage and strength.

Saleh was trained at Al Kubba military camp in 1992 at the age of 18 years. He was transferred from this military camp to the military camp in Tripoli. From there he was transferred to the area Alweigh and then to Wadi Aldoom on the border with Chad, where he participated in the war with Chad. He saw that senior officers of Gaddafi's troops treated young soldiers disgracefully and when he defended them, he was reprimanded and punished by placing him in the sewage disposal tank. These officers were giving young soldiers hallucinogenic pills.

When he returned from the war he entered a psychiatric clinic for treatment for the effects of those pills for more than a year to recover his strength and nature. One of the events he hated in this bitter war was how they suffered from severe hunger because of the severe shortage of bread; authorities gave them flour and ordered them to bake it by themselves (with their own hands). They were looking for something to bake on and they couldn't find anything except a rusted plate thrown in desert. When they picked it up, they found the corpse of a soldier. Saleh panicked, ran, and shot into the air. He didn't sleep for three days until his friends started to read Qur'an to him to calm him down.

They were left in desert of Chad till one member of the officer's family brought Saleh back to his family.

For these circumstances, Saleh was without pay or a monthly income and no financial compensation from the previous failure of the government. He had no job, no marriage, no home, no car nor any future. He became strongly critical and disgusted with the system until the February 17 revolution came. He went out with the protesters using all his strength. On the day when the protesters were trying to take over the katiba in Benghazi, Saleh was together with his brother Ahmed defending Benghazi side by side. When Ahmed was hit by bullets from mercenaries, he ran towards Jalaa Hospital carrying him in his arms. Ahmed died four hours later. Saleh came back to the family house, the blood stains over his clothes and hands and he didn't wash for three days.

A few days after the funeral, he returned to the protesters and they wanted to go to Ajdabiyah. On March 19, when Gaddafi's soldiers entered in Benghazi, he was among the first defenders on the front line. He carried weapons and supplies by small fishing boat to Misurata and Ajdabiyah, an operation which was vital to the success of the campaign against Gaddafi's forces. He was martyred on the evening of May 2, 2011 at Bawabet Al Arbaeen when he was on his shift rotation as a guard.

17th Of February
Rainbow From White Ashes

Pido, Benghazi, Libya

We wanted Liberation
You gave us Annihilation
In your destruction
Stand our Salvation

 Our hearts only beat for freedom
 Our hearts only beat for victory
 Save your stupid speeches, we don't need 'em
 Your delusions are contradictory
 We only want freedom and liberation for eternity
 And your brutal regime will be crushed by our fraternity

You killed the souls of innocents and silenced many others
Raped our sisters and slaughtered our brothers
For 42 years you shed bloodbaths
And still want to rule and command us

 You fighting back in hopeless
 Done are the days of your lawlessness
 The Libyan lives that you have poisoned
 The Libyan people have chosen

We do what we must
It's now you or us !!!
There is no "try"
We either win or we die . . .

 These are your last days
 Our souls won't waste!
 Not the blood spill in vain!
 May be cursed your name

The blood that will set Libya free from your shadow of darkness
Now we're singing the anthem of victory with all the strength we can harness
That set our hearts free
And free Libya will be

 Never again shall you ever kill for your pleasure
 Entertained by the rape or profit from Libya's treasure

Libya is one
Forever United
Crowded streets are cleared away
One by One
Hollow heroes separate
As they run
Wise men wonder while strong men die

Breaking Dawn of Freeedom

Pido, Benghazi, Libya

Tripoli's smiling again
Breathing Freedom through the youth's veins
Everywhere you look, you'll find an Independence Flag
Rather than them green rags
From the east to the west all you can see
Faces smiling, hearts loving and souls feeling free
Libya now is more like a free soaring bird
Aiming high in the sky and sending message to the world
We are free Libyans and we'll keep going on
We'll keep rising up with the freedom we own

It's the Breaking Dawn of Freedom
Hidden in a corner of the World
We were left Unknown
But that's a different Story
We're the new face of Bravery

No doubt on whose side we're at
You can clearly see the ground we stand
It's Red, Black and Green
With a Crescent and Star in between

How I Became A Freedom Fighter

Mustafa Billhassan Eamon, Al Marj, Libya

When my father was shot, it felt like the bullet struck us both. I grabbed him and held him. I held him for the entire four hours it took him to die.

"Do not tell Dedra!" were his last words. "Do not tell Dedra…!"

I am Mustafa Billhassan Eamon. I was born in Al Marj city, in eastern Libya, to a Libyan father and an Irish mother, Dedra. Mum is from Belfast in Northern Ireland, but her parents are from Dublin, and her grand-parents are from Romania... so, I am mixed ^_^. But I feel Libyan, and I love Libya so much.

My dad was a civil engineer who built homes. He had a small company of his own in Al Marj city. He was a peaceful man who loved order and beauty. Some

Mustafa Eamon with fellow Freedom Fighters from the "Martyrs of Zawiya" Brigade (about 2000 fighters and 70 generals, most from Benghazi and Al Marj) returning home victorious to Al Marj on Libyan Liberation Day, 2011

times I worked with him in his business. I am 25 years old. I graduated from the Police Academy in Tripoli in 2004. I worked as a policeman and I know how to fire a gun to ensure peace. When I was 20, I was a striker in the Libyan National Football team.

On Sunday, February 20, 2011, my dad was shot for doing nothing. He was shot right outside his home. Gaddafi brought thugs and murderers to instill fear in those who dared to demonstrate against him. My dad wasn't demonstrating. The mercenaries were paid to terrorize, to break the people's spirit by committing acts of violence against anyone. My dad, my hero, was one of their victims. The day he died I lost my innocence and another part of me that I do not know what to call.

I am Mustafa Billhassan Eamon, and the day my father died I became a Freedom Fighter.

On Sunday, February 20, my little brother Khalid and I both became two of the thousands and thousands of men fighting for freedom in Libya. Khalid and I fought Gaddafi's forces for four months, from Benghazi to Ajdabiya to West Ajdabiya to Brega. But after the death of Major General Abdel-Fattah Younis, I left the front lines. My little brother fought almost all the way to Sirte. On September 2, almost his entire unit was wiped out by a grad missile in Hawara. Only two Freedom Fighters survived with injuries. Khalid was one of them. He had shrapnel wounds to his neck, arm and leg, but he made it. Only one of his friends also made it. The rest of his friends were martyred.

While Khalid was still fighting, my American friend in Florida was calling me. She was very scared for me and my family. She invited me to a wonderful website where I found members from all over the world. They were older, but they were great. I joined them discussing the meaning of freedom and the meaning of peace between all races and all religions. For this I would like to thank all these wonderful friends who were there with me. I'm here and invite them to visit Libya next summer. I thank in particular my American friend in Florida who is a great human being.

Today, Libya is free and I am slowly getting my life back. I am a FIFA agent, and I have a girlfriend named Sandra. About my girlfriend :) FUTURE WIFE :)… She is Irish. She was born to an Irish mother and a Lithuanian father. I love her so much, but she can't cook Libyan food. That's just like Mum when she first visited Libya in 1980. But even though she can't cook it yet, Sandra already knows all our food, so I am not worried. I will help her learn when she lives in Libya with me next summer. I already have a nice house picked out for her. She said to me: "I will live with you in Libya or on the Moon. I don't care, as long as it's with you." That made me feel as if I am a king.

I am Mustafa Billhassan Eamon, and I still think about my dad all the time. I am happy in free new Libya, happy with my friends, but when I go to bed, I remember all the moments with my father. I remember all the happy moments, because I don't remember him ever being angry. I just remember all the happy moments and the beautiful times we spent together in Libya and in Ireland, or even while working with workers from Serbia and Bosnia.

Now I think that my father is watching from the sky. I know he is happy because Libya is free.

But I am sad, because he cannot share this joy with those he loved.

Hugging brother Khalid, Al Marj, October 2011 during the Libyan Liberation Day home coming of the "Martyrs of Zawiya" Brigade

My Nation Will Remain Free
"I held my Kalashnikov in my left hand and my guitar in my right hand"

Masood Bwisir, Businessman, Benghazi, Libya

My name is Masood Abdul Salam Mohammed Bwisir. I am 40 years old, married, a businessman from Benghazi and I have loved music since childhood. I formed a band about two years ago. When I saw the announcement on the Internet, which asked Libyan people to join peaceful demonstrations for our legal rights on February 17, I looked forward to joining my people demanding their rights. Therefore, my band and I went out in the demonstrations on Omar Bin Al Aas Street in Benghazi and we felt we had achieved our dream. Then we were brutally attacked by men wearing yellow construction hats. At this point the demonstration divided into two groups. The first group went to the Juliana Bridge and the second headed towards the courthouse. I was with the second group and, after the attack, we de¬cided to sit in front of the courthouse.

After the barbaric attacks against us, the other young men and I decided to begin sit-ins in front of the courthouse. We participated in processing explosive charges, which were made of small amounts of TNT, usually used in fishing. This was in an area called Al Sabri. Most of us were civilians, but we were joined by some dissidents of the army and Special Forces which were lead by Colonel Naji Al Mogra¬bi. He helped us use a tank to demolish the walls of Al Fadeel Bu Omar katiba. The destruction of the Katiba and the liberation of Benghazi were achieved after that.

When the front lines opened, we headed towards the west of the country armed with our faith and the desire to liberate the country from the oppression of the tyrant, Gaddafi. We did this, despite the lack of military experience in battle and the lack of weapons. This brought us within the range of heavy weap¬ons shelling, missiles, Grad rockets and mortar shells. I thank the Western and Arab press for their help in delivering the news and images of this to the world despite their surprise at a group of lightly armed untrained fighters confronting a well-equipped army that had heavy weapons. We were always asked how we could be fighting an army of this size in light of a limited prospect for victory. Our re¬sponse was al¬ways the same. We said, "We do not give up, we win or we die. We have great faith in God and we know that God grants victories." We were sure that God was with us and victory was inevitable.

On the battlefield, I held my Kalashnikov in my left hand and my guitar in my right hand. My mes¬sage was peaceful from the beginning of the revolution when we sat in front of the courthouse. There I sang: "My nation will remain strong, my nation will remain great, my nation will remain free and my nation will remain at liberty." The members of my band, Faisal Fakroon, Mohammed Shoaib, Omar Al Aneezi and Waled Alagouri and I participated in the battles for liberation. We always sang on the front lines, "My nation will remain free."

I want to convey the message of our revolution of peace, the revolution against mass murder. The voice of the guitar is stronger than the voice of bullets and it brings peace while gunshots bring death. I want to convey the message that we are not Al Qaeda, but we are moderate Muslims. We are doctors, engi¬neers, lawyers, musicians and teachers. We were civilians forced to take up arms in response to injustice. I always sang this song to raise the morale of the revolutionaries. The press always looked for the possibil¬ity of extremist warlords on the front lines, but they always found my friends and me singing to defend our honor and our homeland.

We sang our song in Ajdabiyeh, Brega, Ras Lanuf and Bin Jawad. During this time two of our band members, Faisal Fakroon and Mohammed Shoaib were captured in Brega. Thank God that when Tripoli was liberated, they were released and we all went together to Sirte. Mohammed was then wounded by three bullets, but he is now in better shape, thank God.

Along with taking part in the battles in the east, I also participated in the fighting along the front lines of Misurata. We traveled to Misurata by sea. The first time was on March 5. The second trip was by fishing boats, the Shahat, the Irasa and the Al Sarha. These boats were equipped with relief supplies and medical equipment. During this time the Port of Misurata was mined by Gaddafi and they threatened to bomb any vessel that entered the port. We received a warning from NATO not to enter the Port of Misurata. We waited in the fishing port of Benghazi for ten days until an Italian minesweeper was able to clean the port of Misurata of mines. Then we were able to deliver the relief to Misurata, which was surrounded by Gaddafi Kataib.

I stayed in Misurata for a month and a half. The heroes from the eastern cities of Libya arrived to help their brothers in Misurata. Then Gaddafi knew that all Libyans were of one heart and were all brothers. He could not separate us – we would live or die together. We were able to achieve victory on Tripoli Street, Al Karareem, Taurgha and other places until finally Misurata was liberated.

I returned to Benghazi to join the battalion of Ahmad Ahwas. We started out with a group of 200 people consisting of Special Forces, infantry and fishermen from the Sedi Ekhrebesh area who had experience in dealing with TNT. We landed by sea in Al Shaab port in Tripoli and were able to secure the port. We met our brothers from Tajoura and man¬aged to form a defensive line. I must say here that on our arrival in Tripoli, we found that the city had already been liberated by its own heroes. We only joined in the celebrations and helped in securing the city. Then I went to Sirte to take part in the battles there. I was injured by a sniper bullet in my right leg and had surgery to remove the bullet.

I thank God that He honored us with this victory. God bless our heroes, our revolutionaries. I feel sad for the loss of the lives of our martyrs and ask that God will admit them to paradise, heaven, and I ask for a speedy recovery for our wounded heroes.

Peace upon you all.

Libya In My Blood And The Other Way Around

Libya in Absentia, Benghazi, Libya

A few years ago, I miscarried a baby. Here in Libya, we name and bury miscarried babies, so my blood is literally in the soil of this country. I am not Libyan, but my home and my life are in Benghazi. Libya is in my blood and my soul. Of course I did not know it then, but that baby, unlike my other children, would be spared the terror of living through a war.

That terror began with the very first voice of protest against a government that knew no other way to treat its people but complete and total repression. The voices came from the children of parents who had witnessed so much repression that their only hope for a better future lay in the wished for frailty of their aging dictator and in his supposedly reform-minded son. When the youth of Libya called out for reforms in their government, this reform-minded son suddenly inherited the mantle of dictator and, with his father and brothers, set their army of foreign mercenaries against their own fellow citizens in such a vicious and violent repression that the world could not stand by and witness evil of this scale.

In Benghazi, the protests began on February 15th. Each night we heard the sound of gunfire and tanks and saw the sky lit with red anti-aircraft tracer fire. Each day we buried more brave young men and watched our city burn. We held our young children and sent our sons, brothers and husbands to fight with stones and knives in an impossible battle against an army that had been preparing over forty years for this day. Within a few days, a middle-aged father of two girls, who I believe saw what their future would have been if Benghazi was not liberated, made the ultimate sacrifice. He used his car as a bomb and exploded the wall of the garrison leading the way for its fall.

Benghazi was finally free! We mothers took our children and grandchildren to the city courthouse, where this had all begun, to support our men. We walked to the garrison where so many had died with the threat of death from the skies, and we soon learned to make posters in English to beg the world for help against this threat. We volunteered in hospitals, made food for fighters, sewed flags, baked cakes to sell to help fund the fight for freedom, and found our voices. We finally saw the bright sunshine of freedom in Libya, but it was not over yet.

The war had taken its toll on us; some of my family including myself were sick and not getting any better. Gaddafi's troops had fought their way back to Ajdabiyah and were headed for Benghazi. We knew the men had a better chance without trying to take care of the women and small children, so we prepared to leave in small groups. On March 16th, my youngest children and I left with one of my married daughter's family and my other married daughter was to leave in a few days with her family. We could not stand to go any further than Egypt or stop watching the news to find out all we could of the situation in which we had left our loved ones.

This situation was tearing my heart out. My pregnant daughter and her family were still in Benghazi when I finally got an internet connection and read on the Al Jazeera English blog that Gaddafi troops were only 50 kilometers out of Benghazi. Even after having had no real sleep since we left home, I was wide awake with terror and praying for their protection. The morning news showed scenes of my city being attacked by Gaddafi soldiers and there were no phone lines working to check on family who had stayed behind. At 4:45 in the afternoon, the news finally reported the coalition implementing the no-fly zone and attacking the column of tanks driving down the roads that I knew so well. I was relieved, yet terrified because I knew from the reports that the tanks had come into areas very close to our homes and I had no way of knowing what had happened to my family.

Two agonizing days later, my daughter called me from the border town of Salum. She and the women of her family were safe and she would be with me soon. She arrived exhausted and sick with worry. One of Gaddafi's fighter jets had followed the line of cars fleeing the city. The wait at the border had taken twelve hours and there had been a small riot of the African refugees caught there. However, worst of all the last sight she had had of her husband was of him using his new machine gun to protect them from Gaddafi loyalist snipers patrolling the neighborhood in cars and shooting anyone they saw. She would wait for days before a connection could be made through phone and internet and she could know he was alive and safe.

The hardest thing that I had to do as a mother was yet to come. My son, who had escorted us safely to Egypt, had to return home to Benghazi. We knew that it was safer now that the no-fly zone was in place, but he was still returning to a war to do what he could for his people. I did not cry until he was out of the door.

Now it was time for me to try to continue the battle any way that I could from where I was. Internet had been cut off in Benghazi from February 19th, but in Egypt it was working. I have lived in Libya for a long time and I know what life is like here, so I know when the western media is being fed a load of crap. I am also a native speaker of English, so I can put a few sentences together and send some emails. That is what I did. I bugged everyone I could think of: governments, NATO, TV news stations and newspapers. I watched the news in English and read what I could find online and I pointed out every time the Gaddafi regime was playing the media for their own purposes, which was every chance they got. Many people used machine guns as weapons in this war, but I used my laptop.

I was not the only one fighting this way. I found the most wonderful community of people on the Al Jazeera blog. So many people, who unlike me had no personal stake in this war, were fighting for the people of Libya. I feel honored to have lived through an historic time, a time that I hope will make an important change for humanity. I hope that Libya will lead the way for democracy and peace in North Africa and the Arab countries. I hope that friendships forged in this crisis will be sustained and will help make this world a better place.

One of my daughters with her two children. The photo is taken in front of the courthouse in Benghazi where things began. It was taken during protests before the no fly zone was enacted while we were still not sure if we would be destroyed.

I Can Say Loudly "I Am a LIBYAN"

Dr. Osama Jazwi, Anesthesiologist, Hawari General Hospital, Benghazi, Libya

My name is Osama Jazwi. I am a doctor and a Boy Scout leader. This is how I always introduce myself to others.

On the 17th of February I was on my weekly 24 hour duty in the operating theatre at Hawari General Hospital in Benghazi. When we started to receive injured people, it was more of a shock than anyone can imagine.

We stayed there for more than five days straight, working on the wounded with tears in our eyes from seeing the cruelty of the inflicted wounds that we were dealing with. We received some of the police pretending they were hurt, but I think this was their way of getting out of obeying the orders to slaughter their own city's people.

During the days before the fall of Benghazi, I got a lot of calls from my relatives in the east asking about the situation and saying, "Why is it taking so long for you?" I told them, "We are

Dr. Osama Jazwi on guard duty in Hawari neighborhood on the night Gaddafi's forces attacked Benghazi March 19, 2011

being killed here. We are facing bullets with bare chests. We really need guns." So, I found myself inside the operating room making phone calls and arranging to get some guns to Benghazi to take over the last fortress in the city, the katiba, as we call it.

I was also getting news from my scout friends all over the country, and asking them, "Have you revolted? Are there cities under people control yet?" I found myself becoming a source of news in the hospital about what was going on in other cities.

One day I went with an ambulance at 3 a.m. to check some Turkish workers stranded at the airport. We found ourselves cleaning the runway and making calls to others to get rid of some ammunition scattered on the fields there. Then I started to make arrangements to bring boy scouts to hospitals to fulfil the duties of nurses and medical helpers who were unable to report to work.

After Benghazi was taken by us, everything was stable but there was no order in the city. So, as a boy scout, I found myself taking charge of one of the traffic lights after getting out of the hospital. I think car crashes at intersections have killed a lot of people, too.

The city regained some order and everything became quiet. The hospital became boring and hollow for me. It really agitated me, actually, being there but doing nothing. So, I decided to go to the front line on 6 March. I prepared my car as an ambulance and loaded it with some medications and supplies I got from the hospital, and I asked a doctor friend to join me in this mission of being a doctor to the Freedom Fighters at their location at the front. We reached Ras Lanof. We survived a rocket attack from Gaddafi's jets. We barely escaped from Ben Jawad in the first traitors' ambush. We were among the last people to evacuate the Brega clinic. We had rockets landing around us and we almost got stuck behind enemy lines. But God embraced us with his care and we were able to escape.

One of the funniest things that happened to me was this. I was treating a patient and there was someone with him. I did the physical examination for him and, planning to transfer him to the next main hospital,

I asked him his name. The name was familiar. I looked him in the face and he was my cousin and the one beside him was my twin brother! We all had not recognized each other at that time!

I joined a brigade and became the doctor there doing the physical check-ups for the new volunteers and fighters. I have also been responsible for pro-Gaddafi prisoners and mercenaries. I survived two assassination attempts on my life inside Benghazi city before the attack from Gaddafi's army. I have worked at the field hospital on a few occasions and joined the ambulances in the front line.

On the 18th of March I took a weapon and did guard duty in my neighborhood. I faced the attack on the city by doing an intelligence job from a roof-top. It was my job to locate attackers' cars and tanks and give the information to my brigade fighters. I joined the attack on the pro-Gaddafi sleeping cell in Benghazi city as a fighter and medic at the same time and captured some who tried to flee from the battle place.

I went to Misurata to get the injured into our hospitals on board ships. I joined the air ambulance bringing wounded to Benghazi from the front and taking some wounded abroad to Tunisia. Every chance I got, I went to the front and stayed there for a few days with the field hospital. Lately, I have quit doing the job of giving anesthesia to patients in the operating theatre and I have stayed in the surgical intensive care unit where I can do greater good than I can do in the operating theatre.

Some asked me: "Why you are doing all this?"

Does that need an answer?

It is my country and my people. It is the first time I feel belonging and pride, the first time I can say loudly "I am a LIBYAN!"

It is the feeling of freedom. It is my duty to my people. I will do it again over and over to stop the killing, to feel freedom for the first time, to preserve this feeling for our future generations, and to make Libya a better place for our sons and daughters.

One month before this blessed revolution if you had asked me, "What is your dream?" I would have said, "To get the hell out of this country, because I have no future here."

But now it is the opposite, it is a new Libya and there is hope.

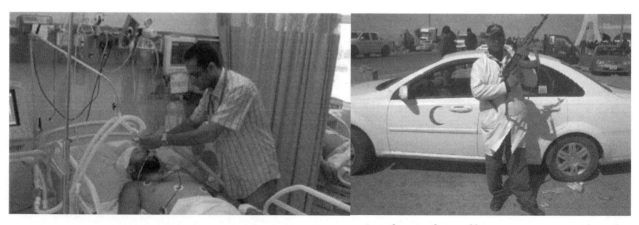

Dr. Osama Jazwi in Surgical ICU, Hawari Hospital, treating wounded FF, August 2011

Standing in front of his own car-converted-to-clinic at the checkpoint in Ras Lanuf, March 3, 2011

Arriving with Patients by Ambulance Chopper to Hawari Hospital

With Boy Scouts during Lunch Break in Hawari Hospital

Collecting unexploded shells scattered around the ambulances to hand over to Freedom Fighters, Red Valley near Sirte, Sept. 2011

My Imprisonment for More than 12 Years

In the name of Allah, the Most Gracious, Most Merciful,
from the victims of the tyrannical Gaddafi regime

Najib Awad Muhammad Dneini, Benghazi, Libya

The victims of Libya's authoritarian fascist regime, the regime of the tyrant Gaddafi, are numerous. Among them are Libyans from different walks of life. This tyrant ruled Libya for more than four decades characterized by marginalization and exclusion. He restricted freedoms, spread poverty and disease, and destroyed such fields as education and healthcare. He also suspended the constitution. Everything was planned in a systematic and malicious manner. Talking about one of the victims of this period of coercion, oppression and arbitrariness, my story embodies one of many of Libya's children and youths, who were arrested by Gaddafi and his accomplices. When we demanded freedom of choice and expression of our legitimate choice, our views were quashed by an iron fist and bullets.

To begin, my name is Najib Awad Muhammad Dneini. I was born in Benghazi on Shamsa Street in 1953. When I was arrested in April, 1976, I was just 23 years old. I was the third child in my family, which was quite a large middle-class family. My immediate family consisted of my father, mother, five sisters and four brothers – eleven people in total.

Like many Libyans at that time, I used to help my father so that our family could have a decent life. In the evening, I attended an all-male school in Benghazi, and during the day I earned a living using my father's truck as a contractor at one of the companies (Al Nasr Company). My monthly salary was approximately 1,200 Libyan dinars. My family was wholly dependent on this monthly income in order to make ends meet. My arrest, which happened in April 1976, followed by my imprisonment for more than 12 years until my release on March 3, 1988, had a significant impact on their lives and the stability of their living conditions.

I will describe the events, my reasons for participating in demonstrations and my subsequent arrest and long imprisonment below.

In April, 1976 the students of Garyounis University in Benghazi began to demonstrate against the regime. They demanded the right to choose and form student unions in universities. They wanted to avoid in their student unions having people who worked with the regime. Also, the students were opposed to the military training program during the study period and the militarization of schools and universities. They supported the military training after graduation.

Faced with these just and legitimate demands, the tyrannical government responded by excessive force, repression, imprisonment and hangings of many Libyans in the squares of Benghazi, Tripoli, and other defiant cities. There were no fair trials; this was done in a surreal terrorist manner. The events then moved from university campuses to the streets and many ordinary people joined in. I was among them and I saw all these protests as legitimate demands. From a national perspective, our country was in danger because of the restrictions imposed on the freedom of opinion, as well as the militarization of schools and universities.

The students, united with ordinary people, clashed with security forces and the police. This forced these peaceful protesters to take up stones to defend themselves because the security forces were using weapons and live ammunition against the unarmed students and residents.

That time I was arrested and later on released. When I returned home after a few days, First Lt. Abdullah Al Sanussi and General Hassan Ashkal came to my home and arrested me. I was arrested and taken to the headquarters of the Revolutionary Guard in Benghazi, where I was tortured and interrogated. I was also accused of provoking chaos in the streets, attempting to demolish the monument to the memory of Jamal Abdul Nasser, and participating in the events which took place in the city. After three days, I was transferred to Ajdaidah prison in Tripoli, then to internal security headquarters in Tripoli. First, I was interrogated at the state security division headed by Sulaiman Al Baruni. Then I was transferred back to Benghazi, to Al Kuwaifiah Prison, where I remained for six months without a trial.

I was later sent to the People's Court, which is a special court led by Captain Ahmad Muhammad Al Zwai, Lt. Abdal Salam Buqilah and Lt. Sulaiman Al Misrati. This was an ordinary trial, and there was nothing exceptional about it. However, the trial was not fair because it did not guarantee the right of legal action. The court provided its own defense, which was worthless. The courtroom rejected our request to be represented by our own lawyers. If this request had been accepted, the sentence would have been different. The judge was not fair to us; the following day he sentenced us to ten years in prison. I spent three years in really poor conditions, without any access to healthcare. After three years, they transferred me to Tripoli, to Hisan Al Aswad Prison. At that prison, family visitation was restricted to once a year, only two people were allowed inside and the time was limited to five minutes. Compared to Al Kuwaifiah Prison, the treatment here was much worse. There were 12 prisoners in our small cell about five by seven meters. There was one small washroom inside. For many years, we were not allowed to go outside to the prison yard to see the sun. We did not know what was happening inside or outside the country. There were no newspapers, no magazines, no television, and no radio to provide us with any news or information. The quality and the amount of food we were given was poor and insufficient. The health conditions were extremely bad and virtually nonexistent, which led to the spread and exacerbation of diseases such as tuberculosis and arthritis, among the prisoners. There was no treatment provided to any prisoners, and we experienced the worst kinds of torture. Later in 1984 we were transferred from Hisan Al Aswad Prison to Abu Salim Prison. We remained in Abu Salim Prison until we were released during what is known as "Asbahu subhu"- ("Dawn began") in 1988, a day when some political prisoners were granted amnesty).

Each day in prison resembled every other long and dull day. A complete day in prison was like this: Early in the morning at 7:00am the prison commander came to count the prisoners inside the cell. There were 12 of us in the cell, which measured 5x7 meters. There was a toilet inside. Then the breakfast was brought, which consisted of a small piece of bread, a cup of tea and a one-liter carton of milk for everyone to share.

At 2:00pm they brought lunch, consisting of a bowl of pasta or rice with a cup of tea. Then the guard came again to count the prisoners inside the cell. In the evening dinner was brought, consisting of a bowl of soup and a cup of tea.

As we were not allowed to have books, radio or television we usually spent our time talking or walking inside the cell because we were not allowed to go outside to the prison yard for many years. At 9:00pm the guard came once again to ensure the count was correct. If anybody tried to speak to other prisoners in the neighboring cells, it resulted in punishment in the form of beatings and not getting sanitary supplies, such as soap, toothpaste, etc. We were not allowed to wear any clothes except prison clothes. If there was any revolt or rebellion against the regime outside the prison, we were punished and they tortured us during meal time.

After I was released from prison I found out that my father, may God have mercy on him, had passed away as a result of grief and anguish. My mother had suffered a stroke because she was constantly worrying about me. I had also lost my chance for an education; all my classmates had completed their studies and obtained positions within the state sector. As for me, I did not have a job. The private company where I previously worked had closed. I did not receive any compensation from the government, be it a job or housing for me and my family, which consisted of six people. In addition, as a result of twelve years that I spent in prison, I suffered from physical as well of psychological disorders.

Since the date of my release from prison (March 3, 1988) until now I have not been able to obtain a job to provide a decent life for me and my family because I did not complete my studies. I do not have a professional certificate that would provide me with a chance to obtain a position in a relevant field.

My great hope is first in the glorified and exalted Allah and then, the new Libyan state after the revolution of February 17. This was among our most important demands: to achieve freedom, justice and a constitution.

I hope they will reward us for all those years we spent in prisons under the rule of the tyrant, and provide us with an opportunity to obtain a job and housing. These are the most important pillars for building a decent and stable life, God willing.

Gaddafi's regime released prisoners from Al-Kuwaifiah prison, Benghazi, so that they would join thugs and mercenaries, People's Guards, Revolutionary Guards and members of the Revolutionary Committees in terrorizing and intimidating the civilian population. This attempt to subdue the peaceful demonstrations failed February 15, 2011

Benghazi citizens celebrate Liberation Day in Al Keesh neighborhood 23 October, 2011

The Arabic inscription above the English words "Free Libya" reads: "The Victory Square".

Salma Mohammed Milad Alsabri

Written by her Doctor in Charge
Osama Alshaikhy, MD, Consultant Neurologist, Benghazi

Salma Mohammed Milad Alsabri was born on 18 September 1992, in Benghazi.

Salma came into this world after a caesarean section due to her having a large head caused by a high cerebrospinal fluid pressure within the brain (Hydrocephalus). She was subjected to surgery within a week of her birth to find a link for the exhaust of cerebrospinal fluid between the brain and the peritoneal cavity within the abdomen (Ventriculoperitoneal shunt).

Enrolled for regular medical follow-ups, Salma enjoyed a quiet life and continued her studies successfully.

During her return from her school on 20 February, 2006, during the events at the Italian Embassy in Benghazi when the security forces were trying to disperse the demonstrators, Salma was hit by a bullet in her head and was taken to Jala Hospital for Accidents and Emergency where urgent surgery was undertaken.

Since then, Salma has been subjected to many surgeries to change the shunt within the brain. These have been needed because of blockage or malfunction or bacterial infection. Other complicating matters have increased as her secondary epilepsy has led to her heart being full of tension, forcing her to take antiepileptic drugs on a regular basis.

Over successive days and years the life of Salma changed from a Libyan girl in the prime of life dreaming of a bright future, into a sick girl spending most of her time between clinics and hospitals. This has had a bad effect on her psychologically and on her behaviour as a young girl.

On Wednesday, 26 October, 2011, Salma was subjected to another surgery within Hawari General Hospital, but unfortunately suffered convulsions repeatedly. This led her into a complete coma which lasted for days during her stay in the Intensive Care Unit.

This is the story of a girl who found herself a prey to disease since childhood but did not care about that much, and insisted on living normally supported by the family. But she was surprised by a change in the course of her life caused by a stray bullet. As a result, Salma found herself unable to study, attend social events or enjoy a normal life.

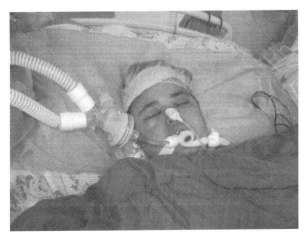

Postscript

After Dr Osama Alshaikhy's report was written for this book, we were kept informed of Salma's situation as the effects of her injuries gradually overwhelmed her strength and her enthusiasm for life. Then, on 22 December, the following email message came from Benghazi:

"I just want to tell you that Salma Alsabri died on December 18, 2011, at 12 noon."

Confidence in a peaceful and happy future is shown poignantly in a painting by Khalid Al Sadeq, completed in June 2011 and exhibited in "17 February Revolution – Libyan Painters" during February 2012. The words on the wall are from Masood Bwisir's "My country will be free". We have placed our photo of this painting with Salma's story as a memorial to her and to other young people who were injured or killed during the painful years of Gaddafi's Libya, and as a hope that there will be no more "Salmas", that the safety and freedom of innocents in the new Libya will be assured.

We Will Never Forget Those Who Helped Us
In The Liberation Of Our Beloved Libya

Colonel Ali Mohammed Al Shamekh, Military Air Surveillance Benina Air Base, Benghazi, Free Libya, November 4, 2011

When Gaddafi overthrew King Idris on September 1, 1969, I was a child with small dreams and aspirations for the future and I had realised none of them. As I was growing up, my dreams slowly diminished until they completely vanished. My decision to join the air force was not so much a voluntary one, because the system cornered me into making it. Because of Gaddafi and his irrational ideas that confused and puzzled the Libyan people, especially the youths, Libya had become a place

Col. Ali with granddaughter Latifa, May 2011

where he could carry out his experiments and bring his twisted theories to life. He abused and misused all media, which he totally controlled, and used them to spread his poison through our country and at the same time, he used them to glorify himself and his evil family.

Upon his arrival in power, the tyrant called for freedom, equality, justice and good principles, of which none have ever been practiced or achieved, and that naturally disappointed the Libyan people very much. All freedoms and rights ceased to exist. Even the most fundamental freedom, freedom of speech, was banned. He imprisoned all his opponents and assassinated dissidents abroad, an act that he preferred to call physical liquidation.

Gaddafi deliberately marginalized the Libyan army, fearing they would execute a coup against him, and so he began to plunge it into losing battles in Uganda, Chad and Egypt.

Gaddafi's paranoia began to grow and develop and as a result, he became very eager to create problems and incidents throughout the world – in Africa, Asia and Latin America – and in neighboring countries.

He also began to form undercover security services to protect him and his family, focusing on his sons, cousins and the ones who were close to him and whose loyalty belonged only to him instead to their nation. He earned the loyalty of the people heading his security by lavishing them with huge amounts of money and by giving them important and powerful governmental positions.

In the early years of Gaddafi's reign, several members of the national army questioned his leadership, and there were several attempts to oust him, but he had tightened his grip on the country through his security forces, bodyguards and his revolutionary committees. It was almost impossible to oust him until February 17, 2011, when news of the revolution in Libya spread via the Internet. Thus, February 17 was set as the day the revolution began. This date was the missing piece required to trigger the revolution and make all the people of Libya along with all the honest and virtuous people from the national army go out and protest. It was a great honor for me to join the glorious revolution from its very birth.

The feeling which awakened inside of me when I joined the revolution was very strange and unknown to me. I had been waiting for this day for so long that I did not imagine that the opportunity to participate in overthrowing the tyrant and to liberate my beloved country would ever come.

It all began at the Benina airbase in Benghazi. The reason I mention it, is that I am one of its employees and I work there as an air traffic controller, with the rank of colonel. I will do my best to depict as clearly as possible the events that took place as well as the events that I personally participated in.

On February 17, a brigade from Sirte, under the leadership of Saadi Qaddafi, one of Gaddafi's sons and Qaddafi's right-hand man Abdullah Senussi, arrived in Benghazi. They were sent to take control of the Benina airbase. I, along with other officers and soldiers, were surrounded by the battalion and no one was allowed to enter or exit the base. Hence, due to the fact that we were unarmed and outnumbered, we weren't able to offer any resistance, but a volcano of anger boiling in each of us, was about to erupt.

On February 20, orders were issued for the withdrawal of all available combat aircraft from Benghazi, as well as the withdrawal of all fighter aircraft from the Nasser airbase in Tobruq, to Sirte. There were four MIG 23 aircraft and five MIG 21s.

On the same day, a group of young unarmed protesters attacked Al Fadeel Bu Omar Katiba in Benghazi, a notorious building that was known to be the tyrant's symbol in Benghazi. Ammunition of the mercenaries in this battalion began to run scarce, so orders were issued that the helicopter was to provide the battalion with ammunition from the stores at Al Rajma. When the MI-8 helicopter landed, pilots somehow managed to disable it. Fortunately the battalion was not supplied with extra ammunition, and thus it was easier for us to defeat it. Another two MI-35 combat helicopters which had been sent from Sirte to attack the freedom fighters in Benghazi and Baida were disabled and seized and later in the revolution were used by the freedom fighters from Benghazi to repel attacks from Gaddafi's brigades.

After the collapse of Al Fadeel Bu Omar Katiba, protesters went to the Benina air base. We followed the latest news and events through mobile phones, but we had to remain very vigilant and cautious. We weren't afraid for our lives but of the fact that if some information leaked to Gaddafi's men, our revolution could be jeopardized. The protesters had managed to enter the airbase after a confrontation with the mercenaries who then fled along with their leaders, Saadi Qaddafi and Abdullah Sanusi. The Benina airbase was completely liberated and so was the city of Benghazi.

On February 23, I had the honor of personally participating in delivering a statement on Al Jazeera satellite channel from Benina air base joining the revolution, which was aired on the channel on February 25 by Colonel Mohammed Hussein Warfali (who later died in the battle for Ajdabiyeh on April 9, 2011). It was the first open declaration of a military unit joining the revolution in Libya. This was a serious risk as it was not known, at the time, whether the revolution would be successful or not. But I was determined to do something and this was the last chance for me – it would be either victory or martyrdom. This was the feeling everyone around me had.

The following days were filled with very difficult emotions varying from anxiety, hope and sometimes fear of failure of the revolution. But the feeling of victory was present inside me since the beginning because we are the owners of these rights and we are the owners of this just cause.

After the liberation of the eastern cities we started to work preparing to confront the tyrant forces and to assist other cities in the west and south. The Benina base became a beehive, where the technicians and engineers began working on the renovation and equipping of combat aircraft with the scrap existing at the base.

Due to the desire of everyone for change and the success of the revolution, and through our great determination, these heroes were capable of extracting four MIG 23s from scrap and putting them back to work. The heroes at Nasser air base in Tobruk did the same, as they were able to renew and equip four MIG 21s, arming them in a record time. They also managed to collect weapons, ammunition and rockets, which were scattered in several cities and several places. This required tremendous effort. Every passing day I felt proud of where we were with increasing certainty of victory day after day.

I was careful at the outset of what might work for victory. Because my business as an observer was not needed (because there were no flights at that time), I gave up my basic career and went to help in any other activities. With the help of some officers, soldiers, civilians and protesters, we managed to lock the runways at the airport and to prevent the landing of aircraft carrying mercenaries. I began to form defensive positions on the base and the airport against any possible attack from the forces of the tyrant. These positions were carried out by young protesters and civilians who volunteered to defend the base, and have been credited for the valuable disablement of aircraft which later raided the base and were not able to achieve their goals.

Here I would like to mention the role of these young heroes who volunteered from the first day. Some of them did not know anything about weapons and war, but I found they were insistent on defending the base and Benghazi.

I began teaching about the formation of defensive positions and training those who did not know anything about weapons. I was struck by their ability to learn at such a rapid pace. Those days created very strong friendships with them; I hope they continue forever.

In the successive days we started following what was happening in the cities of western Libya. Revolution was all over Libya, in most cities in the south and west like Zawia, Zintan, Misurata, the cities of the Nafusa Mountains, Tripoli and Sebha, but in each city or region there were special circumstances such as geographic location, the number of battalions in them, or the amount of available weapons and ammunition to the protesters. But the revolution and the resistance did not subside and the cities become liberated one city after the other.

In the month of March 2011, a large military convoy loaded with mercenaries, with around hundred tanks to back them up, headed towards the east of Jofra and from Sirte to Benghazi, with the task of regaining control of Benghazi and the whole eastern part of Libya by which the revolution would have been suppressed. They were armed with heavy weapons and the orders that had been issued to them by the tyrant were to kill, rape, burn, destroy and erase Benghazi from the map of the world. These tactics, which had been used by the tyrant throughout this revolution, were called "scorched earth tactics" – which meant total annihilation of anything in the way. But the land of Libya had never been sterile, and the proof of that is the birth of heroes who fought against this ruthless and evil war machine and somehow managed to stop and destroy it at the Benghazi city outskirts, before it further entered the city.

The news of progress of these convoys arrived, and it was necessary to take a decision whether to attack before they had reached the city. We started preparing for the attacks. It was not an easy decision to make. Everyone was excited, especially the hero pilot Al Mahdi Rasheed who was crying from the intensity of his enthusiasm to take off and attack. The only thing we were waiting for before launching the attack, was the NTC's final decision. On March 14, 2011 we began preparing the runway, clearing any obstructions and obstacles, making it ready for use again.

I went home around 6:00pm to take my wife to my parents' house, asking her to spend the night there, and I tried as hard as I could not to give away the fact that something was going on. I told her that I would return to my workplace in order to replace a colleague, while the truth was that it had been decided that on March 15th, the attacks on convoys would commence. I was not among the pilots, but it was my job was to arrange a safe takeoff and landing, hence I returned to work at 7:00pm.

At dawn on March 15, the first combat helicopter MI-35 took off from Benina air base in Benghazi, under the command of the Colonel Hussein Warfali, who had previously been dismissed from the air force due to health issues. He insisted on defending his city Benghazi, his people and the revolution.

The risk of this operation was immense.

Due to the absence of communications with Colonel Hussein, and the fact that the time estimated for his return (based on calculations of the plane's fuel reserves) had expired, my colleagues and I began to panic and assume the worst. After a while, I couldn't stand the suspense any longer, so I, along with my colleague Colonel Khalifa Boughrara, went outside to the runway, where Colonel Hussein was supposed to land. After a short period of time, we looked to the sky and suddenly we saw a small dot which later, thank God, turned out to be Colonel Hussein's plane. I looked at the overwhelming joy I felt inside of me, as the first sign of victory!

After that, the MIG-23s took off towards the convoys that were in the region of the city of Brega and between Ajdabiyeh and Awjila and went on to destroy them. The attacks continued till sunset. Before sunset, two MIG21s from Tobruk had joined us in order to aid us in repelling these convoys. The attacks continued for five days from dawn till sunset of March 19, when the rest of the columns of these battalions that had not been destroyed reached the outskirts of the city of Benghazi. At dawn on March 19, our aircraft resumed their attacks on the convoys. In the second wave of attacks, the enemy managed to shoot down two of our MIG 23s. The first plane was piloted by the hero martyr Colonel Mohammed Al Ageeli, while the hero martyr Colonel Fakhri Al Salabi and the hero martyr Colonel Al Mahdi Rasheed were piloting the other.

Regardless of them being my colleagues at work, they were also my dear friends. It was an irreparable and very painful loss, but what kept me from losing my spirit was the fact that they died as heroes and martyrs and that they saved thousands of lives as well as this revolution that had been desperately awaited for decades.

And on the ground, a battle at the western entrance to Benghazi was raging, where the young freedom fighters fought these convoys like lions, preventing them from invading and ravaging the city. Although the freedom fighters were heavily outnumbered, they were somehow able to repel and hold back these forces for so long until French jets intervened at 5:45pm local time. Security Council resolution 1973 had been passed and forces of the tyrant were forced to retreat. NATO took over the mission of enforcing the no-fly zone over Libyan skies and directly prevented a massacre and saved tens of thousands of innocent lives in the city of Benghazi from total annihilation and devastation.

This humanitarian aid and great moral support and friendly attitude, taken by the international community towards us, Libyans, will never be forgotten. We will never forget those who helped us in the liberation of our beloved Libya. It is our duty now to repaint the ugly image that had been painted by Gaddafi that had represented the Libyan people over the past 42 years. The time has come for the world to finally see the Libyans for what they really are, a wonderful and peaceful nation.

I Am What I Am Now Because Of What I Have Experienced

Cherry Mae O. Alvarez, Benghazi, Libya

I am a nurse, and I have been successful in my chosen field. One of my most unforgettable experiences was when I was included in the first batch of Overseas Filipino Worker (OFW) nurses that were sent to work in Libya. Every nurse dreams of going and working abroad, and that happened to be my chance. On April 1st, 2010, as I set foot on the sandy soil of Benghazi, I was full of mixed emotions. I was a novice OFW, and all I was thinking about was to work in the hospital where I had been assigned when I signed my contract back in the Philippines. I just wanted to earn money to send back to my family, to fulfil all my duties and responsibilities as a nurse, to learn the culture and traditions of the people, and, especially, to gain Libyan people's trust and make them believe that we are good nurses.

As time passed everything went well, even though there were many irregularities and promises made that were never kept even though they were stated in my contract. As a Filipino, a foreigner, I really tried hard to understand the Libyan ways and customs and to adapt myself, because I believe that I cannot change or interfere with the customs of the country I am in. I have to try to adjust myself and just go with it.

Living in a foreign land wasn't a bed of roses as some people thought. I shed many tears because of the fact that even a nurse like me, whose only goal was to work hard and to help people, faced discrimination and humiliation. I took every experience as a challenge to prove to my family that I was not wrong to choose to work in this country. I never told them how homesick I felt, or that I was so stressed and shocked with the culture that I couldn't eat or sleep very well. I had to face the fact that here I was and there was no turning back, so I had to move on. I was very lucky with the people that I worked with because they made things easier and less complicated for me, especially the doctors that I worked with in Neuro: Dr. Osama Al-Shaikhy and Dr. Salah Bushhaala.

A few days before the big day of February 17th, 2011, there were rumours going around the hospital that there would be a revolt against the government, but, honestly, I didn't take it seriously. I thought that it couldn't possibly happen because we all knew how hard the people were disciplined by their government. However, I was wrong and it did happen on that date in the evening.

The spark started with people shouting and chanting in the streets in the centre of Benghazi demanding their freedom from their ruler. They began to fight the government's security service. They ransacked the army barracks and burnt government vehicles and buildings. Gunfire and loud explosions could be heard clearly from the hospital. After a few minutes we heard the sounds of ambulance sirens and cars rushing to the hospital bringing patients suffering from gunshot wounds and multiple injuries. There were combinations of open fractures and traumatic amputations with large soft tissue wounds. Many had internal bleeding in the head and torso. But mostly there was a parade of dead bodies coming and coming from where the fighting was happening. This became the everyday scenario in the hospital from the time the revolution began.

When we heard that it was safe to go out and even go shopping, out of curiosity we visited the places where the fighting took place. We witnessed how the buildings, infrastructure and vehicles had been demolished by high powered firearms. We took pictures of these now historic places which will have their place in the history of Free Libya.

One of my most unforgettable experiences was when I was at my flat packing up my things because we were going to sleep at the hospital. Suddenly, out of nowhere, there was a loud noise of gunshots right on our doorstep. I was terrified and, in a panic, I ran into the bedroom with my friend Cathy and we hid in a cabinet for almost 30 minutes. We didn't know who was outside and all I could think of doing was hiding and praying. I was also crying when I remembered what I had seen on the news about women being sex slaves to mercenaries. I just surrendered myself to God. My flatmates, Vinjie and Carl, were holding knives just to be prepared in case someone broke down the door. I tried to contact my other flatmate JM who was on duty at the hospital, but, unfortunately, there was no answer because he was busy attending to the needs of all the people who needed emergency operations. After trying to call him several times, there was a knock on the door. It was our neighbour telling us not to be afraid, that we could go out as it was only our landlord testing his firearms! Whew, what a relief! I had thought it was the last day of our lives. The landlord did apologise for scaring us like that.

That same day, at the hospital, we were about to go to bed when we heard news that Benghazi was going to be bombed. This made me start panicking and crying again, but this time I hid under the bed instead of in a cabinet. The chief of the hospital told us to come out and not to be afraid because the hospital was highly secure.

My family was begging me to return home immediately for my own safety. They told me there were other places for me to work and continue my dreams. But I never thought twice about staying in Libya because I knew that this was the right situation for me to stay and help. I would practice my chosen career in Libya. The people of Libya needed me and they were close to my heart.

I believed that no matter where I am when it is my time to die, it is really my time to die. I also believed in the Libyan people, that they would and could win their battle for freedom and that was why we Filipino nurses gambled and were willing to sacrifice our lives to help them. As long as they need us, we will continue to help them and offer them our hands. We hope they will appreciate our services and that they will give us, justly, equal privileges and benefits.

I have experienced a lot in this war: no communication with my loved ones back home; being bothered, afraid, tired, nervous and uncertain; having no guarantee, even, that I would be alive the next day to continue my dreams; chaos everywhere; sleepless nights and even worse nightmares if I did sleep. But life must go on and I had no choice but to help myself to stand up and be strong and, especially, to stop crying. Facing up to the situation was the right decision for me, and now, when I reminisce, I think only a few people can survive this situation emotionally, physically and spiritually. I am blessed that I did and, right now, I am still surviving and continuing my journey until I find the purpose and reason I stayed.

That's it, a wartime job that became part of my career. Nursing doesn't only challenge our minds but also touches our hearts. I am so proud to be here and to be a part of Libyan history.

These Events Will Never Be Erased From My Memory

Dr. Agela A. Albadri, Consultant Physician, MBChB, MSC, MD
Hawari General Hosptal, Benghazi, Libya

Many are the great and proud moments in all revolutions and especially our revolution. I am not able to tell of all that I saw in my daily life during this revolution, even though much of it is of great importance, but these events will never be erased from my memory. However, it will be sufficient to mention just a few of the events that continually replay in my mind.

The first event illustrates how adamant the youth of Libya were for change, no matter how high the price. In the beginning of the uprising in Benghazi, when the youth began peaceful demonstrations in the streets, they were faced by regime forces armed with guns and live ammunition. Ambulances arrived at Hawari hospital, where I was working as a physician, transporting injured from these first clashes.

Among the first of the injured young men to arrive was a youth of about 20 years of age. His injury was minor and did not require admission to our hospital. I treated him and asked him why he had put himself in danger, facing live ammunition and taking part in an unequal fight with no clear outcome at the time. He surprised me with his clear and concise reply stating that they could no longer tolerate the situation in Libya, they must make a sacrifice for change and they were adamant that they would be victorious. The next day, the same young man was brought back to us again, this time with a more serious injury and he had to be admitted to our hospital. He was later sent abroad to finish his treatment. His second injury occurred at exactly the same location as the first, in front of Al Fadeel katiba in Al Berka, Benghazi.

The second incident that I would like to mention shows how great the revolutionaries' objections to the Gaddafi regime were, as were the objections of all Libyans. It also shows their generosity and kind-heartedness even towards those they considered their enemies. All these characteristics I personally witnessed in an embattled area of Libya known as Zintan. Some of my colleagues from Benghazi and I went to the Nafusa Mountains and the south of Tunisia, to a place called Tataween, in an attempt to aid and help our brothers there during the month of May, 2011.

The ambulances in the western mountains carried both wounded revolutionaries and wounded Gaddafi forces. At the same time as we arrived at the hospital in Zintan, an ambulance arrived bringing injured revolutionaries from a fierce battle in the field. This same ambulance also brought in an uninjured officer of Gaddafi's army as a prisoner. I personally witnessed the way this officer and his colleagues were treated by the revolutionaries and the heads of the clans of Zintan, as they were in the close vicinity of the hospital, which was prepared to help in any way needed.

The prisoners were treated in exactly the same manner as the revolutionaries in regard to medical treatment and kindness. The Gaddafi officer was given water and a chair to sit on. This enraged one of the revolutionaries, but he was calmed by the elders when they explained that the officer was a brother of the revolutionaries and he had been forced by the Gaddafi military to shoot at the population. As this was happening, there was a member of the foreign media documenting all these events. I was sorry that I was unable at the time to fully explain what was happening because of how busy I was tending to the injured.

Al Haja Rajaa Ismail Zubrtay
Mother of Freedom Fighters

Al Haja Rajaa Zubrtay's son Abduladeem Nashad, Ajdabiyah

At the beginning of the February 17 revolution in Libya, the former regime did everything possible to end this glorious revolution by any means: shelling cities and killing Libyans in every city in Libya. No city was spared from its tyranny. Among these cities was the city of Ajdabiyah.

When Ajdabiyeh was heavily shelled, it caused the displacement of many of its people: women, children and the elderly. The men remained in the city to defend it; Al Haja Rajaa remained also. They nick-named her Mother of Thuwar, or Mother of Freedom Fighters.

She refused to leave the city in which she had been born in 1951 and had lived all her life. She prepared Molotov cocktails, and kept a hand grenade and gelato (a type of explosive used in fishing) in her house to defend herself in case Gaddafi's forces broke into it.

She cooked lunch and dinner for the Freedom Fighters. She was always pushing the Freedom Fighters to eat more to become stronger to fight the tyrant's soldiers. She continued to visit thuwar in their barracks to distribute homemade bread, tanur, well known in Libya.

Tanur, Libyan bread

Libya free   Um Thuwar

Mother of Thuwar is a member of several associations and charities, and among these associations, she is a member of the Foundation of "Sheikha Mozah" – Ajdabiyah.

The Story of Libby

Libby, Benghazi, Libya

I first arrived in Libya with my Libyan husband and three children twenty years ago. Being English, the culture shock was overwhelming, so it took a while for me to get over missing my family and the green fields of England before I could even begin to assess the people and the country I had come to live in.

At first I didn't really notice the lack of freedom of speech, the underlying tension – I guess I was busy trying to adjust, tend to my children (who were also adjusting) and get on with living. I did notice that if I spoke about Gaddafi, in any context, people tended to ignore me, not make any comments or pretend that I hadn't said anything. I'm not stupid, I did know the politics of the country, but coming from a place where you could virtually say anything you wanted and voice opinions, I found it really difficult to get my head around the unresponsiveness of people. I did notice the state of the country – the roads were in a state and the sewage and drainage systems were almost non-existent. There seemed to be a lot of poor people around, but also a lot of really rich people as well. Projects never got finished – over thirty years to finish and open a hospital (Benghazi Medical Centre)?

I began to teach, and my first job was teaching people in a Korean company, so I learnt from them how frustrating and difficult it was to try to do business as a foreign company in Gaddafi's Libya. Later I taught Libyans and then I realised just how damaging this regime was for the Libyan people. I taught people of all ages – some obviously pro-Gaddafi and most of them were very nice people. But it was the younger generation that impressed me. There were so many of them who wanted to say so much, but they couldn't. I don't mean politically – they wanted to write songs, poetry, express different ideas, but they suppressed themselves because they were suppressed . I'm not surprised that the younger generation stood up and voiced their anger.

This war was not the first time that I had seen tanks in the streets of Benghazi, or heard gunfire as people were chased from building to building, but who do you say anything to? You couldn't say anything in Libya, and when I used to try to get people to listen in England – nobody cared, or they just thought I was exaggerating. I don't think people who live in a free society (and I know there are people who will scoff at my term "free") really understand what it's like to live in fear of saying the wrong thing to the wrong person. Thousands of people have disappeared and have never been seen again.

I also remembered the sanctions – life was so hard then for most of the people. The Gaddafis never suffered under those sanctions, only the Libyan people, and the poorer they were the more they suffered.

When the demonstrations began in Benghazi, I never thought for one second that these people stood a chance against such a brutal regime. There was a national army in Libya, but only on paper – these soldiers were ill-equipped and didn't have professional training. It shows their bravery that protesters kept demonstrating knowing the brutal nature of these people. I remember standing on the roof of my house watching smoke rising from different areas as people set fire to different government buildings, but only these buildings were attacked and the buildings of well known and hated members of the regime. It was very upsetting when we heard that snipers were killing people as they demonstrated, and this is a fact. The hospitals became more and more desperate as they tried to cope with the growing number of dead and injured. These people had no guns, they were not armed as some people have stated outside – they were just people with huge grievances.

Then came the UN resolution to protect civilians. This was a great relief, but I was really concerned because there were two days before this would be implemented – and I was sure that Gaddafi would take advantage of this time. I watched as the Libyan people celebrated ecstatically, praying that I was wrong and nothing would happen. But it did. The next morning I heard explosions and the sound of jets flying overhead. Only one or two were sent at a time, but that doesn't mean it was any less terrifying. Then came the sound of anti-aircraft fire – and amazingly, because most of these men had never used anti-aircraft guns before, during the course of two days a couple of planes were shot down. And, as we know, some Libyan pilots refused to bomb their own people, parachuted out and crashed their planes. Later they were sent without parachutes to prevent them doing this. Still some took the risk of dropping their bombs in the sea and landing at the airport – really brave people.

The second night as I lay in bed I could hear explosions in the distance and smell an acrid horrible smell. I went to bed fully dressed because I had a bad feeling about what was going to happen. Impossible to sleep listening to the explosions getting closer and the smell getting stronger. Then suddenly there was a very loud explosion – not that near but not that far either. Everyone was awake, but what could you do? We didn't know what was happening – all communication systems were down, but we did still have television. At seven o'clock in the morning there was no news about Libya. What was happening?

I made myself a cup of tea and went outside to drink it. The next thing that happened was most probably one of the scariest moments in my life. Suddenly there was a tremendous noise – I thought that we were being machine-gunned from the air – the house was shaking and vibrating. Three missiles rattled over the roof of our house. I never imagined that this was what it felt and sounded like – I can't imagine what it would have felt like if they had hit. I don't know where the tanks were that fired those missiles, but it proves that they were just firing indiscriminately – I live in a residential area. The rest of the day was spent listening to the news that tanks had entered Benghazi, but these few tanks were taken out by the special forces army and civilians in Benghazi. These special forces were the soldiers of Benghazi who were previously given orders to attack the civilians who were protesting outside of the Benghazi army camp. They refused to carry out these orders, and defected and attacked the army camp in Benghazi, armed only with Kalashnikovs – they didn't have heavy weapons or tanks – (Gaddafi had made sure of that) and they entered the camp with the civilians. Then came the shooting. People loyal to Gaddafi had risen up at the same time, but they were met with resistance from the army here. Many of them were shot or escaped or went into hiding. So I sat in my house listening to the gunfire just outside, watching television. The meeting to implement the resolution in France – Sarkozy and Cameron so slowly walking up the steps. Screaming at the television "get a move on, we're dying here". Then some more bad news; my nephew had been shot by a sniper and died. He'd been married for six months and left a young pregnant wife. I ventured out later as the gunfire had subsided and went to his funeral. The day had been surreal and now the heartbreak of this. What could I say to my sister-in-law – her youngest son had just died. What could I say to his young widow? How would I have felt if it had been one of my sons? I still choke up when I remember that time.

The next morning, I think it was about eleven o'clock, we heard the sound of jets flying overhead. We rushed outside and saw a squadron of jets flying very low and heading west. I didn't feel scared, but I was curious. Later, my son told me that NATO had destroyed a huge convoy heading in our direction. If it had reached us we would have been finished – it was bad enough with the few tanks that had entered. It is said that ignorance is bliss and this is so true, because if I had known what was coming I think I would have gone crazy.

Then the young lads started to head west in pick-ups – off to liberate Libya. I could cry now when

I think how naive everyone was to think it could be so easy, and so many young lives were lost for nothing. Nobody imagined that Gaddafi had the arsenal of weapons that he did have, but we should have known. He had forty-two years to prepare for this. I think one of the most chilling things was listening to him ranting and threatening people (especially Benghazi) on television, because one thing that Libyans know through experience is that he never made idle threats. So when he threatened to flatten Benghazi, we knew that he meant it. He might have seemed like a clownish figure to people outside, but they had no idea of the fear that he was still capable of instilling in the Libyan people.

Despite all of this, I have to say that the air in Benghazi seemed to change overnight. Something was definitely "in the air" it was as if the Libyan people were emerging from a giant nightmare – which they were. They were actually smiling (they really didn't do a lot of that) and slowly, or not so slowly, they began to express themselves in writing, singing and painting.

Of course the war dragged on. Thousands of young men went missing in Tripoli and any town or city that hadn't been liberated. Many still haven't been accounted for. And the freedom fighters kept on dying and getting injured. All because one selfish, arrogant family couldn't or wouldn't admit that the Libyan people didn't want them anymore.

Now Libya is free and the people are trying to find the path to democracy. From what I have seen so far, they will succeed, because Libya has remained united despite what some pessimists say. Of course there's a long, hard road ahead. People can't live for forty-two years under a tyrant with no proper government, no self-respect, no money, no proper healthcare system, corruption on a major scale and suddenly act like a country that has had democracy for a hundred years.

If the world gives the Libyan people a chance, the world will benefit from these people.

The main entry to the katiba Al Fadeel in Benghazi February 21, 2011

The Injured Mind of a Freedom Fighter
Adam Mohamed Ramadan Amer, Beida, Libya

The story is written by Adam's brother Khames Mohamad Ramadan Amer,
Sunday, October 9, 2011 at 10:15am in Hawari General Hospital, Benghazi

Adam Mohamed Ramadan Amer was born in 1972 and he is unmarried as are a lot of Libyan men his age because they were subjected to the unfairness of Gaddafi repressive regime.

When the uprising began in Libya, the people of Beida came out to protest peacefully for a change in government and they were met with live ammunition.

On February 17-18, 2011, Adam saw how the dictator's soldiers killed 17 young men aged between 16 and 25 years whose injuries were to the head and chest. After more than 400 young men were injured in the city of Beida, he realized the intentions of the regime's soldiers. After he heard that mercenaries and soldiers had been sent to kill and vandalize the city, he couldn't control himself, so he and many other young men confronted them.

Adam's father is a retired old man and his mother is getting old too, plus he has seven brothers who all came out to protest against the 42 years of unfairness. Adam was part of the Ali Hassan Al Jaber Brigade. His vehicle was hit by a rocket and Adam was hit in the head, and now suffers from memory loss.

While I was writing this letter, I received information that Adam's cousin fell in Sirte and another of his cousins also died, leaving a widow and seven young daughters – the oldest of whom is twelve.

All of these sacrifices, Adam and all the other revolutionaries, were for the freedom of Libya.

The young men of Libya demonstrated for freedom and democracy and for a better life and future. Even when the regime tried to blackmail and pay people to stop protesting they never stopped because they wanted a better life with freedom and not money.

We are happy that we can tell the world that freedom is the most important thing.

Translation of the Arabic text: Breaking news: Al Jazeera cameraman Ali Hassan Al Jaber was martyred after the team of the channel was exposed to an armed ambush in the Hawari area near Benghazi.
(The Al Jazeera team was returning from Sloug on March 12, 2011.)
Adam was a member of the Ali Hassan Al Jaber Brigade, which was named in honor of the martyred cameraman. In another story in our book, Dr Anas Toweir tells of attending to Ali Hassan Al Jaber in Hawari General Hospital.

War Through The Eyes Of A Child

picas 70, Portugal

When I was a young child in the South of Angola, I experienced something I wish no child ever had to. It was Christmas time in 1975, and father promised me help to build a small brick house in the backyard. I was waiting for him to come home in the afternoon, but he never did. Instead I heard what I thought were fireworks and my mother came out and hurried me into the house with my older sister. My mother closed all the windows and ordered us to go into the bathroom, as this was the innermost part of the house, and the safest. From all over we heard shots and small explosions. Suddenly we were in the middle of a civil war, between FNLA and UNITA, and our house was on the frontline.

During the day my mother crawled to the kitchen to bring us old bread, and that's what we ate for three days and three nights. The nights were awful. Turning the light on would mean an almost certain salvo of automatic weapons fire, so we had to stay in the dark. During one of the nights when the firing was particularly intense, an RPG blew up the corner of our kitchen, and my sister began to cry. I wanted her to stop, so I told her not to be worried because I was with her and wouldn't allow anything bad to happen.

On the third day, the fighting stopped, as one of the parties had defeated the other. What used to be my playground was full of empty shells. That afternoon my father returned safe and sound, but he had to give his Land Rover as a bribe. It was quite a joy for me to have him home! But in the next days I was not able to sleep well. About one or two weeks later a tank column from a neighboring country came to our town and I was very happy because it meant safety. We all went out to the streets to greet the soldiers. To me they looked like knights in shining armor. But one month later they retreated and we had to run. When they retreated, we had to leave for Walvis Bay in Namibia, just with our clothes on. We travelled a 1000 miles by fishing boat, women, sick men and children. I couldn't eat a thing for days; I didn't know what was worse: the seasickness or the smell of saltwater intermixed with the engine oil. This dark chapter of my life, deeply marked by blood, is etched within my mind.

I knew things would be much more difficult in Libya than in Tunisia or Egypt. After I watched Gaddafi's February 22nd speech on Al Jazeera English, my memories flooded into my mind again. My instant recollection was the old instinct: when your children are threatened, the immediate thing you want to do is to protect them — it doesn't matter who the protectors are. So I thought that Western countries should protect the Libyan children — otherwise the Libyans would ask for protection from other groups, no matter who they were.

On February 26, Mr. Ali Ibrahim Emdored, Libyan Ambassador to my home country, Portugal, cut ties with Gaddafi. On that same day the United Nations Security Council, where Portugal has a non-permanent seat, unanimously adopted resolution 1970, imposing an arms embargo on Libya. UNSC also then began its initial deliberations on helping the Libyan people, and the possibility of implementing a no-fly zone. In both cases, the contribution of the United States would be of paramount importance. Without it, the task would have been practically impossible.

At that point, I thought things would go easier: with all the international pressure, Gaddafi would eventually give up.

Then the Gaddafi counteroffensive started on March 6, and suddenly his regime's forces were gaining ground towards Benghazi again. I remembered my childhood, and how the children in Benghazi would live through the same scenarios I had faced.

Meanwhile, the Libyan foreign minister, Moussa Koussa, visited three European capitals trying to break the isolation imposed on the regime. One of these cities was Lisbon. I was worried about the position of the Portuguese government, because it had very good relations with President Hugo Chavez of Venezuela, and Chavez was Gaddafi's best friend. In fact if it were for the oil it would be better for Portugal to do nothing. But Portuguese Foreign Minister José Amado, refused to officially receive Moussa Koussa, and the meeting was held in a hotel. Portugal kept its commitment with the international community and clearly stated that "Gaddafi must go."

I was so relieved! Not for long, though. On the March 16, Ajdabiya had fallen to pro-Gaddafi forces, and Misrata was under heavy attack. I turned to the websites of both the English and the Portuguese language media leaders, and posted there in favor of Western intervention, but the communities in general seemed very hostile towards the idea. Then I went to Al Jazeera English Libya blog, where the mood was totally different. I registered there and begun to post as "picas70".

At the time there were rumors a no-fly zone resolution was in preparation by France and the United Kingdom for the United Nations Security Council, but judging by previous UNSC votes I didn't expect it to pass. I was particularly concerned with Russia, China, Brazil and South Africa, although I expected given the excellent relations between Portugal and Brazil, that Portugal could influence the latter not to vote against it.

Against all odds the resolution was approved on March 17, without a single vote against it! The UNSCR carried a historical phrase: "Authorizing 'All Necessary Measures' to Protect Civilians". It was quite a joy! President Sarkozy stated after the vote that there were planes already in the air. But the question became: how would Gaddafi react? And if he didn't stop the attack on Benghazi, would NATO act fast enough?

After the first ceasefire declared by Gaddafi's government on March 18, and before the air strikes started, Gaddafi gave his last television interview to Portuguese reporter Paulo Dentinho of RTP TV. Portugal was now heading the Sanctions Committee against Libya stated in UNSCR1970. In that interview, Gaddafi restated his usual: all his people loved him, and the ones who turn in their arms would be forgiven, and that he was ready to negotiate, and so on. I was very apprehensive.

The next day, the reason for my apprehension unfolded as I watched horrified on AJE the attack on Benghazi, the MIG23 shot down, and the most-asked question on AJE Libya blog was: "What are they waiting for?" The attack was stopped by Freedom Fighters from Benghazi, as a Portuguese TV reporter stated: "Here they have smelled the sweet smell of freedom." As news came of the first air strikes and later the images of the destroyed tank column we could breathe again.

As Gaddafi loyalists were slowly being pushed away from Benghazi, I thought it was safe — my main concern became Misurata. But on April 9 Gaddafi troops were again in Ajdabiya. I couldn't understand how that was possible and feared the worst, as Gaddafi's forces continued to advance westward too. I feared that, as happened when I was a child, the international community would eventually give up. I wrote on AJE Libya blog: "How can I look myself in the mirror if the international community let the Libyan people down?" The trolls rejoiced, and one of them answered me: "Break the mirror." They were very enthusiastic as it seemed that even with NATO intervention Gaddafi would reach Benghazi. As Gerhard Heinz latter explained, this was a trap to make Gaddafi forces concentrate resources in the east, thus alleviating the western fronts, from where the attack on Tripoli would come. It was a planned stalemate.

With the eastern front stabilized the worries came from Misurata and the mountains, where living conditions of the civilian population became dire. Each day on the AJE Libya blog we faced the desperate situation in Misurata and in the mountain villages. Then on May 10 Freedom Fighters took Misurata Airport, and it was a great day for AJE blog, while the trolls couldn't believe it. In the next days, FF steadily advanced on the outskirts gradually relieving the city from the attacks it faced for nearly three months.

Now the focus changed to the Nafusa Mountains where many water wells had been poisoned with diesel oil. We even tried to design a simple water treatment system to deal with it, in the Koussa.info blog. Each day we looked to mcc's maps, on Koussa.info, to see FF advances in the mountains, while the mainstream media kept talking about a stalemate. At that time, thanks to Gerhard Heinz, we had already understood that the attack on Tripoli would come from the mountains and Misurata/Zliten.

After many Tweets of uprisings in Tripoli, and doubts about Tripoli residents' loyalties claimed by media reporters at the Rixos, I must say the fall of Tripoli wasn't a surprise, only the time and speed of it weren't expected.

With Gaddafi on the run, the mood of Trolls on AJE Blog changed. Now the outcome of the revolution was well known. It is a shame that it would still take so many lives before it was over.

Salheen Taher Al Jwher, a 16 year old medical student who lived through many turbulent days in 2011, photographed in the port area of a peaceful Benghazi, late October, 2011

> *"Think not of those who are slain in Allah's way as dead.*
> *Indeed they are living in the presence of their Lord and are provided for."*
> *The Holy Qur'an*

Kais Alhilali: Martyr Painter
born in 1979 and martyred on March 20, 2011

Naima Al Obeidi, Benghazi, Libya

Kais was born in 1979 and he and his four brothers and sister lived with me after I divorced their father. He was my second oldest son. His brother Hussein had to give up his studies (he was studying at the Faculty of Engineering in Bani Walid) in order to take care of the family, and Kais left his studies as well in order to help his older brother so, unfortunately, due to the lack of funding, they weren't able to complete their education.

Kais supported us by doing various jobs such as working in a restaurant, at construction sites and in many freelancing activities. When his elder brother Hussein died on the 4th of February, 2004, at the age of 26 years, May God have mercy upon him, Kais took responsibility for caring and providing for us, as his father had remarried.

Kais loved to draw since he was a child. He drew wherever he was able to: on the walls of his room and on the bed made of wood, on paper and on many other surfaces. When he was in school, he drew a drawing for the annual exhibition, which is held at the end of every school year. This made his principal, the late Mr. Ahmad Al Snussi, notice his incredible talent. So he took Kais to Ahmad Anwar, his neighbor, who was working in the local radio station and who hosted Kais in a program called "The Best Times". Kais then drew a painting of a soldier who was holding a rifle and was standing with one foot on a rock. He was very creative and most of the time he didn't need a picture or a photograph to prompt

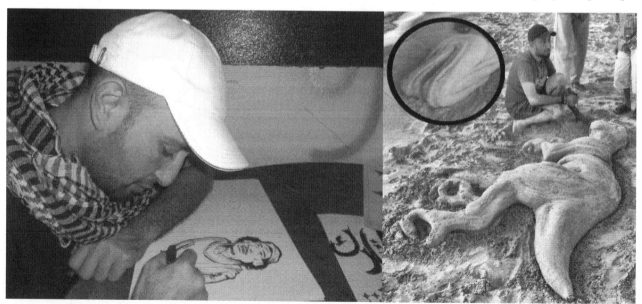

him as he drew or painted as he generally relied on his own imagination.
Kais loved animals very much. His favorite animal was a horse and he loved to draw horses as well.

He could draw a horse starting from one of its legs and finishing the whole horse in one line, without stopping. He drew horses in different positions: running, eating, and with both front legs up in the air. He also liked to draw other animals, especially lions and tigers. When he was only in 2nd grade, he often drew, with a sponge technique, various cartoon characters such as the popular UFO robot character named "Grendizer".

Despite the fact that people weren't very interested in his talents, he kept on drawing and painting in various places such as shops, football clubs, restaurants, resorts and schools but the pay was very low, hence it was not enough for supporting an entire family. So I decided to help him. I started working as a teacher in a private school, teaching Drawing and Handicraft. My salary was extremely low, approximately 120 Libyan dinars a month (less than 100 US dollars) but after a couple of years I was fired from the school because I didn't have a degree in Art. I have got the social help for divorced women, but it is only 60 Libyan dinars per month!

When Kais received a message via SMS in which he was asked to attend a demonstration which was to take place on the 17th of February, 2011, I said to him: "There will not be a day of the 17th". But with great insight he replied: "There is no Eid without Kabira".

(*Kabira is the day before Eid. Eid al-Adha, or Eid al-Kabir as it is named in North African countries, is the festival of sacrifice that honors Abraham's willingness to obey God even if it meant sacrificing his son. Translated, Kais' reply to his mother was: "There is no festival without sacrifice".*)

Kais drawing on a roundabout March 20, 2011
He was killed later that night at 11pm

Kais drawing on the monument The Pipes of the
Artificial River – his last drawing March 20, 2011

Since the beginning of the revolution Kais was frequently away from home, along with my other son Adam, who also still lived with me. They went to the Courthouse and carried banners that supported the revolution. They also helped with the burial of the martyrs who were killed by Gaddafi's thugs.

A group of friends, of whom Kais was one, founded a charitable organization called "Martyrs of the Revolution of 17th February" and collected donations for the families of the martyrs, for the transportation of the wounded to Egypt for further treatment, and for helping the people from all over Libya who had fled their homes because of the fighting and come to Benghazi. He actively participated in the demonstrations and he drew various caricatures of Gaddafi and his sons on banners and distributed them among the protesters so that they could raise them in the air as they demonstrated. He hoped that justice will defeat the darkness that had been spread by a regime that didn't care about its people. He spread that idea through his drawings and paintings. He also drew the ideas of other people who, like him, wished to express their feelings of freedom.

The 20th of March was the date when Kais was martyred. At around 11pm he was hit in the neck and head at a checkpoint made in the neighborhood named Tabalino. He was in a grey car which had taken him from his house that afternoon to draw a caricature of Gaddafi on the pavement of the roundabout and to write on the monument, the Pipes of the Artificial River, these words: "The Square of Misurata's Martyrs".

May God have mercy upon Kais, our martyr hero, who was not afraid to stand up to the tyrant and to mock him.

My beloved son, I am very proud of you and so are your brothers and your entire family. It is because of you that I performed the Hajj and visited Our Prophet Mohammad's (Peace Be Upon Him) Mosque and returned home satisfied. I hope I will perform the Hajj again but with no martyr. All your life you wished that the world would recognize your art and now in your grave you have become a famous hero and a martyr and your name will be remembered in our history forever. God Almighty has heard my prayers and killed the tyrant and his sons Saif Al Arab and Khamis and Mu'tassem and hopefully soon I will see the death of his son Saif Al Islam and the rest of his children.

Your mother

Naima Al Obeidi

Postscript

On March 25ᵗʰ 2011 The Australian newspaper reported the murder of Libyan street artist and revolutionary Kais Alhilali, and in the accompanying story included the following details of his life. Kais was murdered an hour after finishing a caricature of Gaddafi on a Benghazi roundabout. He was one of 25 young activists to begin agitating for change in the lead up to February 17. They called themselves the "Furious Nation". On February 20 Kais took part in storming the city barracks, painting Gaddafi hung next to a two fingered victory salute on the walls during the fight.

After reading the story of the painter who charged into a fight with his paint brushes, Australian performance poet Royce wrote "an angel for Kais Alhilali" to remember Kais. The title is a reference to British street artist Banky's tribute piece, "Ozone's Angel" dedicated to 19 year-old graffiti writer Ozone who had been killed by an underground train in Barking, East London on January 12th 2007. A copy of "an angel for Kais Alhilali" was delivered to Kais' mother and printed in a Benghazi newspaper through the efforts of AJE bloggers and their contacts. It is re-printed here with the author's permission.

an angel for Kais Alhilali

according to the article
he titled his final instructions

what if i die?

pre-wrote an obituary

asked us to
cross out the unnecessary words

stop
rewind the tape
let us retrace final steps and strokes
walk the crimson red drip trail
left on the feathered wings of an angel for Kais Alhilali

his Libya grows in that angel's halo
freed by storms brewed in tea cups
and thrown into the laps of tyrants

LET THEM SCREAM

the streets of his city filled with the rhythm of the unheard
the constant beat of a thousand angry footsteps
a thousand angry hands
angry eyes
angry mouths
ten thousand angry fingers curled into fists
raised to the sky
protesting the sound of gunshots
the crunch of metal on bone
not even bullets could stop his furious nation

he painted hushed whispers
those well kept secrets once stuffed under mattresses
hung them on the walls in the sunshine
but the regime wanted to silence his brushes
tear out the bristles with his last breath

check point
point blank
gun shot

a life stolen
shoplifted
walked past security
hidden under jackets worn by shadows

but the paints that make these pictures

DO NOT KNOW HOW TO BE QUIET
gaddafi hangs from the walls of benghazi now
and in those last lines
his friends found the answer to his question:

if i should die?
start riots

and if i should die?
START RIOTS

AND IF I SHOULD DIE?
START RIOTS

The Good, The Evil And The Disinformation

Ingolf Dahl, Sweden

How did I get into this? I have no connection to Libya. No friends, no relatives have ever been there. The closest I have come is when I met a researcher, a Palestinian, who had studied in Libya, and had been forced to view the execution of some of his fellow students. He shuddered when the name of Gaddafi was mentioned. He got "Final exit" stamped into his passport when he left Libya stateless after his studies, and I think he was happy with that. Now he is a Swedish citizen, and that made it possible for him to get a job in Saudi Arabia.

I am a physicist in my sixties. I am a family man with a wife, four children and two grandchildren, trying to take care of my family, our house and our garden. I do some mathematics as a hobby. In the autumn of 2010 I became interested in the WikiLeaks story, and started to follow it in the Guardian and in other places on the web, as I found Swedish media dull, slow, bad and biased. Thus, I was well accustomed to using the web for information when the Arab Spring started with the revolutions in Tunisia and Egypt, and then in Libya.

The conflict in Libya is special in a certain way. It is exceptionally simple to see which side is evil and which side is good. In many other conflicts, both sides are evil to some extent, but both sides can often give some reasonable arguments for their case. The Libyan conflict was started by the Gaddafis showing their inhumane side. They have managed to perform crimes against humanity and break laws of war systematically. Proofs have been presented showing that these crimes have been ordered and sanctioned at the highest level.

The Freedom Fighters have of course not behaved like angels all the time – that is impossible with such a diverse set of people – but there seems to be a common ambition to play fair and to protect civilians as far as possible. So it is not difficult to decide between the evil and the good side.

To be neutral in a conflict like this is a good starting point as long as too little is known, but when more information is available, we might quote Bishop Desmond Tutu: "If you are neutral in situations of injustice, you have chosen the side of the oppressor. If an elephant has its foot on the tail of a mouse and you say that you are neutral, the mouse will not appreciate your neutrality."

In the Libyan conflicts, as in all war, it is said that truth is the first victim. I am always cheated by propaganda lies, but some things I have learnt during this Libyan war. Most of all, I have learnt that lies are often told simply without details. To lie in a detailed way requires professionals. I feel that I have no protection against professional liars.

In Swedish we have a word "grötrim", which according to the dictionary can be translated as "little rhyming verse made up when eating rice pudding on Christmas". Here a "grötrim" about disinformation that I wrote and posted on an Al Jazeera blog:

The war in Libya and disinformation

Truth is always the victim of war
but we are blogging like never before.

But we are not more than a small little cog,
that almost get lost in the media fog.

Propaganda, wishful thinking.

Something is said while eyes are winking.

What is true and what is false,
what is foxtrot, what is waltz?

I try to follow the war on Twitter,
there are some pearls but also some litter.

Is Khamis dead, is Brega free?
Which of Gaddafi's men will flee?

And all agents from abroad
this we know is not a fraud.

If you are a tourist from Belarus
with Sirtean girls you should not make fuss.

In Tripoli was there an airplane crash?
Is the tale true, or is it just trash?

That Younis was murdered was a real shame
but it still is not known who is to blame.

Now listen to what G's TV says
but find the truth in other ways!

From freedom of speech and from truth it is free,
the fourteen channels on Gaddafi's TV

The color of Moon will turn to blue
before they say a thing that's true!

That what is wrong is turned into right
when it is sent through a Nile satellite!

When he as bandit keeps might with force
he distributes lies as "official source".

All the victims that G has caught
and all the mines that he has bought

cause not even a whisper in the media stream,
I think it is true, and I feel I will SCREAM!

*"What is true and what is false,
what is foxtrot, what is waltz?"*

What indeed! Gaddafi, far away in Tripoli, may not have realised the extent of the wreckage of his forces in the east in quite the way it was seen on the ground after a French fighter jet fired on and destroyed the Gaddafi advance on Benghazi, at 4:45pm on March 19, 2011.

The Importance of Brega

From the Editors

The little coastal town of Brega emerged as pivotal in the struggle for Libyan freedom. Because of its oil refinery it has long held strategic value. In addition to Ras Lanuf, Tobruk, Sarir and Az Zawiya, it is one of only five oil refineries in Libya. Once the Freedom Fighters captured Brega and Ras Lanuf, Gaddafi was left with just Az Zawiya to fuel his war machine. And because Az Zawiya rose up early and strongly against him, its operations were disrupted by the raging war.

Brega exchanged hands four times in 2011. Holding Brega had not only strategic value for Gaddafi but also enormous psychological value, especially after his defeat at Misurata. His savage efforts to destroy Misurata thwarted, he seemed still to cling to his last ditch plan to divide the country into two parts, but keep Brega and Ras Lanuf in his pocket. That is where he drew his line in the sand. That is where he concentrated what was left of his elite forces after his forces were repelled in Benghazi on March 19th. That is where he sent his son, "general of generals", Mutassim Gaddafi.

Gaddafi spared nothing in fortifying and defending Brega. He took what was left of the Khamis Brigade after the battles for Benghazi and Misurata were lost, and threw it into Brega. His Belorussian military advisors made sure the troops were dug in and all approaches to the city booby trapped with tens of thousands of anti-personnel and anti-armor mines. His best and deepest bunker was hidden in Brega, and he fired his SCUD missiles from there as his troops were being forced out.

Realizing Brega's importance to Gaddafi allowed NATO and the Freedom Fighters to turn his strength into his weakness and ultimate downfall. If Gaddafi ever realized that Brega was a trap, his realization came too late. With Brega's relative remoteness from Tripoli, NATO used its air supremacy to ensure that Brega's troops could not easily be reinforced. It became a waiting game of attrition. The challenge was to hold back the Freedom Fighters eager to free their brethren while the allied gunships and bombers slowly whittled down the numbers of the loyalist troops.

To the backdrop of the international media's "stalemate" narrative, the Freedom Fighters probed Brega's defenses every couple of weeks, testing whether or not they could advance with a minimum loss of lives. Finally the strength of the Gaddafi troops was spent and, even though they were not yet completely routed, the tide had turned. The next challenge was to clear the thousands of mines that Gaddafi's troops had laid, so that the Freedom Fighters could advance. The task of mine clearing fell on Colonel Saleh Faraj Muhammad Younis and his company. Under constant enemy sniper and artillery fire, and armed with nothing more than metal sticks, household tools and infinite bravery, he and his men risked life and limb to clear paths for their brothers. They did a spectacular job.

Hidden in Colonel Saleh's story are the grueling, nerve-wrecking hours spend disarming tens of thousands of anti-personal and anti-tank mines. The photos tell the story! Brega and Libya were won for freedom because of incredible men like Colonel Saleh, his colleagues, fellow retired officers, and his company.

Battle for Brega

Colonel Saleh Faraj Muhammad Younis Alagouri, Benghazi, Libya

In the name of God the Merciful and the blessings and peace showered upon our Master Muhammad, his family and companions, God give mercy to our martyrs and grant our wish for the speedy recovery of our wounded and the return of the missing.

This account tells the story of some of the heroes of the 17 February Revolution.

I, Colonel Saleh Faraj Muhammad Younis Alagouri, was born in 1960 in Sloug. My specialization is in the field of engineering. I graduated from the Military College in 1981. I obtained the training for the command of an engineering company and engineering equipment, and the postgraduate courses for command officers in 1991.

After the collapse of the attack on the city of Benghazi – that is, the collapse of the attack made by the forces now known as the convoy which was defeated on the 19th of March, 2011 – the dictator's forces started to concentrate in the city of Ajdabiyah and the attempts of the Freedom Fighters (FF) to free the city began. It was found that there was a minefield next to the high voltage electricity pole, Number 140, which is situated before the eastern gate, one kilometer before the city. With the grace of God, we were able to remove this minefield, which was an obstacle to the delivery of electricity to the city of Ajdabiyah.

Then we started doing fortifying engineering to defend the city of Ajdabiyah, but the National Army did not have any equipment. We were supplied with private heavy equipment by the citizens of this region. Our work enabled the FF to gather. As well, it deprived Gaddafi's forces of the ability to shoot on the city, which they had been doing repeatedly in order to destabilize the stability and displace the citizens.

We began to prepare for the Liberation of Brega and started to advance. Then there was an unexpected announcement from Major General Abdel-Fattah Younis, declaring that 40,000 mines were planted and this was disrupting the attack. We, as active military engineers of the engineering corps, formed a company called "Engineering Company 17" and another company was formed by the FF and retired military engineers who joined us in big numbers. They all declared that the mines should not be an impediment to the rebels and started to advance towards Brega from three axes: Imrir Qabs, Al Arbaeen and the road servicing the artificial river.

Imrir Qabs is a small village by the sea and is also the name of a very beautiful area. The villagers had suffered very much under Gaddafi's forces. When the battles started between the FF and Gaddafi's forces, the village was in the middle and it was terrifying for the villagers. When the FF entered the village, they helped the villagers to leave because Gaddafi's forces continued to shell the village.

Al Arbaeen, meaning "40", is named because it is situated 40 kilometers from Ajdabiyah. It is also a very small village. It was fortified by the FF as soon as they had the opportunity to do this, so that Gaddafi's forces could not come closer to Ajdabiyah.

The road servicing the artificial river is the road running parallel to the main road from Ajdabiyah to Brega. It is used only for heavy trucks working on, and maintaining, Gaddafi's project named the Great

Man Made River, but Libyans never use Gaddafi's title of the "Great Man Made River", calling it only the artificial river.

Map of the Brega Minefields   *Col. Saleh and Engineering Company 17 Over a Map of the the Brega Minefields*

These three places were the starting points for our work of clearing mines to enable the FF to reach Brega.

The soldiers, the FF and the retired engineers sometimes worked under bombardment as they secured these areas for a concentration of forces and built earth mounds. Together, we secured the route of the FF forces as they progressed to the city of Brega. We removed 22,000 mines. They were M/A and M/D types. The M/A (mudad-ashas) mines were small AP (anti-personal) mines made in Brazil. They were made of plastic and could not be detected easily, so they were very dangerous. The M/D (mudad-durua) mines were AN (anti-tank) mines made in China.

We slowly combed the sand with rakes to find the anti-personal mines, and poked the sand with iron sticks to find the big anti-tank mines. When we found a mine, we knelt down, cleaned the sand from around the mine and took out the detonator. When we had a bucket full of detonators, we made a hole in the sand, placed the detonators in it, poured in some petrol, set the petrol alight and waited a few minutes for the explosion. It was extremely dangerous to work with such primitive equipment but that was all we had.

It should be known that we worked with very primitive equipment and that in the middle of the battle an explosion resulted in the deaths of:

1. *Ahmad Al Salem Aqeeli*
2. *Abduselam Salem Abdelaziz Alyamani*
3. *Adam Mohamed Alshelmani*
4. *Salah Saleh Abdel Rahman*
5. *Mohammed Abdul Salam Jaballah*
6. *Al Mahdi Alfalah*

Some members of the company received very serious burns and they are:

1. *Colonel Adel Hassan Alashab*
2. *Lieutenant in police- Salem Mohamed Bushdeiq*
3. *Mousbah Jumaa Al Warfali*

We advanced towards Bishr, Ageela, Ras Lanuf and Um Al-Gandil. At the outskirts of Sirte we found the roads blocked by containers filled with sand and earth mounds. The progress of the FF was secured, but at the entrance to Sirte two members of the company were wounded:

1. *Emad Al-Din Saleh Faraj Muhammad*
2. *Yahya Mohammad Mokhtar*

The "Engineering Company 17" advanced and removed 6,700 mines in the vicinity of the city Sirte. As well, hundreds of missiles and projectiles were detonated in cooperation with the Red Cross, but we still need to work in the areas contaminated with items left over from our earlier removals.

There is a lot of pride in the company that made all these supreme efforts in difficult circumstances during the month of Ramadan in the burning summer. Congratulations to all who fought against the tyrant's battalions; and my congratulations to our heroic people who rebelled against the lunatic tyrant who intended only to betray us.

I attach to this story a copy of the original map of the mines planted in the area of the city of Brega.

Long live free Libya, rest in peace martyrs and live proudly heroes!

This account has been written on behalf of the FF "Engineering Company 17".

Just one of the thousands of anti-tank mines planted by Gaddafi forces on approaches to Brega

A few dozen out of the tens of thousands of anti-personnel mines recovered from Brega minefields and disarmed

Engineering Company 17

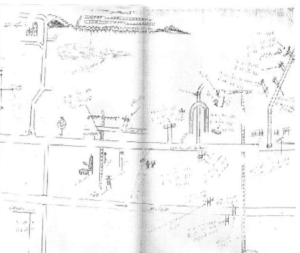

Map of the Brega Minefields

Cleaning minefields near Brega with rakes

> *"Think not of those who are slain in Allah's way as dead.*
> *Indeed they are living in the presence of their Lord and are provided for."*
> *The Holy Qur'an*

Luay Fathi Layas
born in 1982 and martyred on February 22, 2011

Dr. Nesrein Fathi Layas, Hawari Hospital, Benghazi

My brother, Luay Fathi Layas, was a popular and beloved young man. He was born on December 23, 1982, in North Carolina in the United States. He grew up in Benghazi where he finished high school in 2001. He completed a Bachelors degree in civil engineering in Benghazi in 2005. After that, he gained entry to the State University of New York at Buffalo, USA, to study for a Masters degree with civil engineering as his major. He was determined to study outside Libya but he was not granted a Libyan scholarship, so he supported himself in Buffalo by working in a coffee factory and accepting some help from his father. He graduated from SUNY-Buffalo with the degree of Master of Science on February 1, 2010.

After graduating, he came back to Libya and worked as a supervising engineer on a housing project in Derna, on the eastern coast of Libya, to gain experience as a civil engineer and to save money for further study. His goal was to undertake Ph.D. study at SUNY-Buffalo. When he applied for admission, the University offered him sponsorship because they considered he had been a very good student during his studies for his Masters degree.

A few days before the revolution, Luay accompanied his mother to Egypt where she was to receive radiotherapy treatment because it was not available in Libya. After he learned what was happening in Libya he could not wait to come back to join his friends and he told his mother that he had decided to return to Benghazi. He asked his uncle and aunt, who were in Egypt, to take care of her till she completed her treatment. She didn't agree at first but he insisted on going back with his cousin and some of his friends. She said good bye to him but she didn't know that it would be her last good bye to her son.

Luay and his friends traveled from Egypt by car and when they arrived in Tobruk they obtained some weapons and headed towards Benghazi.

When they heard that there were a lot of mercenaries at Al Abraq airport and that the rebels there didn't have enough weapons, they decided to go there to support them and to help the gate keepers around the airport.

His mother called him by phone and he told her: "Don't worry! Benghazi is free". These were the last words Luay said to her.

As they reached Al Abraq by car, another car escaped from the airport. It was full of mercenaries who shot Luay and two of his friends. Luay was so badly wounded that he lost too much blood and died almost immediately after being shot.

My beloved brother Luay was martyred on February 22, 2011, at 3:00am.

May God bless his soul.

How I Came To Participate In The Extraordinary Events

Pie, France

How did I come to be interested and participate at my humble level in the extraordinary events that took place in Libya, of which I knew barely the name up until recently? It's actually a long story.

Around 1975, I changed direction to train myself in computers, first on the very large mainframes that took up space in a room where several families could have lived. Around 1980, I had my first computer, a tiny one, with 1K of RAM. Soon after, I got my first IBM PC, and with it I discovered computer communications, and BBS (Bulletin Board System) precursors of the public Internet. I joined a network, Fidonet, and have created one: a Liberty, Intercommunication and Friendship (LIFnet). These networks are used to communicate through forums with people around the world, including in the former USSR, and it appeared that computer communication was a tremendous vehicle for freedom. At first, my involvement was at a very low level, but then things began to change, and the whole world of communications changed.

The Internet became public, with all the changes one could imagine. LIfnet and other BBS networks were losing interest in favor of a more powerful tool. I joined Microsoft as forum manager, then as a Sysop for the launch of MSN with its forums and chats. There, I tried to show all users that this new tool provided discovery, knowledge of others, freedom, and how to use it in the respect of others. It was also the real beginning of a channel of information independent of traditional media.

But freedom leads to abuses. Trolls are users who believe that freedom is their freedom, and they do not care about others. Worse, they have to damage the freedom of others. Also profiteers of a new system appeared, with strong networks of banditry. I fought against each to the best of my ability.

Then came a big break. In disagreement with Microsoft on the security and freedom of chatrooms, I denounced my contract with this company that quickly sold or closed its preferred chatrooms rather than take the necessary steps for freedom and security. With that came personal health problems and I disappeared from the world of computing and communication.

At the end of 2010, events in North Africa, minimized by the media, caught my attention. It had been a few years since I had followed the news, but I felt that there was something that was about to happen, perhaps, a change to the world, perhaps more than the breakup of the former USSR.

First Tunisia, where I tried to follow as best I could what was happening, then Egypt, where I gained a little more enthusiasm for a people crying out for freedom. Against all odds, freedom has taken a small step in the two countries. With luck, it will eventually grow up and win. The important thing was that the movement was launched, and that other people dared to do the unthinkable: to claim their freedom.

Libya. Late in January, noises start coming from Libya. What did I know of Libya? Nothing! Like many people, it boils down to "Gaddafi Libya = terrorism."

I started to educate myself on the subject, but it was hard to find something about what was happening. On the AJE blog — I started to find some information, and misinformation. Good, a broad compilation of the international press and its archives. I found out a little more information, and probably much misinformation, but of them all, the blogs of AJE seemed most reliable. I learned to walk on Twitter, and above all I learned to sort quite effectively between reliable and questionable information. Like many people on the AJE blog who were at least as thirsty as I was for information, I began to listen to those that I considered quite reliable

Of course, on the AJE blog, I met my trolls of the "good old days", usually very, very, young people, whose only pleasure is to spoil life for others. Probably a new form of the rebellion of adolescence as it can only be exercised vis-à-vis parents and others who have long since given up. There are ways to neutralize, if not shut down, most of these parasites. Some are stubborn and we can only limit the effects of their stupidity. It occurred to me that some of these trolls were better organized and more stubborn than they should have been. Trolls normally play with the disorder they create; some people believe in a truth, embedded in an ideology suited to their vision. Some of those we found on the AJE blogs were really not trying to disturb the communication process, but were trying to divert support to Gaddafi, while most often they seemed to know nothing. At the beginning they came especially to fight the United States, and thus NATO, and therefore any so-called Western opinion, and by extension any free country.

The game was certainly difficult, but interesting, and my sources became better and more structured. I launched into a war against trolls. I did my best; many who have shared this way did even better, much better. Like many, I spent more time on the AJE blog than for any normal activity, and I believe that my small contribution has been helpful in this war and the virtual parallel.

My health problems suddenly slowed my activities for the benefit of freedom, but the troops of the anti-troll professionals had largely grown, and finally my presence was really less critical, at least not at the price. I became primarily a "voyeur", continuing to keep informed of the progress of liberty, and giving occasional thrusts against those professionals in the pay of Gaddafi.

What seemed the most unimaginable was done! The Libyans got rid of their tyranny. The hard part is yet to do: turn this victory into an ode to freedom, and so far, this second phase seems on track.

August 20, 2011: a banner raised high above Libyan crowds who still gather each evening outside the Benghazi Court House and have not forgotten those who helped them gain freedom.

Memories from Tataween

Dr. Emad Al Din Al Gwiri
Resident doctor at the Department of Internal Medicine
Hawari General Hospital, Benghazi, Libya

The City of Tataween

The city of Tataween is located in the far south of Tunisia, and is home to about 7,000 people. It is the largest city in the Province of Tataween which also includes other small villages on the border with Libya, such as Thabh. Tataween is one of the poorest provinces of Tunisia and possesses the least in terms of potential and this is evident by taking a look at the homes and streets, road, vehicles, and facilities. But people living here have shown an enormous level of generosity, hospitality, chivalry and greatness. They proved to be of all these things by not hesitating to host and help the Libyan refugees who were driven away from their homes by the war and the heavy shelling of their cities and villages of Mount Nafusa by Gaddafi. They welcomed them into their small and humble homes and shared their bread and water with them. I have seen a Tunisian family that, despite the fact that they lived in a very small apartment which had only four rooms, accepted into their home a Libyan family of three and they all sat at one table. The atmosphere of brotherhood and affection that I felt among them was incredible and absolutely amazing.

I heard from another small family, a husband and a wife that they had left their home and had gone to stay with their relatives so that a Libyan family could move into their home.

One of my friends told me that one of Tunisian families living in France postponed their visit to the village in order to allow a Libyan refugee family to stay at their home until the war stopped. I also met an elderly couple, who had escaped their home in Libya due to war, and were given shelter and refuge by a Tunisian woman who also took care of them and provided them with medicines.

I can't even begin to explain how helpful, generous and friendly the people of the south of Tunisia on the border with Libya were. They really proved that the spirit of brotherhood and friendship between the Libyan and Tunisian people really exists.

The role of doctors from Benghazi in Tataween

Several doctors working in hospitals in Benghazi specializing in different fields were called on behalf of a charity organization called Ibn Hayyan which coordinated and cooperated with the local council of the city of Benghazi. They assembled a team that would provide medical relief for the Libyan refugee camps in southern Tunisia. The operations began in the beginning of May, 2011 and were coordinated by Tunisian Red Crescent and other charity organizations based in the city of Tataween. Many specialized clinics in several fields such as general medicine, paediatrics, obstetrics and gynaecology, mental illness, dermatology, ear, nose and throat, and eyes had been opened in Tataween. The doctors paid weekly visits to many other cities, villages and refugee camps where Libyan refugees were located such as Djerba, Jarjees, Qabbs, Gimrasn, Bani Kahdache, Alsamar, and the Thabha Remada, and Tataween camps.

The Tunisian Red Crescent branch of the South Btatauan, made a donation to us in one of its headquarters by providing equipment that enabled us to help the Libyan refugees in the Tataween camp. In this camp we had an operating room, a clinic and a small laboratory; all the equipment was brought from Benghazi. We also had a pharmacy from which we were able to provide the refugees with medicines, milk and diapers for the children as well as many other medical supplies. An ultrasound machine was also brought, in case of an obstetrical delivery or some other case that required an ultrasound scan. In addition, several members of the medical team performed surgery at the Tataween Regional Hospital.

Pharmacy

Laboratory

Volunteers from the Tunisian Red Crescent

The president of the medical team held weekly meetings, which included representatives of Tunisian authorities in the Province of Tataween, the Tunisian army, the Tunisian Ministry of Health and the Tunisian Red Crescent, as well as Libyan delegates representing Libyan medical teams and relief organizations operating in Tunisia and on the Libyan-Tunisian border. The main purpose of the meetings was to assess the ongoing situation and, by all means necessary, find a solution and ways to help the Libyan refugees in southern Tunisia.

Relief organizations from Benghazi

There were numerous Libyan associations from all over Libya and they played a large and active role in alleviating the suffering of Libyan refugees. The most prominent of these associations was the Libyan Interim Relief Organization.
Their mission was to ensure that refugee facilities in the city of Tataween and other refugee camps, received everything they needed such as food and clothing during this crisis. They also ensured a safe return and took care of transportation expenses for all Libyan families taking refuge in Tunisia.

I will never forget how important was the role of Tunisian non-governmental organizations which were under the command of the Tunisian Red Crescent who provided help to the refugees in the city of Tataween and many other Tunisian cities. They helped by distributing food and clothes to refugee families and provided assistance on a weekly basis, also covering the expenses of the transportation of refugees to Libya.

The group dinner of Libyan and Tunisian elders

During one of the days of the holy month of Ramadan, a large group of elderly Libyans and Tunisians was invited to a collective dinner, which had been organized by the Daily Tataween Elderly Club in collaboration with the Libyan Organization for Temporary Relief. The atmosphere was filled with love, intimacy and tolerance, as well as brotherhood. For this event, many local women generously cooked very delicious local dishes and a filming crew was present as well along with several guests who were there to express their gratitude to the people of Tataween. The event was broadcast on the Tunisian Satellite Channel as well as on Libya Al Hurra TV. Later on, verses from the Holy Quran were read and women shouted with joy to once again express their never-ending gratitude to the good and pious people of Tataween.

Photo taken before the group dinner including several Libyan refugees and their Libyan Interim Relief Organization and several members of our medical team

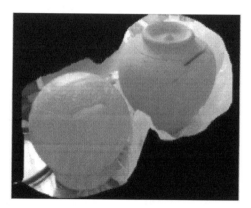

The money boxes

During my stay in Tataween, I witnessed many emotional situations and one of them brought tears in my eyes. It was the time when donations for the Libyan refugees were made. The people who were volunteering and helping were Mrs. Zainab Jouni and people from a British charity organization for the refugees of Libya in Tunisia. The donations arrived from all over Libya. Hundreds of gifts along with money were sent. One particular sight made tears flow down my cheeks – it was when I saw money sent by four children from Benghazi who had collected that money for a whole year. They also sent a letter in which they expressed sympathy and support for their fellow Libyan brothers who were forced to leave their homes.

This is the picture of the letter

Libyan refugee camp in the south of Tunisia

In order to escape the heavy shelling and the unjust aggression from Gaddafi's brigades many families were displaced, especially the elderly, children and women from all cities and villages of Mount Nafusa, which is located in the far west of Libya, near the Tunisian border; the younger people and fighters stayed so that they could defend their towns and villages. Refugee camps had been set up in all Libyan cities near the border with Tunisia such as camp in the city of Thabh – a camp which was under the auspices of the United Arab Emirates and another camp in the city of Tataween under the auspices of the State of Qatar. There was another camp in the city of Remada under the auspices of the United Nations and the Tunisian Red Crescent. We visited the camps on a weekly basis and I was member of the team that visited the Thabh camp. There I saw Libyan refugees– women, children and the elderly– and each family was allocated a tent. In this area, the temperatures were known to reach as high as 53° Celsius

Picture of author and Dr. Salah Boushaalah who was one of the members of the Zhabh humanitarian mission in front of customized satellite clinic tent

The photo of mother of the martyr, my friend Khaleed Taqtaq, and the author

During our stay at the Thabh camp we visited the mother of a Libyan martyr Emad Zackariya, who was martyred in Nalut on May 22, 2011. She is known among Libyans for her appearance in the Libya Al Hurra TV News opening commercial in which she prays for her martyred son. Before entering the tent, one of our colleagues wasn't able to hold his emotions and he began to cry as he remembered the martyred Emad. After couple of minutes we entered the tent and were surprised by the tranquility and patience of how warmly Emad's mother welcomed us. She praised God's name and said that her son is a martyr and that he is in Heaven now. We also spoke to a child whose parents were killed in the war.

We also met the father of one of the martyrs, who showed us a letter from his martyred son's friend who explains how incredibly brave his son was and how he wasn't afraid to take a bullet from a sniper who was shooting at his people and at his city.

This is the picture of the letter

Picture of the author with some of the members of the scout cam at Tataween camp

Boy Scouts from Benghazi

The atmosphere I saw in the camp was excellent. I met young people who were always smiling and were very well mannered and always ready to provide assistance to anyone in the camp. They invited us inside one of their tents and welcomed us in the friendliest manner possible. They were a division of Boy Scouts from Benghazi and their commander was Walid Al Gunein who volunteered for that position in order to provide the children with recreation and games. The Scouts also received some Islamic instruction. Classrooms with seats and benches had been set up in separate tents for the purposes of educating the children and also to help them get through pain and suffering that this war inflicted upon them.

The Boy Scout camp collected charity for needy Libyan families and also helped in the distribution of various necessities to people. These young scouts were a perfect example of the support that Libyan refugees in Tunisia received from their countrymen from Benghazi.

A trip to the western mountain

When I passed through the Tunisian-Libyan border and entered Libya from the far west gate of the town, I felt very proud when I recalled all the scenes of the battles that took place for control of this vital crossing, and how the freedom fighters defeated Gaddafi's troops. Finally, the crossing was safe. The Zhabh border passage was a vital artery for the supply of mountain areas with food, medicine and gasoline, for providing the freedom fighters with arms, and for ensuring a safe passage for families fleeing the fighting in the western regions.

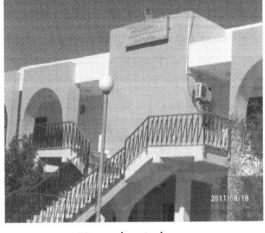

Checkpoint   *Kapau hospital*

When I passed by the cities of Mount Nafusa I saw there was a lack of equipment, and the buildings and roads clearly showed the neglect of Gaddafi's government for this part of the country. Despite the neglect, we saw the generosity and hospitality of the people of the mountain, especially in the village of Kapau, which gave us a warm welcome, and we stayed with them for a night. After this, we went on to complete our visit to other cities of the mountain.

We visited hospitals in the cities of Kapau, Jadu, Zintan and Nalut. The director of the Kapau hospital asked us if we could provide medical assistance to his people in the fields of dermatology, paediatrics and gynaecology for as long as possible. He particularly asked for our help in dermatology because they hadn't had a dermatologist for a very long time. The words that my colleague told me after he heard the director's plea still to this day echo in my ears. He told me: "It is only now in Kapau that I finally felt that I could contribute to this revolution even though I spent months in south of Tunisia helping refugees." He also told me that many people were suffering from scabies due to absence of water and that they had no dermatologist who could prescribe the right medicine for it.

I noticed that some of the hospitals in the western mountain were almost devoid of medical specialists because these areas relied on foreign workers who returned to their countries following the outbreak of the revolution. I saw Nalut Central Hospital, which is one of the largest Libyan hospitals, but given the acute shortage of medical personnel and despite the availability of medical supplies, it was almost devoid of people.

Photos showing Nalut Central Hospital

With this small token, we wished to express our thanks and gratitude to people of Tunisia for their unselfish contribution to our revolution and for the precious help they offered to the people of Libya. We especially wish to thank the Tunisian Red Crescent Organization from Southern Tataween. Our medical personnel presented our Tunisian friends with a memorial shield in which the flags of Tunisia and Libya were carved in, in order to represent a special bond of friendship and brotherhood between our people.

The memorial shield

The author with the volunteers of the Tunisian Crescent in Tataween and with Dr. Ramadan Al Maghreby the head of the mission and with my other colleagues Dr. Ibrahim Amzika and Khaled Taqtaq.

"Think not of those who are slain in Allah's way as dead.
Indeed they are living in the presence of their Lord and are provided for."
The Holy Qur'an

Idris Mohamad Abdallah Al Masdour
born in 1969 and martyred on July 15, 2011

The story is told by the martyr's sister Hawa Al Masdour, Benghazi, Libya

When I grabbed my pen to write about the revolution, it seemed the words flew onto my paper before they flew into my mind. I was writing the story of people who value honor and heroism, those who carry medals of bravery on their chests and those who were chosen by God Almighty for martyrdom.

This is the story of the love of my heart and it makes me proud when I say that I am the sister of a martyr and the mother of a hero.

Idris Mohamad Abdallah Al Masdour was born on January 23, 1969 in the city of Ajdabiyeh, after seven sisters. His birth was a gift from God that gave the family the greatest joy; our only concern was to give him love and care. Our love for this child grew stronger and stronger and he was not like any other child. Because he grew up among sisters, it was obvious he was a manly character, kind, generous, brave and feared nothing but God Almighty.

He was a student of "Al Jala" school in Ajdabiyeh when our father died and despite his young age, he took responsibility for our home and family. His responsibilities were growing. He finished his studies and started work in the ethylene factory in Ras Lanuf. He was an example of devotion and dedication to his work. He was brilliant in English and computer operations. This made him the target of conspiracies by colleagues including the manager, driven by jealousy. In addition to that, he was a religious man who respected Islamic values and morals. He was excluded every time the administration considered people for overseas scholarships because he did not have the influential people behind him to promote him and his future. They continued writing reports against him. Ras Lanuf is a small city full of tyrant thugs and imams were afraid to preach in its mosques. He was an imam and he preached with no fear and it was a sensitive issue for the now annihilated regime. He was gutsy and his speech to the people was straightforward, always daring to tell the truth. He felt that one day he would be in trouble with the government security forces as he was clear and bold. That day came in 1977 when the security forces surrounded him and he disappeared into the darkness of Abu Salim, the jail for political prisoners, where he went through all types of torture, but with no fear in his heart. Once he said to the guard who was interviewing him: "Although I am blindfolded I know your voice and from your kicks I know your shoe size. The days are yours, but the future is mine and if one day we meet outside (Allah willing) you will know then who I am and you will regret that you interrogated me." The days passed in the prison and he used the time to memorize half of the Holy Qur'an.

After his release we celebrated our beloved's freedom. After that we convinced him to leave the Ras Lanuf complex since it was full of Gaddafi loyalists. He moved and started working at Zweitina Company. Since it was close to Ajdabiyeh, he moved with his family to settle there. He had four sons and one daughter named Jumana. He was neither satisfied nor happy at work because he was a man who respected good work routines and feared God through all his actions. Again he was excluded from all training courses and scholarships. Once again he was among very few that fulfilled all criteria for trainees to be sent to England for a special technical course. But once more security clearance was the obstacle that prevented him for joining the group going to England. He went to Tripoli many times and repeatedly told them to either jail him if they had something against him or to give him clearance to leave. One of the officers in the security forces sympathized with him and granted him the clearance, telling him: "I wish all men were like you." He went to England and in addition to the course he was sent for, he enrolled for two more related courses at his own expense because he was a man who valued time and education. He did really well in his courses and was honored and a golden watch was given to him. He was seventh among all participating students from all around the world. He came back home. Our mother died and he became our mother and father, kind to the young and old for his way was the candle that lit all the dark corners of our home. Tribal interference in our town and all social mistakes and misleadings did not appeal to him. Employing people and filling positions based on tribal strength or relation with influential people made him leave our town and work. But one day the phone rang and it was a surprise. His boss called asking him: "Where are you, Haj Idris? I did not see you for a long time." He told him that he realized that he lost a good man and he offered to return him to his previous job. After a few calls he decided to go back to Ras Lanuf to his old job where he could go hunting and diving, which were his loved hobbies. The days went by but he carried hatred for the tyrant Gaddafi that did not seem to fade.

My beloved brother had an account on Facebook and he visited the web site of people taking part in the uprisings. He came quickly to Benghazi to participate in the downfall of Gaddafi on February 17. He met with my sons and told them to go out and strive to remove the regime. He asked us not to stand in his way, but on the contrary, he had all our support and we all longed to have our vengeance and to see Libya free. My son Emad was closer to him and accompanied him even though he was much younger. They went together and fought together till Benghazi was freed. Then they went to Ajdabiyah, then to Ras Lanuf, and finally to Bin Jawad.

Because he was a man of strong instincts he asked Emad that day to go back home to sleep and when he returned, they would start moving towards Sirte. During that time freedom fighters were ambushed in Bin Jawad and some of his companions were killed. This made him more determined to fight. He was a good narrator (speaker) and he used that talent to help fighters get strength and patience. He was followed by a group of fighters wherever he moved. The fire power of Gaddafi's forces was increasing; bombs came from airplanes and artillery shelling and they had only semi-automatic Kalashnikov rifles. He got angry because it was chaos. He went to Benghazi where he joined Omar Al Mukhtar Katiba for training and became a technician for BMB tank maintenance. He gained the respect of his colleagues and became their commander.

Once he told me: "I wore a military uniform and after I saluted to the commander of the camp, I asked him for a spare part to fix my vehicle, which I named after my daughter Misha." Then someone confronted us and said: "I do not want the freedom fighters to enter this place anymore." Idris said to him: "These freedom fighters removed Gaddafi from power and they can do the same to you." The man was astonished by these words.

Idris chose among the freedom fighters the good ones who were ready for martyrdom and he became their commander. They called him "The hard man".

On July 13, 2011 they were in a training camp in Zweitina, a city near Ajdabiyeh. He asked his companions if any of them felt like eating any particular type of food and each one had just to name it. One asked for asban and the other for asida. He brought them what they asked for and he also brought them the water of Zamzam.

They all moved to the 18th kilometer on the outskirts of Brega. Idris prayed and asked God for "sha-hada". On 15th July, 2011, they moved towards the city of Brega, but Gaddafi's mercenaries monitored them and shot their vehicle with a heat sensing rocket. Idris and eight of his companions died. They died fighting, moving forward, knowing that Allah promises a place in heaven for martyrs who fight for their faith and their country. May Allah accept these martyrs who paid a high price for the purity of Islam and the freedom of Libya.

Live long free independent Libya!

Idris Al Masdour with a falcon

On the tank , pointing to its name "Misha", nicknamed after Idris' only daughter

"Think not of those who are slain in Allah's way as dead.
Indeed they are living in the presence of their Lord and are provided for."
The Holy Qur'an

Navy Colonel Tawfiq Bashir Alfakhry
born in 1970 and martyred on October 11, 2011

This story is told by the martyr's sister, Ghalia Bashir Alfakhry, and brother, Sayeed Bashir Alfakhry, Libya.

This Revolution started with the call to all Libyans on the internet, on the pages of Facebook, to protest on 17th of February. It was the spark which, on 15th of February, lit this Revolution. Libyans came out to demonstrate asking for simple human rights, but the regime's response was an attack on Libyans and it confronted these peaceful demonstrations with live bullets.

When honest Libyan men in the army saw this, they were outraged at the shedding of the blood of un-armed youth who rebelled at the injustice and tyranny, the poverty, the unemployment, and the robbery of their legitimate rights to live in dignity. Due to all of these reasons, the honest army officers made the decision to side with the will of their defenseless people. When they decided to defect from Gad-dafi's army, our brother, the martyred hero Col. Tawfiq Bashir Alfakhry, was among them. Tawfiq was a commander of the navy divers' Katiba during Gaddafi's regime, and he was serving with the oil port guards in Brega when the Revolution began.

Tawfiq sent his family away from the city of Brega with his youngest brother to the city of Benghazi.

On 19th of March, the day Gaddafi's forces attacked Benghazi, Tawfiq was one of the first fighters who faced the army corps. He distributed explosives handmade by people living in his neighborhood and other weapons, and he and his companions secured the western entrances to the city. After the fall of the Fadeel Abu Omar Katiba in the city of Benghazi, the remnants of Gaddafi's battalions escaped towards the city of Sirte, and Tawfiq and his colleagues started fighting against Gaddafi's forces on the Brega road, using ambushes to push back cars loaded with mercenaries and men in yellow helmets.

Afterwards, Tawfiq returned to Benghazi with his colleagues to secure the city's port. As well, they helped international and local organizations to organize the departure of many foreign nationals who wanted to leave the country. He and his men were involved in the tasks of receiving relief aid, organiz-ing fishing boats to take the relief aid and weapons to both Misurata and Zawiyah, and receiving the fishing boats coming back with people fleeing Misurata. They took part in humanitarian efforts to help refugee people from Ajdabiyah, and Tawfiq provided accommodation for them in his own house.

After the liberation of Ajdabiyah, the battle for Brega started. This battle took much longer so they decided to help the western front. Fishing boats were again used to transport revolutionaries and weap-ons, but this time to Tripoli and the Nafusa Mountains. Other fishing boats were carrying Zodiac rub-ber boats to Zawiyah to be used in navy operations. At the end of April, Tawfiq and his men moved to the Zweitina area to protect the company there and to assist in the advance to the Imrir Qabis area. In Zweitina, they helped to secure the oil field using camels for transport as the terrain in this area is very difficult, and they discovered a mass grave.

Then, they spent approximately four months in hit-and-run battles, going back and forth by sea using Zodiac rubber boats, in the region of Forty. When the battle for the liberation of Brega began, they entered the second and third residential areas and, after a fierce battle with the dictator's forces, they entered the industrial area. Before the liberation of Brega, they were exposed to attacks from behind and this led to the martyrdom of one man and the wounding of two noncommissioned officers.

After the liberation of Brega, Tawfiq and his men proceeded to the areas adjacent to the city of Sirte, following the fleeing battalions of Gaddafi's forces within the city. When the battle for Sirte began, they kept fighting to ensure that progress along the path to liberation was maintained. In the house in which they stayed, they found caches of gold and weapons. Tawfiq looked for the owner of the house who turned out to own a jewelry store and so Tawfiq handed over the gold to him as it was clearly the man's personal property. At one stage in the fighting, Tawfiq and his men converted a four wheel drive pickup into an ambulance because there was a shortage of ambulances in the front line.

By this time, Tawfiq had become a member of the committee negotiating between the revolutionaries and the tribes of Sirte and Harawa. The revolutionaries set a deadline and after that the liberation of Sirte started. The navy divers were asked to enter to the centre of Sirte. During fierce fighting on the roofs of buildings when Tawfiq was covering his Katiba of navy divers for tactical withdrawal, he was shot in the head by a sniper. The bullet stayed inside his brain. During his days in Hawari hospital, the hospital was overcrowded with friends, relatives and colleagues who were worried about him. He was loved by all of them. Tawfiq died after four days. He was married and left a wife and five children.

Tawfiq died a willing martyr and believed that God will bestow this blessing on him. He believed that to God we shall return. His family, friends and battalion buried his pure body on 12th of October, 2011, and said farewell to him with ululating, shooting in the air in honorary fire and takbir.

All of Tawfiq's brigade members continued to fight and were among those who defeated the tyrant and declared the victory of the Libyan people. After Gaddafi's death, all of them came to his home praising the Lord and chanting. For them, this was the day on which they could offer and accept condolences for their commander and friend, the martyr hero Tawfiq Alfakhry.

Col. Tawfiq Alfakhry at sea; and in Imrir Qabis near Brega where he was stationed from May until the liberation of Brega, August 2, 2011.

Helping Zintan

Radwan, 22 years old, Ajaylat, Libya
A petroleum engineering student before the Revolution

At beginning of the 17th February Revolution the town of Zintan was under siege by the Gaddafi forces. By early March, 2011, Zintan had no food, no electricity and no gas. Gaddafi had cut all the life support to the town. In a few weeks NATO would start its operations to save civilians in Libya. But in early March, Zintan could not count on any help from above. We had to do something to help them.

Zintan is up in the Nafusa Mountains, 160 kilometers southwest of Tripoli, only 130 km from us. In our home town of Ajaylat my friends and family hold a meeting, trying to figure out how to help our brothers in Zintan. They need gas for their cars, they urgently need food, but Gaddafi troops control the roads in and out of Nafusa Mountains. They arrest anyone trying to get in or out. Arrest or worse. But there is a back road through the desert. It is so ancient, unpaved and rough, the Regime forces never think somebody will be crazy enough to brave its kilometers of bumps and axle-breaking holes. But desperate times call for desperate measures.

We divide ourselves into three groups. The first one is to take the food supplies. The second is mine, in charge of running the fuel. The last bunch collects funds, asking trusted people for monetary donations. Turns out, a guy in the first group has an ace up his sleeve. He tells me he knows the man who owns a nearby gas station, and the owner can provide us gas for Zintan. The problem is, how do we get it there? If we use a normal fuel tanker, the Gaddafi forces will spot and kill us instantly, or, worse yet, capture us alive.

Then I get an idea! Well, it's not completely mine: I once saw a man in Benghazi transferring fuel in a water tank mounted in the bed of an ordinary pickup truck. My cousin has a truck like that, so we're all set. We just can't transfer fuel on our first trip. We have to make a dry run first in case the Gaddafi forces are monitoring the dirt road after all. The dry run is with water. We fill the tanks with water and hit the road, hit the road hard. It is a road from hell, bumpy, slow and difficult. 130 kilometers take us five hours to make it up the mountain, but when we arrive, it is worth it. Even though it was only water in the tank, we still completed our first mission successfully.

The next day we fill the tank with the gasoline and made calls for the Zintan people to meet us. Five hours later, our first tank of fuel is delivered. Then another. The first week goes by, and we are making runs to and from Zintan without incident, delivering gas and food every time for our brothers in the mountains.

But the good thing doesn't last. After that first week, I notice that there are guys following us around the city. They look as though they are taking turns. I know it's bad news because I recognize that one of the guys is from Gaddafi's feared secret police. Three years ago, my father pointed that guy out and warned me to watch out for him, to be careful. We have to figure another way. We cannot let Gaddafi's men capture us red-handed, and we've still got our mission to run.

Our truck has been spotted, so we can't use it. We have to change vehicles, but there are no other trucks, so we use my passenger car. The best it can do is some smaller containers in the trunk, but it's still better than nothing. For the next twelve days we make the Zintan trip in my car, then I figure, we have thrown the Gaddafi guys off the scent. I figure, it is safe to run the pickup again, nobody will notice us and we can deliver more fuel. We make a delivery using the old pickup, and it goes without a hitch. I figure, we're out of the woods now, and the next day my friend makes the run into the mountains alone. He doesn't come back, and a day later I learn that he was captured!

I am freaked out by the news. My uncle calls me from Tripoli and tells me to come to his house to stay. I say, "Okay". He is an MP, a military police officer, and I stay with him while he figures out a way to get me to Tunisia. Three weeks later two men from Libyan Intelligence take me to Tunisia safely. Two days after I arrive, people call me and say they need my advice about the local council of Ajaylat. The NTC (National Transitional Council) runs the whole country, but every city must also have an LTC, their local transition council. Each LTC's duty is to run that specific city in coordination with the local branch of the MTC, the military transition council. They make ID cards for the Freedom Fighters and organize them to be more like a professional army.

Ajaylat LTC needs me in Tunisia for two reasons. The first is to make contacts with my father's friends in the NTC in Tunisia to help us organize our LTC. My dad cannot contact that TNC himself because he is banned by Gaddafi from travel outside of Libya. The second is to create a web page for the Ajaylat LTC so the world can find out that even though our town is surrounded by the Gaddafi forces, the residents fully support the revolution.

For a while, I help my LTC from Tunisia, but I miss my home. I decide to go back. I call my uncle and tell him, "I've got to come back no matter what happens because I miss my girlfriend. She has cancer. I have to go and see her." Finally my uncle says, "Okay". He arranges for me to come home with the same men that got me to Tunisia.

Six months later, Libya is free. My girlfriend is fine now, and doctors say she has a 60% chance of living. My plan is to marry even if she has a 0% chance of living.

Zintan- a well in front of the hospital

A Journey of Self Awakening Thanks to the People of Libya

Suzanne Jones, England

Dear reader, I was born in 1974 in England to an English mother and Libyan father. When I was a mere 40 days old, my Libyan family were granted special permission, only this once, to leave Libya to see me.

That was the last time I had physical contact with them, until in the 1980s when another family member fled and sought asylum abroad. I was never taught Arabic. Libya was never discussed. Because Libya was never discussed and kept away from me, when I did come into contact with another family member I viewed them with suspicion.

Then in 1999 I had a child. Somehow this made me want to find my family in Libya. We found each other and kept in contact via letters, emails and occasional phone calls. But Libya was always out of reach and never a dream of mine to go and visit, funnily enough, until three years ago. I was on holiday in Southern Spain and it dawned on me that over the horizon, somewhere, was Libya. At the very beginning of February my aunt asked when I'd be coming to Libya to meet her and family as she would have to ask the authorities if I could visit. I was aware of what was happening in Egypt and Tunisia at the time, but I don't think my family in Libya knew. So I made up an excuse that I couldn't afford the trip.

Then the uprising started. I remember watching that first stone thrown in defiance at a tank in Benghazi, on the BBC. I then discovered Al Jazeera English very quickly. I couldn't get hold of my family in Tripoli. But there was a live blog up and running in March on Al Jazeera English. Oh what a wonderful tool it became for me! I have met so many wonderful people. Libya was not only brought into my home but also into my heart with such great force it reduced me to tears of joy, fear and hope. As an online community of freedom bloggers we cheered and still cheer in unison at all the wonderful people who have been so courageous and brave, giving their lives to free each town, city and village from Gaddafi's shackles. Then a new blog was formed and I was allowed to be part of it. This enabled us – people from around the globe from different cultures and religions – to strengthen our bonds. There have been many dark times for me on this particular blog, then someone has said something that has instantly put the smile back on my face. There have been some very funny conversations, including on Al Jazeera English. What a wonderful resource of humanity these two blogs became! Laughter, anger, debates, petty arguments and access to latest events that were not in mainstream media shaped our community's identity.

For seven months I no longer had any contact with my family in Libya. It was terrifying not knowing if they were alive or dead. But my uncle who lived abroad was able to make contact, and was a lifeline in communication. I met many other Libyans on the two blogs. I was welcomed with open arms (so to speak)! Because of this uprising I have discovered a part of my identity which has been lying dormant since I was a baby. Thanks to the brave people in Libya this part of me is now flourishing. I have learnt more about Libya in the last seven months than I did before, in my entire lifetime.

On August 29th I finally got the Skype message I'd been awaiting for the seven months from my family in Libya. I cannot put into words the relief and happiness I felt. It brought me to my knees. They were waving the free Libya flags with great big smiles on their faces. I met so many cousins and uncles and wives, I couldn't keep up with who they all were. We are going to have a very large family reunion next year in Libya. I cannot wait to be a part of my heritage which has been hidden throughout all of my life. Thank you to the fighters who liberated Tripoli.

It is with great thanks to the people of Libya that this can happen. I am sad that so many people had to give up their lives for people like me to enjoy such rights. I am so lucky to have met such wonderful people along the way in the last seven months on Al Jazeera English and other blogs. Next year if you see three very sunburnt people wandering around Libya looking a bit lost it will probably be me and my little family!!! Thank you again people who fought in Libya and those who have supported Libya. Makes me realise there are so many people out there with love in their hearts.

It doesn't matter where we come from on this planet, we all share the dream of being free and treated fairly by others. You have made that dream come true for Libya.

Flags, families and a poster seen in Libya on February 17, 2012, a day when Libyans celebrated their country's freedom and remembered those who had been injured and martyred in winning the opportunities for Libya's renewal.

42 Years of Life Under the Tyrannical Regime

Abdelaziz Ali Al Shaari, Consultant Physician, Hawari Hospital, Benghazi, Libya

I was 15 years old when Gaddafi came to power. People accepted him, put a lot of faith in him and hoped for a better life. However, his true intentions for this country and its people slowly began to emerge and he proved to be nothing more than a greedy, evil and arrogant dictator.

I was a student at the Alexandria Faculty of Medicine, in Egypt, when a group of students in Benghazi took to the streets demanding basic freedoms and human rights. Gaddafi's response

to the demonstration was a fierce and merciless crackdown. His men imprisoned, killed and publicly hanged dozens of innocent students who had asked for nothing more than the freedom and human rights that by birth belonged to them. The public hanging in Benghazi was on April 7, 1976, and that day was celebrated every year for decades as a national holiday. To mark solidarity with our fellow students in Benghazi, we occupied the Libyan consulate in Alexandria and many other Libyan students in Cairo occupied the Libyan embassy there.

When I went back to Libya during my university vacation, Gaddafi's security men brought me in for interrogation twice and took away my passport, thus preventing me from resuming my studies for several months. I kept asking for my passport on a daily basis but was always sent away. I even thought of crossing the border on the donkeys that were used by smugglers between the two countries! Then I met a lady who lived in Tripoli and was a close friend of the wife of the chief of internal security of all Libya. I went with her to Tripoli and met the chief who gave the order by phone to the Benghazi branch to give me my passport. This is how I was able to return to my studies in Egypt.

I graduated in 1979, and returned to Libya to start work as a senior house officer at Hawari Hospital in 1980. Then, a total lockdown of the country began. All private shops were closed by force and public markets with abnormally obsolete supplies were opened. For example, you would find only yellow shirts size 40 and shoes in non-identical pairs. The situation was horrendous. Often, they would give you a plastic bag to buy without you even knowing its contents. It was impossible to buy even the simplest product. Children forgot the taste of chocolate and how a banana or an apple looked. The only explanation we received for the misery we were put through was that the USA had, without any viable reason, imposed sanctions on us, whereas the real truth was that Gaddafi himself had imposed sanctions on his own people.

In 1981, I received an order from military headquarters, along with a few colleagues, to go to Chad as medical support to the Libyan forces for three months. We were nothing but a tool used to realize the dictator's insane visions and dreams. The cost of these dreams was thousands of graves for the Libyan soldiers killed in this absurd war. Gaddafi sent the national army to Chad to weaken it because although he had reached power through this army, he always feared that he would be removed from power by this same army. After the war in Chad, Gaddafi destroyed all their heavy weapons and did not offer the army military training inside or abroad. He started to create brigades led by his sons and his family members. He spent billions for training inside and outside for this select group, and the most modern weapons were supplied to these brigades. He brought orphans from sub-Saharan African countries, raised them and trained them in military camps all over Libya. He did it all because he had two aims. The first was to oppose the Libyan national army, already weak, in case any of them staged an uprising against him. The second was that he tried to control African countries because his dream was to be president of a united states of Africa and he used to mention this in his speeches.

When I came back, Libya was in a very sad and poor condition. There were humongous queues for basic necessities such as bread, meat, cooking oil and clothes, and those with very strong connections and friends who worked for the government fared best. I was sent again to Chad in 1985 and in 1987, one month after my son was born. I told my wife to go with our son to her country if I did not come back after a month or two.

In 1984, my older brother Wanis returned from the USA after receiving his Ph.D. from Ohio State University. Several days later, a group of dissidents and oppositionists entered Libya through Tunisia to execute their plan of assassinating Gaddafi. They reached Gaddafi's Bab Al Aziziyeh compound in Tripoli, but somehow the operation failed; several were killed and the rest were captured. Later, as retribution for the attempted assassination, Gaddafi hanged several people in the streets of Benghazi and in the Benghazi sports dome, having no decency at all to respect the Holy Month of Ramadan. Shortly after, on May 19, 1984, they arrested my brother Wanis as well, because he was a member of an opposition group called the National Front for the Salvation of Libya. Four years passed, without us knowing whether he was dead or alive.

On March 3, 1988, Gaddafi, in what turned out to be a publicity stunt called "Asbaha Al Subhu" ("Dawn began"), drove a bulldozer and broke down the first wall of the Abu Salim prison to release some prisoners. They had been chosen before and were waiting behind the wall. The previous day, Gaddafi had told a general session of the public committee in Sirte that from the following day there would be no more political prisons in Libya and that anyone who had someone in the prison should go to Tripoli to wait for him. Hundreds were released, but thousands remained imprisoned inside. My brother Wanis was among those still imprisoned. The committee Gaddafi formed before to judge which prisoners should be released found that my brother stuck to his beliefs in spite of the suffering and torture they had inflicted on him. They decided to keep him imprisoned for 14 years more.

I will never forget the day when we were finally allowed to visit Wanis. The doors of the prison opened and I saw prisoners entering the room which very much resembled a zoo. The space between the bars was so small that I couldn't even put my hands through to hug my brother. Wanis' younger son Ali was with me at the time and he saw my brother and asked him, "Are you daddy Wanis?" – Ali had been born just after Wanis was imprisoned. After 18 years of unjust imprisonment, my brother Wanis was finally transferred from a small prison which had taken away so much of his physical strength and wellness into a much larger one – Libya where, because of his past, he was unable to find a job. This educated and cultivated person, who spoke several languages, was even denied a teaching position at the university although there was no one there who could teach the subject in which he had specialized. Wanis died on March 10, 2006 – four and half years after he was released from Abu Salim Prison.

For all the years my brother was imprisoned, my entire family was prohibited from leaving the country, not even to perform the Hajj, the holy pilgrimage to Mecca. For years I did everything I could to leave the country, but in the end, all I could do was watch my colleagues receiving scholarships and going abroad to improve their professional standing while I remained trapped in Libya all because my brother was a political prisoner and didn't support Gaddafi's tyranny. In 1987 when my son was nine months old, my wife and son were to travel to Yugoslavia so that she could visit her family but I was forbidden from leaving the country. My son was also prevented from leaving the country, because he bore my family's name "Al Shaari". What harm and damage could a nine-month-old baby have inflicted upon Gaddafi's regime?

Many times the Education Department gave approval for me to go abroad for additional training, but every time internal security told me not to dream of it, even, because all members of our family were on the black list. Luckily for me, a famous professor from Belgrade, Vera Perisic, came to work at our hospital for one year. When she heard my story she offered to help me get permission from the University of Belgrade's Faculty of Medicine to undertake a Ph.D. in hepatology under her supervision. When I finished my thesis, Professor Perisic and an examining committee from Belgrade came to Benghazi and I defended my thesis in front of them. As I was still not allowed to travel outside Libya, I could not attend the graduation ceremony in Belgrade University so Professor Perisic received the diploma on my behalf and brought it to me to Benghazi in 1987. Some years later, I was able to leave the country and from 1991 to 1997 I studied in Belgrade to become board certified in internal medicine as a specialist.

Other members of my family were also prevented from travelling abroad to continue study in their chosen fields because Wanis had been a member of the National Front for the Salvation of Libya in the USA. Our brother Hassan was investigated several times and prevented from going abroad for postgraduate study in Industrial Engineering; our sister Fatum and brother Mohamed were both prevented from going abroad for postgraduate study, Fatum in Biochemistry and Mohamed in Information Technology; our brother Faraj was studying Civil Aviation Engineering in the UK but when he came home to Libya on leave, he was prevented from returning to finish his studies; and our brother Mahdi took the precaution of not coming back to Libya until he had finished his studies in Telecommunication Engineering in the UK.

Yes, Libya was a prison indeed. Before the Revolution of February 17, its wealth and resources were confiscated and held by Gaddafi, his family and his hypocritical associates. Its people were not free and Gaddafi's policies meant an extremely rich country was made extremely poor.

On February 17, 2006, the youths of Benghazi, persuaded and advised by Gaddafi's secret intelligence agency, gathered in front of the Italian consulate to demonstrate. Suddenly, Gaddafi's intelligence forces began shooting at the unarmed protesters killing approximately 30 of them. The demonstrations lasted for three days and while it raged on I, stayed at the hospital where I work to treat the wounded. On the last day, Gaddafi sent his special forces to suppress the demonstration.

When the revolution began in Tunisia, and then in Egypt, we began to support it and secretly dreamed of creating a revolution of our own, but that was just a dream because we knew this couldn't happen in Libya. The Libyan national security system comprised the following: internal security, external security, the security of people's revolutionary committees, the Revolutionary Guards and military intelligence and these were just the major components.

On February 15, 2011, the hospital, where I work as a medical consultant and head of the intensive care unit, began to receive many wounded young freedom fighters after the young people of Benghazi took to the streets in peaceful protest and were fired upon with live ammunition of various calibers. I saw many horrid scenes such as spilled brains, open skulls and many dead. With every person killed that we buried, our rage and determination to overthrow the tyrant grew stronger. As a result, the people and national army in eastern Libya organized themselves. The young people's protest was held to demand a trial of those responsible for the killing of 1,276 political prisoners in Abu Salim Prison in 1996. One of those prisoners had been my uncle Maraey, who was imprisoned on October 20, 1995, and murdered in the massacre less than one year later – as my father has told in his story in this book, "Victims of Gaddafi the Tyrant" – so the sight of the young people's wounds was heartbreaking for me.

Within four days all brigades and battalions in Benghazi were destroyed and eastern Libya was finally liberated from slavery despite the fact that Gaddafi's forces had better weapons and many armed mercenaries. After that, a National Transitional Council was formed which was later recognized by many countries.

Oh, how great is this nation! One of many examples of the heroism of Libyans is a respectable old man from the city of Ajdabiyah. He had five sons fighting in this war. Three of them died at my hospital and each of the other two lost one of their limbs. And there are thousands more such heroic stories that prove the bravery of Libyan people.

I have been asked how people were able to maintain their honor and personal integrity during 42 years of corruption and injustices. This is my answer: I have maintained my honor by keeping away from any position or powerful post in the country. I knew that if I were included either I would become like them or they would destroy me. So I kept working only in my profession taking care of my patients and living my life in the shadows. During Gaddafi's time it was not an honor to be in a position of power and most honorable people posted in important positions either quit after a while or were fired because the regime's policy was for the planned destruction of the country.

After all the suffering in this dark era I am so happy that my children and the children of my friends and contemporaries will live in a free country.

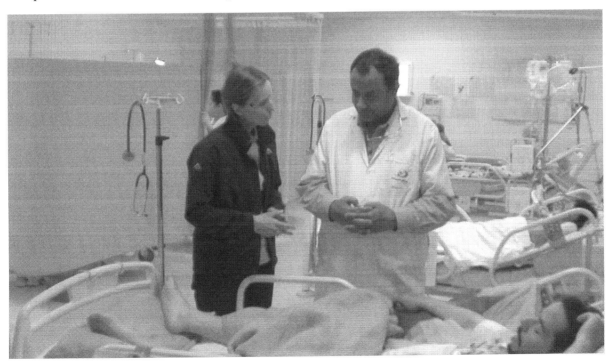

Dr. Abdelaziz A. Al Shaari goes over patient treatment

To Libya with Love

Viviane/Asldkure, Switzerland

Dear Libya,

A few days ago you were finally cured of this terrible illness you had been dragging for more than 40 years and now you are going into rehabilitation. I was elated when I heard the news last Thursday. It seems there is only a tiny infection left and hopefully it will be dealt with successfully in the not too distant future.

While you were in a coma, very few people cared for you around the world. Very few people knew about you. I, for one, knew nothing of you, or so little. Lots of sand. Lots of desert. And a clown!

Then something happened in Tunisia. The people got rid of their president before I really understood what was going on, and within the month Egypt erupted. For me, this was the turning point. I was hooked on watching a whole country being shaken free from the bottom up. And there you were, between Tunisia and Egypt, crippled for more than 40 years by this terrible illness called "fear".

Now, all this belongs to the past because eight months ago your sons and daughters decided that it was time for you, too, to become healthy and free again. They came to the rescue from all over, from your houses, your cities, your villages and hamlets, some of them even came from the other side of the world. And those who could not come to your bedside decided to get together and support with all their heart and with all their love those who were with you.

I have a bunch of crazy friends who live all over the world. I have never met them. I stumbled on them one day while looking for some news. I was happily surprised to see there were so many men and women of different cultures whose only connection was their care for you and your family. It took a little while, but they accepted me and I have been with them ever since.

One of these friends (is he the most crazy of all?) suggested we write about you to let the world and your family know how much we care and how much we admire you, how much we love and admire your sons and daughters, those who died fighting this curse which had brought you down on your knees, and those who have survived the terrible battle you fought to become healthy again. Because, you see, we have been so worried in the past months.

But today you are on the road to recovery. Your family says that it will take time and patience, and we know that. Despite the risks of relapse, most of your children are set on your complete recovery so that in a few years you should be up and around in a better way than before.

One day, in the hopefully not too distant future, I will come and visit you! I look forward very much for this day. You see, I will want you to show me all your beauties, your gardens and your cities, your parks and your sea, your desert and your mountains. I would love to visit an oasis!

I look forward to eating in your kitchen, to sitting in your garden, to singing with your daughters, to laughing with your grand-children, to listening to your sons. I will tell you about the colours of early mornings in my mountains and the shades of colour when the sun plays in my forests. I will tell you about my voyages, the worlds I've visited, my family and my friends.

But most of all I will listen. I will listen to your tales of harsh sun and endless deserts, of life in the cities and in the villages. I will listen to the stories of heroes and of happiness regained. I will listen to your children's dreams, their music and their songs! One day all will be well. Until then, I shall continue to pray with all my heart for you and all your family!

Women and Children

From The Editors

The photographs published in our book were supplied to us by our authors, and by their family, friends, and colleagues. Photographs of women and children deserve a special place in our pages to remember the Libyan women and children who lost parents, sons, and daughters; endured uncertainty and heartbreak; prepared meals for transport to fighters at the fronts; provided encouragement and love; were wounded by random fire; carried ammunition in their handbags; joined demonstrations day after day; helped direct traffic in the absence of their fathers; visited the injured; left their homes rather than submit to the old regime; and made the flags that became Libya's new symbols of hope and purpose.

A little girl (left) and a multitude of children (below) in a Libyan refugee camp in Tataween, Tunisia – a camp to which women, children and elderly men fled to escape the Gaddafi regime's early advances and reprisals in the Nafusa Mountains and western cities.

Hawa Al Masdour is one of millions of brave Libyan mothers, wives and sisters who supported the February 17 Revolution. Born in 1963, she has six sons and three daughters, and has written three of our stories. Her four eldest sons were among the first protestors in Benghazi and one was wounded; another son lost a leg fighting on the front line; for months her husband, Col Saleh Al Agouri, cleared mines in Ajdabiyah and Brega; her brother was martyred in Brega.

Congratulations to the Brave and Pious People of Libya

Maisa Motawaj, Matron, Hawari General Hospital, Benghazi, Libya

I am a Syrian nurse who has worked in Libya, in the city of Benghazi, since 1992. I have seen the suffering of the Libyan people and the hardships that they were experiencing on a daily basis, and I also have seen that a very large part of the population was crippled by poverty and lack of employment despite the richness of their country. They were also very mistrustful of each other. But a day finally came that would make all fear and terror disappear from their hearts. The voice of justice had never been louder, thanks to the youths 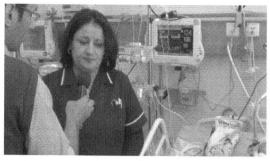 that had enough of living their lives in fear and terror. They stood up and decided to take their future out of the hands of the tyrant and they did that by taking to the streets demanding their most basic human rights. What were the consequences of their peaceful protest which they hoped would grant them at least a tiny bit of those rights? These young people were met with a fierce crackdown from the oppressive government and were fired upon with live rounds that as a consequence left many of those unarmed young people dead or badly wounded.

On February 17, 2011, the Libyan people rose up and made the world witness a very patient, courageous, determined and willful uprising. While the revolution was taking place, the diplomatic missions evacuated their nationals from the city of Benghazi back to their countries for their safety. I refused to leave and preferred to stay and help the injured and to be as useful as I could possibly be, especially because of the fact that all the medical workers Libya relied on were of foreign nationalities, and had gone back to their countries. I asked myself, is it fair to live for more than nineteen years in a country, and to be close to its people – like with your family – when everything is perfect, but when the time comes that your help is required more than ever you just leave them as if you have no conscience or moral obligation to them at all? I also believe that all of our lives are in the hands of God.

I decided to stay and share their destiny and started to go to work on a regular basis. I used to come back to the hospital in the afternoon and stayed there till the middle of every night. I always returned home to make sure that my two daughters, who eagerly waited for me, were safe. Fortunately, my workplace is very close to my house. But the truth is, while working in the hospital during the revolution, I saw a side of Libyan people that I have never known to exist. I felt an atmosphere full of intimacy, love and tolerance among all levels of Libyan society; and I wonder where were these feelings hidden for so long?!

For instance, when you now go to the grocery store, the seller greets you with a smile, which I had seldom experienced before. He tells you that if you didn't have money but you need something you may help yourself to whatever you need and that it would be his pleasure if you did so! Oh God how beautiful is this feeling of unity and brotherhood that arose among the Libyan people. Even the neighbours are wonderful and cheerful! One of the neighbours makes bread every day and distributes it to everyone.

These are only few of the examples showing that the Libyan people deserve the best quality of life there is. They are the best people I have ever known and I am happy to be living with them in their beautiful country.

I also hope that I have at least, to some extent, fulfilled my duties towards them. My feeling of brotherhood towards them is very pure and sincere.

I hope that after complete liberation this country will experience nothing but progress and prosperity, and that peace will prevail in all Arab countries and all the world. Congratulations to you, brave and pious people of Libya, and be aware that many of the challenges lay ahead and are yet to come and with each day gone, you will have to prove yourself more and more.

Hawari General Hospital, Benghazi, March 10, 2011. This photo and others published in this book have been kindly supplied by Hani Al Aureebi, Benghazi, a photographer at the Hawari General Hospital.

The wounded thuwar going abroad for further treatment. Hawari General Hospital October 24, 2011

Freedom...

Johanna Sandberg alias JossanSE, Sweden

... is something that most of the time many people take for granted, at least in my part of the world. I was born and raised in Sweden, a small country in northern Europe, but also a country that has not been in war for over 250 years. I am a citizen who is never afraid of anyone and especially not of government institutions such as the police or political institutions. I do not even mention our military because they only protect our country and are run by us. I find myself a citizen in a democratic country and I try to influence the things I do not like, on peaceful roads through public opinion.

When I, in February, realized what was happening in North Africa, I became extremely delighted and happy. FINALLY! I never thought I would experience that day when oppressed people in these countries would rebel at this scale. In Egypt and Tunisia the dictators fell, and Libya was next. The situation was slightly different among these countries since many of the countries in the West had historically and contemporarily "supported" Gaddafi's regime and many felt shame.

When the Freedom Fighters occupied land and the resistance grew, there were many there, and I wanted to try to help as much as I could by acting to get my own government to help out – to put everything in the past and help the people of Libya today, here and now. Sweden sent planes to support NATO and it made me enormously proud. I feel proud that we in Sweden support freedom even if we are not a nation in NATO.

Spending hours upon hours on the Internet and in chat rooms and on Twitter, became a reality for me and I had, for the first time in my life, the opportunity to chat with people from Libya. After a week, in early February I realized how small the world is and how wrong I was in my opinions of people. This gave me even more power and I wrote to everyone I knew and wanted to get people to support the Freedom Fighters who gave their lives every day. And by that power of the people and all the people on the net who fought Gaddafi, I never in all these months ever believed that Gaddafi would have power again.

When fear is gone there is power left. Libya was free and I grew as a person and Libya got freedom, and I have friends and knowledge for life, and knowing also that the "little" man can affect the world.

Now that Libya is free, and I will try to help support my friends and look forward to visiting this beautiful country in the future.

The freedom and the future is you, dear Freedom Fighters!

Punishment in Gaddafi's Libya

From the Editors:

During Gaddafi's time in power in Libya, many families suffered because a family member did something that upset Gaddafi. As the Gaddafi regime was driven back and finally defeated during 2011, the world became increasingly aware of the extent to which suspect individuals and their families had been interrogated, arrested, imprisoned, tortured or killed to satisfy Gaddafi's mania for self-preservation and control.

As a number of the stories in this book affirm, the families of Gaddafi's victims were mostly silent about what they knew was happening, fearing that more family members would be persecuted or imprisoned. One such family was that of Fathi Al Shaari who masterminded an unsuccessful plot to kill Gaddafi in 1981. When Fathi's family heard that stories were being gathered for this book, they brought the story of their family to a relative asking that it be included, for they knew that their experiences provided one example among many of Gaddafi's methods of control.

Their relative, Ali Ahmed Al Shaari, is a member of another branch of the Al Shaari family and he, too, had family members who had been victims of Gaddafi's reign of terror. Their stories are also included in this book.

The family: Al Shaari

Written on December 4, 2011, in Benghazi, Libya

In the history of peoples it traditionally happens that, when there is injustice and tyranny and authoritarianism, there occurs intellectual, political and social panic and division of the people into categories. Some of them "kiss the feet" of the ruler, and one so-called "hero" walks in front of him and another one behind him. Who did not do so, his fate is this: prison or torture, exile or escape to other country to find safety and develop his mind.

We have been plagued by the dictator's undefined and unjust behavior, and by his anonymous history. He swayed the people and did what he wanted. He imprisoned many members of the Libyan families, men and women and even children under fourteen years of age. Among these families is our family.

The story of the family Al Shaari began with the lieutenant pilot **Fathi Al Shaari** and some of his friends who were from the same Al Shaari family. They founded an organization to attempt to assassinate the tyrant in Benghazi in 1981 at the opening of the market Alroissat, the so-called "general market". But God did not bless his attempt. Since then, a series of arrests of his family's brothers have occurred, starting from December 4, 1981.

Fathi Al Shaari (born in 1954) was imprisoned and sentenced to death but it was not done. He was transferred from Abu Salim prison in 1997 to an unknown place and since then we have had no news of him despite the attempts to find out, and now we consider him to be missing.

Fathi's brother, **Ahmed Abdulhamid Al Shaari** (born in 1950), was considered to be a witness of the assassination attempt and during the investigation he was accused of not reporting his brother. He was sentenced to five years in prison but he was not released after that and the period of his imprisonment was extended for one year and three months more.

Another brother, **Suleiman Abdulhamid Al Shaari** (born in 1958) was sentenced to seven years imprisonment. Suleiman's wife was investigated, tortured and put under psychological pressure even though she was nine months pregnant and had with her the other child who was only one and a half years old. When she gave birth during the period of investigation, she was separated from the baby and she received no care for her health conditions. Instead, she was put under increased pressure, despite her condition, to confess and provide more information even if the details were lies. Finally, she was released by the same simulated and unconstitutional court which sentenced all the family.

Fathi's uncle's son **Abdallah Ahmed Al Shaari** and his son **Nasser Abdallah Al Shaari**, were each sentenced to seven years in prison. **Ayesha Abdallah Alsenki**, wife of Abdallah and mother of Nasser, was investigated, humiliated and put under psychological pressure. At the end of the investigations she was found innocent. Two other sons of Abdallah were also punished: **Nabil Abdallah Al Shaari** was sentenced to death in absentia, as he had fled to the U.S.A.; and **Najib Abdalla Al Shaari**, who was less than 15 years old and was in Britain at the time, was sentenced in his absence to five years imprisonment.

Three of Abdallah's brothers were also punished. **Othman Ahmed Al Shaari** was suspended for four months and then was released as he was not a resident of Benghazi and was not related to Fathi Al Shaari's case. The late **Yusuf Ahmed Al Shaari** was imprisoned and interrogated for four months. This left Yusuf in a bad psychological state. When he was released, his health was ruined and he did not live long. **Ali Hamad Al Shaari** was sentenced to death in his absence as he was a resident in Egypt, again by the same unconstitutional and illegal court.

The family of Abdallah's brother Ali Hamad Al Shaari also suffered. Ali's oldest son, **Muhammad Ali Al Shaari** was imprisoned and investigated while in prison and then released after almost two years but he remained under house arrest without work for five more years. A second son, **Mohsen Ali Al Shaari**, was imprisoned and interrogated for two years and then spent the rest of his term under house arrest, also without a job or any income. A third son, **Rafaa Ali Al Shaari** was investigated more than once and then suspended from work and mistreated in Ras Lanuf even though he had nothing to do with Fathi's case. A fourth son, **Mustapha Ali Al Shaari**, who was the captain of a merchant navy ship, was investigated more than once and mistreated. **Abdulkadir Omar Murad** (a half brother of Muhammad, Mohsen, Rafaa and Mustapha) was imprisoned for about two years without investigation and then released. He stayed in house arrest for five years.

The family of Assaad Mansour Al Shaari, the son of another of Fathi's uncles, also suffered. His son **Farag Assad Al Shaari** was arrested in 1993 and was sent to Abu Salim prison where he was assassinated in the 1996 incident of the Martyrs.

The family Al Shaari stayed without income because many members of the family did not work.

When visitors knock at your door at dawn, it is certain that they knocked at a door before yours and they will knock at a door after yours as the doors of the prison are opened (and waiting for the new prisoners).

Libya 2011: Through the Eyes of an Individual

Joris Diepstraten
19-10-2011, Tilburg NL

There is a difference between choosing sides and choosing life.

Many times I have thought about this very same question.
"What is it that drove me to support a country, a region, a whole continent?"

Saying that I saw this coming doesn't help one bit.
Pointing the finger while shouting "I told you so!" will not do any good.

What I noticed early on in the conflict was how hard it was to keep the two sides apart, like in any civil struggle: it's hard to show neutrality when you're shown brutalities, while showing support for the cause when shown acts of compassion and love.

When I was a child and Gaddafi was shown on TV, I remember that I was amazed that they did not show any of his people. In most news reports you got to see the leader's statement first, then the opinion of the people second. In this case, as with other dictators nervous about opinions, the people rarely got to talk.

The Amazigh with their language and customs, were discriminated against. I could see similarities and differences in the Netherlands between the Dutch and Friesian people, as there were in Libya with the Amazigh. The Friesians have their own language and are encouraged to speak and develop it by the state and the people. In Libya, that difference in policy made me cry.

That a hanging was like "a day out" to people instead of a brutal punishment of a regime is another reason why I showed support to the peaceful movement of change.

The importation of foreign workers, being paid wages barely over what they earn back home, while being made to sleep in shipping containers was a smear on the hospitality of the Libyan people.

In the first month of the conflict, I was most active. I followed the news and when I was not satisfied by watching re-runs of the same reports over and over, I looked for other ways to become connected to the Arab revolution.

One thing I said many times on the AJE blog was: "When I can be myself in your country, talk about my life and how I want to live it, without fear of prosecution, the revolution will have succeeded in my eyes. You will see me when there is peace because I cannot visit a country that has war — it would not be like a vacation to me."

But, as a mission, a campaign, and being from another country it's really hard to get involved, state an opinion while at the same time rejecting opinions and comments of some participants. I don't want to offend, but I have to keep my distance from people in a war, because I believe those that are there are those who either have nothing or everything to lose, and in my opinion, they are the most dangerous.

It was really hard to reject those opinions. I was called a few times by one side or the other to either come to Libya to "help" or to write in support of them: yes speaking up does have its consequences. I have learned much from people who try to steer a conversation in a particular direction. Each time I write something, I have to stop and think: Is this what I believe and what I want— is it my opinion or am I copying it from another?

To all who asked, my answer is that I write for myself and that helping out in a war would get me enslaved or jailed and would stop me from helping verbally. I have no military training whatsoever. Feeling absolutely no need to kill any human being helped as well.

The 10-15 steady bloggers who were there every day quickly became respected by me — yes, that included some people who were advocating for Gaddafi's re-rising in power.

To give one's opinion, even about Gaddafi, means that Gaddafi has lost.

Even when I got angry, sometimes to my regret, a lot of ice was broken by the virtual battles that took place on AJE. The AJE blog started a dialogue, although it was not always mature in nature. It was the only way to combat people like Gaddafi and his direct and indirect neighbors and friends.

By talking in a calm way, without threats of any kind, but supplying alternatives to a problem and sound arguments for the need to change course — it takes a special kind of people, and my advice is not to suppress them, but to keep them at your side in times of despair.

When it was a peaceful movement for two days, oh how I cheered for them! When I looked into their eyes I saw, and I knew, that the cause was just and its people were peaceful, and that a struggle, no matter what the price, was worth it.

So, to put myself on the line, to the best of my ability, with them, I chose to put all my statements and opinions about freedom and revolution in the world under my own name and with my own picture. Some warned me otherwise, others smiled nervously. Showing fear for what can be is not the way to draw support from people, so this was an easy choice for me. There were a few others that went by their full name and picture as well. You can say a lot if you remain anonymous, but without a face and a name, it is really hard to get support. Being afraid to speak under your own name for whatever reason you may have, is giving power to those that don`t want you to speak, ever. This is one of the first step towards transparency — being transparent yourself.

After one to two months, there came a time of distress for me.

Having spent days and nights behind the computer on the AJE blogs, my mind began repeating questions and answers I gave over and over.

I have lived with this for my whole life, but during this time it suddenly became worse and I had to distance myself drastically. I saw it coming and I knew that there was a risk for me of "burning out".

But it was well worth it in my opinion, to try and keep informed about the cause and to give ideas and opinions. A risk is not a guarantee, and if you are prepared, no obstacle is too great.

It is a shame it had to come to a war; this would not have been my choice, my choice would have been blue helmets all around. But I do respect their decision to do it alone with help of a NFZ. The fact that the world made that decision within a month shows the strain and danger the Libyan people were in at that time.

Many videos were shown and some will always haunt my mind: the woman who had boiling water poured over her head; the first casualties who were brought in with comrades who were crying; the man who fell in the sand during the first battle of Brega.

Others I will cherish: the sound systems with the Libyan anthem deep within Tripoli; the first free radio station Libya Al Hurra; the freedom tea song; the Amazigh standing on the plateaus defending their villages.

Many people have died. Most people who did speak out in defiance were sitting ducks, but they did so anyway. They are the best Libya had to offer the world, these are the best any country has to offer.

To actively pursue and assassinate those who stand up is to put a noose around your well-being as a whole. Perhaps, that is the greatest reason to see people, brave people stand up, and then to be beaten down by bullies (grown-up bullies who do not know any better than to use violence). That pain, be it as a child or as an adult, is the same and that was shared with me during those moments and forever.

I am sorry for what happened to you all, and I have a great wish to see you all live with self-respect and with an active global participation in politics and the economy.

How that will be shaped, is up to you all.

Photos taken among the crowds in Tripoli still welcoming their hard-won freedom, September, 2011

"When I looked into their eyes I saw, and I knew, that the cause was just and its people were peaceful, and that a struggle, no matter what the price, was worth it."

A Global Community Participates, Real-time, in the Pursuit of Freedom

Robert Franza MD, USA

It began with Egypt.
Went to AJE because US newstainers provide zero reality ...

What is this Disqus? Never used it before ...

Libya is suddenly a place I realize is going to be pivotal for humanity.

Begin checking AJE daily ... okay, hourly ...

Ah, a Libya live blog with Disqus comments.

Begin reading comments ...

The music of Coldplay 'Yellow' is accompanying my reading these comments, and then 'Clocks' ... this becomes a routine, a remarkable match of beat and sentiment to the passion and incisive 'going tactical' by a regular participant in the Libya live blog ...

Something is definitely happening here ...

So, I venture to offer a comment ... then another ...

The dialogue is open, inclusive ...

Easily I recognize these folk, with few exceptions, really care; they are informed, highly diverse, humorous, passionate. The blog is clearly also attracting some who are pitifully inept and probably in desperate need of whatever pittance they're being paid to disrupt ... but they fail, they try, they fail ... the pattern persists even till today ...

Days pass; many brave Libyans die or are injured; irrespective of the inexorable reality that they are going to overcome every obstacle to their freedom, there is an even deeper reality.

We are most likely never to see, touch, hug, laugh or cry in physical contact with one another, but we are forming bonds and sharing emotions just as profound as have ever happened between or among humans. We transcend geography, time zones, language, race, beliefs, backgrounds. We transcend every known barrier and form a community.

We have a dialectic based on love, respect, a willingness to place life on the line, a desire to give all that each of us is capable of giving to express to every Libyan – and to every person on earth striving for their inalienable rights – that we care, we are present with one another, we will persist until our human race evolves to a norm of uncompromising equality.

The Destruction of Business in Benghazi

The story is told by Muftah Suleiman Dneini, the son of the late Suleiman Dneini, Benghazi, Libya

The crimes of Gaddafi are too numerous to count. He was always trying to marginalize and destroy all national forces in Libya. At first, his system started to destroy the intellectuals then the merchants and the owners of private shops and lastly the private industrial factories.

I am going to try to tell the story about one of the first factories in Benghazi city and how this factory began. Also, how its owners improved it so it would be able to keep pace with industrial development in the rest of the world.

The owners of this factory, the Dneini Carbonated Water Factory, went to visit Italy and Germany and learn about the technology and development for this type of industry.

In 1956, Mohammed, Suleiman and Hassan Dneini agreed to construct a plant for soft drinks in the city of Benghazi under the name of the Dneini Carbonated Water Factory. Work began in which bottles were cleaned and then packed with soft drinks and this process was continued until 1965. In that year the company signed a contract with the German company Sinalco and continued operations under the name of the German company.

The factory was improved with the help of Sinalco. It was updated with new machines and became automated. A used bottle was placed at the beginning of the process; and it was automatically washed, filled and sealed ready for use by the end of the process. There was however a problem with the water supply for the factory because the water supply for Benghazi was very salty which necessitated the purchase of a machine for desalination of the factory's water supply.

This was a major shift in the manufacture of soda water in Benghazi, and production and development continued until November 3, 1979. On this date the factory was seized by the government, which the owners did not agree to, on the excuse of one of the laws of The Green Book, which states: "There are no wage workers; all workers are part owners of the factory." Following this, there was no work done in the factory for over two years and the factory was looted, vandalized and destroyed. The rights of the original owners were lost.

In 1985 Suleiman Dneini, now deceased, requested the return of the building and the site upon which it was built. The state required him to write a pledge that he would not claim compensation for the loss of the factory, which he signed. When the factory was handed back, he found that the buildings and ma¬chines were in very poor condition and were unusable. They had suffered from rust, looting and neglect and had to be disposed of as scrap.

This was not the case for Dneini only. Many factories in Benghazi were looted and destroyed by Gaddafi's govern¬ment. Gaddafi placed his favorites as the heads of these factories. Dneini Carbonated Water Factory-Benghazi was one of the first factories in this city.

The Path Which Lead Me 2 Libya

MCC, Germany

The revolution in Libya which brought down the Gaddafi Regime was part of the Arab Spring, which is also now being called an "internet-revolution". And there is a reason it is called that. Using Twitter, blogs & Facebook was very important in enabling the people to get information about revolution activities and to share this information with others. The internet was also a prerequisite for me in deciding I was able to support the revolution. To pay tribute to the internet & its importance, I decided to write my story in a style similar to that which I used on blogs and Twitter.

I am a 27 year old male from Germany, born in the year of 1984. So I was born when Germany was divided into East & West. I also have relatives in the former DDR, the Eastern part of Germany which was ruled with an iron fist of a brutal regime from 1949-1990. We have had our own revolution which ended in the fall of the wall of Berlin & Germany being re-united after more than 50 years. 4 me there is no doubt: Every single human should be free. If ppl who want 2 be free, r suppressed by their govt, the ppl should fight this govt.

When I was a teen I learned about how people in Africa and in the Middle East r suppressed by brutal dictators. So I also learned about Gaddafi – the dictator whose brutal regime ruled the North African country Libya. From this moment on I knew that the Libyan people must be helped. They must be free. But how can someone do something 2 help people who r many, many miles away?

The answer was: Be patient – wait 4 your moment. The moment came many years later in 2011.

Here is how I found I could help the people of Libya in their struggle 4 freedom.

It all started with the beginning of the Arab Spring. I followed in the German and international media how the people freed themselves from the tyrants in Tunisia and Egypt. I was so happy after these people achieved their freedom.

One day in February I was at the home of a friend to setup her new laptop. The TV was running while we worked, and the news channels showed reports about the Arab Spring. The reports suddenly were not about Tunisia or Egypt. The headline in the news said these magical words: "Uprising in Libya."

We saw reports about the attacks of Gaddafi forces on unarmed protesters in several Libyan cities. After this day I followed any news ticker I could find 2 try 2 get news of the Libyan revolution. I ended up following the news ticker from N-TV – which seemed to me to be very up to date. One day N-TV suddenly stopped the news ticker – BUT they gave their source – Al Jazeera. I switched immediately 2 the internet page of Al Jazeera English and searched the page for every bit of information on Libya. By searching I noticed the many blogs on the page & started 2 read them. From this point, the blogs began to consume much of my time – every day.

First I only read the postings in the blogs but I noticed people who posted very interesting & informative stuff. I noticed there were a lot of people who had much love for Libya & its people – freedom-loving people. I also noticed, there was another group – the trolls. These people posted a lot 2 destroy hopes of Libyans & tried 2 discredit the brave Freedom Fighters. After some weeks I decided 2 register & post on the AJE blog & try 2 support the Libyan people, using the internet. I wanted 2 communicate with these people all round the world who supported Libyans in their fight 4 freedom. I wanted 2 tell these trolls that they were wrong in what they were doing.

Later, some of the bloggers decided 2 create a chat page where invited people could discuss and analyze things outside the AJE blog. People all around the world joined this group – so did I. The day I joined the group I would consider one of the best days in my life. I was in contact with many people whom I now call my friends.

The group grew fast & Libyans also joined the group – these were historic moments. It was so amazing to see them speaking freely about what happened in Libya and how they were affected by the Gaddafi regime – 2 learn their stories. They could speak freely, without fear of being monitored by the regime's intelligence services.

I had no gun 2 help the Libyans in their struggle 4 freedom. My weapon was the internet – one of the most powerful weapons in the world. I posted information on the blogs and I also created maps based on satellite images of the Nafusa Mountains and other areas of Libya, which I steadily updated through information I got from news pages, tweets & many other sources. This provided a good way 4 the people 2 follow the developments on the fronts in a detailed view. People watched, more or less patiently, how the green dots on the maps, which represented areas held by Gaddafi forces, turned into red, the colour which represented an area liberated by the fighters of the NTC. Soon we all became "armchair generals" & we couldn't wait till the colour changed from green 2 red. Our group called this process the "squashing of the green peas".

We witnessed the liberation of the Nafusa Mountains and the liberation of Benghazi, Misurata & many other cities which resisted Gaddafi's army, the fall of the capital Tripoli on August 23rd after FFs captured the "home of the Beast" – the dictator's Bab Al Aziziyah compound, the first goal & the first victory of the Libyan national soccer team as part of a free Libya on September 3rd, and, finally, the end of the regime with the death of Gaddafi on October 20th. On October 23th, Libya was declared liberated from the more than 40 years rule of the Gaddafi regime.

I will never forget the day Libya became free.

I will never forget the people I met in these nearly eight months in the blogs & the chat page.

Libya will forever be part of my life.

Al Jazeera TV news was viewed around the world for many months. Here, Libyan crowds watch and listen as it is projected onto a wall of the Benghazi Court House August 23, 2011

120

The Price of Freedom: Written on Saturday, January 28, 2012

In the Name of God the Merciful

Mukhtar Ahmed Al Mukhtar, Agricultural Engineer, Benghazi, Libya

Libya was liberated from the clutches of Italian colonialism after a bitter struggle. Many sacrifices were made by our ancestors and our brave fathers throughout the thirty years of jihad and glorious struggle against our Italian occupiers. Libya became independent on December 24, 1951. A constitutional monarchy was established and the country became a sovereign and free nation governed under the Constitution and just laws agreed upon by all the sons of the Libyan people, who soon recovered from their wounds, reconciled with one another, and united their ranks.

The country had begun to rise from the ravages of war and the fighting which had taken place on its territory during the Second World War, and was moving forward in progressiveness and prosperity towards a bright future as the government embarked on rebuilding the country. The civil state government and institutions were established and working to achieve democracy, to establish principles of justice and equality between the Libyan people, to maintain security and stability, to promote education, to provide health services, to improve living conditions, and to eliminate all instances of poverty, ignorance and disease. They also worked to build a strong national army to protect the homeland and its property. They were establishing the

Mukhtar Ahmed Al Mukhtar with his grandson Ramadan

required roads, infrastructures and public housing, and extending electricity, water, sewage and telephone networks with the goal of enabling Libyans to live in dignity and practice their democratic activities with freedom. The judiciary was independent and working impartially and honestly. The press was free and making constructive criticisms. The houses of representatives were watching progress and seeking to become accountable in governing. There were some wrong practices being committed by some ministers and officials in the forms of financial and administrative corruption, and the spread of intervention and nepotism in some corners of the state. But nonetheless, things were going very well and life flourished in Libya, especially after the discovery of oil in 1959.

In 1969, a handful of young Libyan army officers overthrew the monarchy and government in Libya through a military coup planned and supported by foreign entities with strategic and regional ambitions. That handful of army officers seized the country without being familiar with its administration and its crises. Soon, their leader – Lieutenant Muammar Gaddafi – began to liquidate other members of the coup one after another, either in suspicious and unclear incidents or through fabricating false accusations against them. Having eliminated most of his collaborators, he became himself the government. He began to destroy the country and the people. He annulled the constitution and the laws in place at the time, dismantled the national army and its arsenal of weapons, and corrupted the judicial system requiring all to consider and obey only his orders. From the beginning, he crushed all patriots who opposed him and all university students who rebelled against him. He set up gallows in public places, universities and sports stadiums, and he threw thousands of Libyan activists into prisons and detention centers. Thus, he gagged the mouths of all who spoke the truth about what was happening. He even had his security people chase many of those who fled the country. He liquidated and killed in front of the eyes of the world. The world watched his crimes but moved not one bit.

Despite all of this, Libyan activists continued their struggle against the tyrant inside and outside the country. Some of the honorable officers tried to overthrow his regime, but his intelligence and security people – backed by certain Western countries – thwarted all attempts to remove him from power. The tyrant continued to take revenge against the Libyan people and to practice all kinds of injustices and tyrannies against them, humiliating honest people and abusing and wasting their nation's wealth. Many crimes were committed: the well known Abu Salim prison massacre in which more than 1,200 prisoners were killed in a few hours; the crimes associated with the Libyan Arab Airlines aircraft incident in 2006; other crimes associated with Libyan Arab Airlines aircraft in which hundreds of innocent people were killed; and demonstrations at the Italian consulate in 2006. Other crimes of genocide of the people of this area were committed but I cannot mention all of them because it needs too much space.

The suffering of the Libyans from injustice, oppression and tyranny continued over four decades until all the people rose on February 15, 2011, in peaceful demonstrations in Benghazi demanding an end to the systems and practices of the dictatorship, and the return of freedom, dignity, the constitution and democracy to the country. This revolution spread through the rest of Libya: Beida, Zintan, Yefren, Tobruk, Derna, Ajadabiyah, Zawiya and the rest of the Nafusa mountain area, Misurata, Al Marj, Khoms, Zuwara, Kufra, Jalo, Auwjila and the rest of the areas in the south of Libya – all these places rose up in support. The dictator opposed this immortal revolution with suppression, harassment and killing. He wished to crush the Libyan people. He had in his hands fighter planes, tanks, guns, battalions and mercenary African soldiers. The Libyan people were saved from the disaster and the bloody slaughtering, which Gaddafi wanted to commit, by the decision of the international community to stand on the side of right and issue the United Nations Security Council Resolution 1973, which stated the firm commitment to the protection of civilians.

Youth and the heroic men of Libya arose and took up arms to defend their families and their honor, and to protect their property. They went to liberate the country, to eradicate this tyrant and his criminals, to liberate areas: Gharyan, Tarhunah, Sebha and Tripoli. They encircled him in the city of Sirte until he was arrested and received what he deserved for his criminal actions.

Again I say, the Libyan people rose up in the city of Benghazi on February 15, 2011, in peaceful demonstrations in which all who participated acted for the homeland. We were opposed by the police forces. We resisted with sticks and stones, and then thousands of other Libyans joined us. The day after, demonstrators from all parts of the city came out, and we tangled with the remnants of the revolutionary committees, the police forces and the people with yellow helmets in the squares and the streets until they turned to flee. The number of people prepared to stage a sit-in in Freedom Square in front of the Courthouse increased. I wanted to encourage the enthusiasm of the demonstrators so I brought my uncle Haj Mohammad Omar Al Mukhtar, the son of the Sheikh of Martyrs, Omar Al Mukhtar, to Freedom

Square on February 19, 2011. We reached the podium with great difficulty because of the excitement of the people at seeing him present. The takbir became louder and the people's morale increased. Everyone knows that these demonstrations were the people's revolution and that crowds flowed from everywhere.

Inside the corridors of the Courthouse, consultations were underway about the continuity of the revolution and the demand to abandon the regime's systems. We agreed to continue our revolution. So, we were burying the martyrs in the daytime and demonstrating in the night until we were able to attack the katiba and break into it. We liberated Benghazi from the chains that had tied the city for many years. The young people came from every direction. Many volunteered and took up arms to liberate the homeland while others joined in by giving a hand in the hospitals, helping to organize the traffic, establishing charity organizations for the relief of the people of the Nafusa Mountains displaced at the Tunisian border, and receiving and bringing relief supplies to Libyans in Benghazi displaced from Misurata, Zawiya, Ajedabiyah, Brega and Ras Lanuf. All Libyan men, women and children participated in this revolution. They donated money, food and clothes, they cleaned the neighborhoods and streets, and they sent arms, ammunition and food to the fronts. They received displaced people into their homes and handed them food and medicine. They guarded public property, banks, enterprises and government departments, and they accompanied journalists and correspondents as they gathered information for broadcasts and satellite TV. We all played our part in encouraging unity and national solidarity, working to overcome all difficulties, providing charitable assistance, visiting the rebels on the fighting fronts to raise their morale, and organizing seminars and meetings that contributed to the clarification of the goals of the revolution and the dissemination among the people of information about the new political culture.

Thus, every Libyan citizen inside or outside Libya did as much as he or she could to guarantee the success of the revolution and to continue the effort until, first, the rest of the homeland had been liberated and, then, the building of the free Libyan state has been achieved. We have been able in a short time to form a Transitional National Assembly to represent the people of Libya to the world, to assign an executive office to administer the country temporarily, and to establish local councils in the liberated areas to run the business and public services that people need.

Thanks to God, our martyrs and our brave wounded and heroic thuwar have enabled the Libyan people to have victory over the tyrant and his criminal thugs. Libyans are now free to roll up their sleeves and build their country's democracy on the basis of laws that guarantee them public freedom and the rights of participation, dialogue, respect for human rights, citizenship, and the separation of legislative, executive and judiciary powers.

Free Libyans still sit-in at Tree Square in the city of Benghazi to correct the course of this revolution when the Transitional Council deviates from its goals, for example, in delaying the conduct of elections, lacking transparency, postponing the return of the judiciary, hesitating on the issues of building the national army and national security, failing to remove from the state's offices at home and abroad those who are climbers or elements of the former regime, and not responding to other claims and rights advocated by the people. If the Transitional National Council does not pay attention to such matters, it may face a new people's revolution that results in the fall from favor of a TNC that continues to disregard the goals of the revolution and the people's hopes.

Long live undefeated and free Libya. Long live the heroic Libyan people. May Allah the Merciful grant immortality and glory for the martyrs, the wounded and the missing.

I Know How It Feels To Fight For Your Freedom

AK47, Brazil

My friends are fighting for freedom – some with guns, some in hospitals as doctors and nurses, some with their guitars and mikes, some by drawing graffiti on the streets at night, all of them hoping, praying, and risking their young lives 150%. All they all want is to be free, to live a normal life. Not knowing how to help them, I am feeling useless.

Like others in my situation, I join Libyan Youth Movement and Libyan Revolution Support on Facebook, trying to help by spreading the real news instead of the "psychogreen stew" served daily by the Libyan State TV. Mass media stops, uncaring, stops covering the Uprising, leaving me hungry for info. I can only find some decent info on Al Jazeera English. I am following Libya Live Blog and trying to share any possible news with my Libyan friends via Internet and phone. Getting through is becoming more and more difficult, and I can tell, my conversations are being recorded. It dawns on me that I may put my friends in danger, so I now try to avoid calls. Some of the people I was calling had already stopped answering the phone, and worrying about their lives becomes an agony.

On March 3rd the net is cut in Tripoli, and I won't be able to communicate with some of my friends for more than 6 months. I am really nervous and desperate about the situation. So soon after March 6th I join the AJE blog, and I start posting – "AK" is born. Anything that I find useful from my sources, I try to share on the blog. Here on the blog I am finding more than just real news and info, but also open arms, wonderful people who are willing to share and listen and explain. There are also a lot of idiots who are trying to convince me that people who I know and love are basically terrorists. I can see that Psycho Gaddafi hands reach even Al Jazeera.

In April I am invited to join the newly created koussa.info site. There are real fighters there, people from all over the world united by a common goal - free Libya. So there I am able to openly share my worries, hopes and ideas. When my friend goes missing in Libya and another one is wounded, when friend of mine is killed – at those terrible times when I couldn't get through to anyone in Libya and couldn't take it anymore, feeling down and losing hope, I find the support I need among my virtual friends on koussa. info. The strength of the group is amazing. We are starting to realize our combined strength and use it to do something real to help Libya.

Soon I start posting the musical work of my friends from Benghazi on the koussa.info Forum – projects from the band The Guys Underground and also other guys. I feel very close to them, even though I know these guys only through Internet. They are already breathing Benghazi freedom. They are happy, but their happiness is tempered by the knowledge that their friends and family members are still fighting, still dying for freedom. I try my hardest to share their wonderful songs, their artwork about suffering and fighting and hopes for a better future with the world. Even though I can only be with them virtually, I lend them an ear at hard times to cheer them up...many times we cry together when news are terrible... many times we give each other hope and strength that soon Libya will be free...

When I learn a story of a terrible rape in Misurata, about Gaddafi using rape throughout Libya as a weapon to demoralize the Revolutionaries, I cannot sit by. I feel compelled to do something. I am filled with overwhelming anger and the urge to act. With support of friends from koussa.info, I create a petition to TNC urging for action and offering our help. We collect signatures from all over the World and from within Libya. Via my dear friend I have it delivered to Dr. Salwa Fawzi El Deghali's table. As of today, there is still no answer...

Meanwhile, in July, some of my Tripoli friends (now refugees) start to reappear online. Most of them log on from Tunisia and Egypt, but also from Italy, Hungary and Emirates... Two friends are still missing, and I am worried: one girl can be nabbed by the secret police for her Facebook activities and another guy for his anti-Gaddafi graffiti and street art. At last, I am relieved when I see they are alive and safe. But what about my pregnant friend ??? I remember when she told me the news of her pregnancy back in March, happy and worried at the same time about her husband, her uncle, and the rest of her family. She had to get out of Tripoli and run to Tunisia, then to Egypt and then finally to Dubai where, I learn, she just gave a birth to a beautiful healthy girl! I am also happy to hear back from my other dear musician friends from Z+Z metal and another friend ready-to-be-a-dentist ...

Online I exchange the latest info about our friends in Tripoli and the breaking news and hope and hope and hope and wish for this to be over. I listen to their stories. I soak in their anger. I love when they protest in Egypt in front of the Libyan embassy. I treasure my chats with my other friend who is safe in Budapest. Together with him we worry about his missing Freedom Fighter brother. Sometimes I am able to talk with my friend , who is on standby in Tunis, waiting to be called to fight. Because he is so young, he can only help by driving, by delivering fuel to Nafusa. But he is ready, waiting to return when Tripoli calls. I will never forget when he told me he was going back to Libya. I was proud and scared at the same time.

In August, the Freedom Fighters finally reach Tripoli, and the capital rises up! I am getting calls from all of my Tripoli friends, and I call and call, and together we all cry with joy! I scream over and over: FREE! FREE! FREE! I can't seem to tire of it! In September our koussa.info group puts together a booklet of personal notes of encouragement and thanks for the wounded Freedom Fighters in Benghazi. I am so very proud to take a part of this project! In October we witness a much wanted END of Libya's psychotic dictator, followed by the declaration of liberation of Libya a few days after. Libya is now a free country, heading towards its first free elections. Soon, Libyans will finally get to decide their future.

You may want to know who I am and why do I care so very much about Libya. I come from the Czech Republic, and in 1989 I was participated in the Velvet Revolution. I know how it feels to fight for your freedom. I know what it feels like to face the Special Forces with bare hands. I know what being beaten up is like. And I know how wonderful it feels to go for the first time to the elections and freely decide what you want for your country. Libya - my fingers are crossed , good luck! :-)

Masood Bwisir, the epic Libyan "Guitar Hero" and author of My Nation Will Remain Free inspires a group of Freedom Fighters during the war.

> "Think not of those who are slain in Allah's way as dead.
> Indeed they are living in the presence of their Lord and are provided for."
> The Holy Qur'an

Pilot Brigadier Al Mahdi Rasheed Mohammad Al Sameen
born in 1959 and martyred on March 19, 2011

The story is told by the martyr's brother Mansour R. M. Al Sameen

Father: Rasheed Mohammed Al Sameen, born in 1898 in the city of Benghazi. He died in 1986.

Mother: Lelahum Salem Qashouta born in 1922 and she was Rasheed's second wife. She died in 2002.

Rasheed married Lelahum in 1956 in the city of Benghazi and they lived in Mohamad Al Sameen's grandfather's house which is located on Al Shams Street, in the Al Hasheesh District.

They had four sons. Moussa the eldest son, Mansour, our beloved martyr Al Mahdi and Jumaa.

Our beloved martyr Al Mahdi began his early education at the July 23 Elementary School in the District of Sabri after his family moved from Al Shams Street to Al Daraey Street in Sabri in 1968. After acquiring his elementary school certificate, he finished his first and second year of Al Nahda (Renaissance) Middle School, after which he finished his two remaining years and received his middle school certificate from the Sheikh of the Martyrs Omar Al Mukhtar School, formerly known as Al Ziraeya School (Agricultural) in the Sabri District. In 1977, after finishing middle school, he was enrolled in secondary school for aviation as they were looking for middle school graduates in aviation and thus our hero Al Mahdi enrolled in secondary aviation school at Maitiga Airbase in Tripoli.

He completed his secondary education in 1980 and then entered university where he studied aviation science and graduated with the rank of flight lieutenant. In 1980, he went to Russia to acquire training on MIG combat aircraft and he returned home as a fighter pilot. Our hero martyr Al Mahdi married Nafeya Dneini, a Libyan, who graduated from a public secondary school and was employed by the Libyan Association of the Blind to transcribe texts into Braille.

Martyr Al Mahdi had six daughters: Rosa, a student of medicine, born in 1986; Munya, student of faculty of veterinary science, born in 1988; Ruwand, student of secondary school of engineering born in 1995; Marah, student in middle school born in 1997; Reetaj student of 5th grade elementary school born in 2000 and Mayar born in 2006. This is the family of the martyr hero Al Mahdi Rasheed Al Sameen.

Our hero martyr, the pilot, took part in aerial operations against tyrant's forces along with the martyred Brigadier Fakhri Al Salabi. In the first attack, they destroyed naval frigates. In the second attack, they bombarded a column that included heavily equipped tanks, infantry and mercenaries along with many other weapons of destruction, which were heading towards Benghazi for the sole purpose of carrying out scorched earth tactics against the people of Benghazi. In his third and final flight, in which the hero Al Mahdi was martyred, he attacked the tyrants' forces and the killing convoy but the plane was damaged by a missile fired by the tyrants' forces. Our hero defended the rights of citizens; tyrants always defend the unrighteous (bad). Despite the fact that our two heroes, Fakhri and Al Mahdi, could eject as their plane was burning, they saw that they were flying over a residential area and they sacrificed themselves to save the people from disaster. Fakhri and Al Mahdi wanted be sure that the plane was above a safe (empty) place before the plane crashed. They tried with great effort because the plane was burning as the motor or the wing was hit (we do not have this information). When they finally steered the plane away from residential areas, the plane crashed in an area known as Quwarsha and thus our two heroes became martyrs. With that unbelievably unselfish and heroic act they prevented a catastrophe and saved thousands of lives. They paid with their lives for the liberation of a country which they loved more than their children and themselves.

Al Mahdi's daughters, may God bless him, Munya and Ruwand, told me everything about his missions of transporting planes and how he and Fakhri returned on foot to Benghazi. They also told me the story when they decided not execute their orders of bombing their brothers and sisters in Benghazi and how they ran away from the base they were stationed at, and how in order to get home they made a very perilous journey. When they escaped from their base in Sirte in order to get to Benghazi, they had to go through the desert on foot and the rest of the way they managed by hitchhiking. Even though they were exhausted and weary from that horrific

Three Martyred Benghazi Pilots: Mohammed Al Ageeli, Al Mahdi Al Sameen and Fakhri Al Salabi

journey, as soon as they returned home, the two of them went as fast as they could back to their base in Benghazi and got into the planes and took off to attack the killing convoy and thus save the people of Benghazi from the oppressors who were readying themselves for an annihilating assault.

Oh Libya, these are your sons, who defended you and paid with their lives. Brigadier Al Mahdi Rasheed Al Sameen didn't hesitate in giving his life for you and he also didn't think of his daughters, his wife or his family because his only concern was the liberation of his beloved country and success of the February 17 Revolution. And as I said earlier he has six daughters as beautiful as flowers and I said to Roza, Munya, Ruwand, Marah, Reetaj, Mayar and his dear wife that their father and her husband gave them a beautiful medal of honour which they will wear close to their hearts and of which every Libyan will be proud and that in the eyes of the Libyan people he will be always remembered as a great person. The names Al Mahdi, Fakhri and that of pilot Al Ageeli, God willing, will be mentioned in many other stories which are yet to be told and written.

Their names shall be written in golden letters by history.

May peace and God's mercy be upon you our hero martyrs.

endless nights of the nameless

Def_izit, Austria

The lot is not yet gone – so are we still here – not really still – but as long as it's needed – until it's gone.
The lot – can now dare to think – it would leave – no one here

But there are signs – it would be over soon

– day after day – here and there
There are always some – often more – drinking coffee or tea – some beer –
while others a glass of wine.

One hand on the mouse – typing the other – many do smoke –filling

ashtrays
waiting to be emptied
Until it is gone, the lot – along the freedom blogs – we trail through
the network
So many tears – dropping like blood – women's on sheets – and men's on
the soil – all fighting the brood.

And some brothers and sisters – awaiting the end – could come and see
us –
when the net let allows them

****
Dreaming the heaven – been dreaming

– the heaven so near
Awaken, remembering the heaven

– until one day no longer comes help from
a dream

Awaken to win heaven – the heaven of freedom – one day it will be
To gain it – this heaven of freedom – it is not heavenly
How far it is in reality the way – at the end the dreamed-of heaven

The desert is dry and hot – or it's raining – not other the mountains
are.
At night its fine to be near to the sea – preserves from the frost of the night.

Not knowing how long and how far away we´ll be led to the end of this
path
Not knowing how – many will be lost – will the soul be hurt by
cruelty
and sadness

Resisting the hungry – forgetting the warmth of a bed – hoping there
will

be water to drink
But it calls us the courage – for our beloved country – it can't be
continued, only dreamed

One day in late winter – we found ourselves in fighting the evil –
comrades
side by side
Hoping – the sky sends the help we dreamed – the world will hear us –
while
we cried out loud – freedom and God is great
Our scream opened the sky – the scream echoed around the globe –the
world
opened their ears and their eyes
Hundreds of thousands screams were heard – we stand with you – our
hearts
are crying freedom for you

Whenever you look you will see us – one of us will always be there

***

- text the day gadaffi died -

now the G-day is over
i'm waiting for my heart to get silenced
all men can go home
can go to sleep in peace

fathers can go back to take care of their children
men can join their women – holding each other without fear
children can have the peace and trust in tomorrow
and the stars are silencing this first night in peace

i heard
date-palms had tears
fig-trees started crying
flowers jubilant today across the Maghreb

What We Have to Sacrifice for Freedom

Riyadh, Budapest and Libya

February 4, 2011: I'm sitting in Budapest in one of the cafés with a friend from Iraq and we were talking about the revolutions in the Arab world. She asked me if Libya would be the next country to have a revolution and I replied: "We Libyans are too scared of Gaddafi – he would kill us all in a second if we were to do anything."

The next day I was back in Libya and I opened Facebook when I got home. I remember a fight between Libyans and Tunisians on one of the pages and the Tunisians were saying to us that we should rise up and act like "real men", meaning like the Egyptians. I replied that Gaddafi would kill us all if we did anything, because we were raised knowing this was the way of Gaddafi. From videos I saw on the Internet, I knew he was a vicious killer. I remember family members telling what he did in the 70s and 80s and that my father told about going to college and finding people hanged just for thinking differently or thinking that our lives needed improving. That's how cheap lives were in Gaddafi's eyes.

On February 10, I was sitting in a lecture with a friend, whose mother is from Benghazi. He had just come back from there and he told me that they were going to start the revolution on the 17th and everything was going to shut down. I believed him: The city of Benghazi was punished by the regime because they tried to take him down in the early 90s and they failed. From the resulting "punishment", the city became a total mess, trash everywhere, no sewer system, no infrastructure – nothing. We were being pushed backward instead of forward.

Before February 17, we would talk about how it would be almost impossible to have the revolution start in Tripoli – too many people would die if they were to ask for some kind change in the government. We were laughing about the Facebook page which had only 34 people talking about how the streets of Tripoli should be filled with people protesting to take over the system. We always said: "Gaddafi will kill us all."

February 17 came and I woke up and went to college but I was the only student there. It was scary because there was another guy who looked like he was from the "Lijan thawriya", which means "revolutionary committees" , which were really groups of people who loved Gaddafi dearly and who wished death to anybody who opposed him. They were powerful enough to be able to do whatever they want in the country. They "receive" money and are able to purchase cars for very cheap prices just because they are in these "committees".

I went home and started to watch the news and the big channels had nothing about anything happening in the east of Libya. On the Internet I found some videos of people burning a police station so I had my doubts about any revolution. There was one channel taking calls from the east of Libya, in Benghazi, and one caller was telling horrific stories about how people were dying in the tens and he was crying on live TV, talking about black people, "African mercenaries", fighting for Gaddafi, killing Libyan people and raping Libyan girls. I believed what he was saying because we knew Gaddafi would kill and slaughter a whole nation if that would allow him to sit on the thrown as the "king of kings of Africa".

During the next week, the revolution in Benghazi started to expand, and they formed an army which started marching to liberate Tripoli. They went all the way to Sirte, but due to a lack of experience, they were pushed back to Benghazi. On TV, Gaddafi and his son said that they would eliminate and wipe out the resistance (rebels) in Libya, and by that, we knew he meant Benghazi. He sent a huge army and tanks to kill and eliminate the whole eastern region of the country, but luckily, NATO came in and protected two million people from certain death.

In March, we heard that Misrata was putting up a huge fight against the regime as well. They were ambushing and destroying Gaddafi troops every day. No one thought a city like Misrata would put up such a huge fight – they were known to be very good businesspeople, but no one ever expected that they were good fighters as well.

Then Zintan, Nalut, Yefren, Kabaw, Kikla, Ghdamis, Kofra and Ghila'a were resisting too – they all had been against Gaddafi since February 17, and were acting like brothers, despite the fact that Gaddafi tried to separate them by playing the "tribal card" – which didn't work. Everyone was cheering: "Gaddafi go and die; the Libyan people are all brothers." In Arabic, this rhymes.

When we heard of minor disturbances in the Tripoli region and near the city, in my area, people were going out saying: "The people want to take down the regime." But they were easily turned back when the police shot in the air and the protesters didn't gain any additional support.

On February 19, Al Jazeera and Al Arabiya, the two most famous Arabic news channels, started showing images of what was going on and the horrible videos of people shot with anti-aircraft guns, people shot in the head and videos of mercenaries attacking people in their homes. After three days of watching, sitting in front of the TV with my father, we heard that Benghazi was liberated – all the way to the east is too, and everyone there started cheering and urging the Libyan people in Tripoli to go out and protest as well.

We also heard that people in Tripoli had acted and that there were protests there too, and that Tripoli was liberated. Of course we didn't believe it and we stayed indoors because we didn't think that Gaddafi was going to give it away just like that. We heard rumors that Gaddafi was in Venezuela and everybody was out celebrating but after midnight; it turned out that this rumor was false and that the Gaddafi brigades went out onto the streets and started shooting people with anti-aircraft guns. They killed over 300 people in Martyr's Square in one night. The next day a series of arrests occurred and people who were suspected of being out on the streets protesting on February 20 were arrested and never seen again.

After NATO came to help, we thought it would be over in a matter of weeks, but March and April passed, and the front lines were going back and forth. My family and I were in front of the TV watching the news minute by minute, and at the end of June, we began to think that the revolution would take much more time because of the slow progress rebels were making and because of living conditions in Tripoli becoming much worse. Benzene prices were through the roof; cooking gas was almost impossible to obtain; and the prices of everything on sale doubled. It was almost unbearable to live there.

I always said that I never believed anything the regime said – it never told us the truth. Once they told us that the people who were out protesting were on hallucinogenic pills because we live in a perfect world and that's the only explanation for why people would protest against Gaddafi. Some friends started to drift apart and we continued to have huge arguments. People known to be anti-Gaddafi were captured and taken away – just because they said that they hated or disliked Gaddafi.

One day in July we heard awful news about my brother-in-law who was caught by the regime. I was extremely shocked when we got the call from my sister crying on the phone, and we straight away to his house and he was there.

When we saw him, my brother-in-law was bruised all over his face and arms and he said that he was captured late at night by the police at his house. We were blessed that night because my sister and her daughter were sleeping at our house – when they broke into his house he was the only one there. They interrogated him for four hours with a bag over his head. He said that they were drunk and had loaded guns, and they arrested him just because he used to have three friends over for dinner. We still don't know who reported him but he is looking for the one who almost widowed his wife and orphaned his little girl for the simple reason of not knowing what was being talked about behind closed doors.

At the beginning of August, NATO announced "Operation Mermaid Dawn". Most of the cities had been liberated, such as Misrata, Zawia, Zintan, Yefren, Nalut, Kikla, Kabaw, Gadamis, Kofra, Ghila'a, Badr, Tiji, Ghiryan and Sabha, and the rebels from these areas were marching to the capital. By this time, I was watching TV for almost 24 hours a day to follow the progress. Tripoli was liberated, which meant that all Libya was free – except for Bani Walid and Sirte, where the Gaddafis were hiding.

On the morning of August 21, my brother went out and said he would get some bananas for the house. When he hadn't returned by 9:00pm, his wife suspected something had happened as she had tried to reach him by cell phone all day– without success. Finally, the phone was answered, but it wasn't my brother on the other end. The person said: "I'm with the Gaddafi brigades and the carrier of this phone got shot in the leg and now he is in the (Tibi) hospital. I have his phone now so don't call again."

We were free but my brother was still missing. We were glad about the liberation but at the same time, sad because one of our family members was missing. He was married with a child on the way. We looked everywhere for him. Every time we heard that prisoners or bodies were transferred from one place to another we checked, but my brother Munir was never there. We went to morgues and the prisons of the Gaddafi brigades, but we never found him.

I know other people who lost a relative in this revolution and now they say if that if they had known that they would lose a relative to the revolution, they would not have supported it. But not me. I lost a cousin (he died in the Abu Salim massacre) and a brother (lost and hopefully not dead) and two friends (one in Sirte and one in Najela) and I'm still happy this revolution happened.

I remember once in June I was talking with my brother and cousin, and we were talking about how things were in Tripoli and how benzene was so expensive and how hard it was to get money from the banks – that life all over had changed. My cousin said: "Don't you guys wish that this revolution never happened?" My brother said: "No we can suffer a little bit for a better future without Gaddafi and for our kids' future." I will never forget that, and for the first time in my life, I loved Libya and for the first time I bought the Libyan flag and for the first time I went out to celebrate something about Libya because I could feel freedom in the air and see the people wanting change. People can now point fingers at bad guys and not get in trouble or thrown in jail. It's not only me who feels this way – a lot of other people have started to feel the same. The love for Libya is coming from within since the revolution started, and little by little I hope Libya will be a better place.

The Long Perilous Road to Freedom
Tripoli-Misurata-Benghazi

Colonel Salem Abdullah Al Rokh, Benina Air Base Media Centre

After the revolution in Tunisia and the beginning of the protest movement in Egypt, the intelligence and security forces in Libya began to take measures to prevent a similar movement from happening in Libya. On January 25, 2011, the day of the Egyptian revolution, officers including Colonel Mohamed Khamis, a pilot, Mr. Juma Al Zaydani, also a pilot and professor at Benghazi University, and myself were summoned by military intelligence and were taken by airplane to Matiga Airport in Tripoli. When we landed, we saw three cars carrying army intelligence officers parked under one of the plane's wings. These officers accompanied us to a place which be-

Col. Salem A. Rockh at Benghazi Court house, May 2011

longs to the military intelligence inside the Matiga air base. Also present was Colonel Adel Al Jahani, a pilot who had been captured two weeks before us.

The intelligence officers put us in two rooms without food or water until the next evening. From there, they took us to one of the departments under the command of Abdullah Senussi (the mass-murderer of Abu Salim Prison). They interrogated us for 13 hours without break and accused us of working as spies for foreign interests by use of the Internet. They brought out "evidence" consisting of my personal e-mails, and photos of the former king of Libya, Idris, caricatures of Gaddafi and political poems about Arab leaders and the coincidental inheritance of power by their sons. The poems included one of the famous poems by Ahmed Fouad Najm, titled "The Donkey and the Mule", and other poems about the massacre at Abu Salim Prison. I had written one of the poems, but I did not confess that I had written it. Luckily, they did not know the names of the blogs which I had participated on. The most important of these was the Al Jazeera blog, in which I had written 170 comments under the name of Obama. I chose that name because I looked up to President Obama and all the changes that he had promised in his election campaign and thank God, in some way he even helped us.

We stayed in the intelligence building waiting for the commander to officially press charges against us, and during that time we worried about what would happen to us. I was very concerned because I had called my wife, even though I knew the calls were being monitored. When I asked my wife about my three sons, she told me that they were out protesting against the brigades. I could hear gunshots through the phone because my home was close to the garrison in Benghazi. I also heard my youngest daughter crying and when I asked to talk to my sons and tell at least one of them to stay at home, my wife told me that they were all out on the streets and God was with them. When I hung up, I acknowledged that my destiny was with God because I was being held in Tripoli while they were protesting and all people in Benghazi were being subjected to danger and there was nothing I could do to help them.

Through this time the killer Abdullah Senussi was busy with the suppression of the uprising in Benghazi. Thank God, we didn't see him until the protests started in Tripoli on February 20 and the revolutionaries attempted to take the Matiga air base. There was a great deal of confusion as the revolutionaries fought with Gaddafi's battalions there. We escaped and retreated from the gunfire to Tripoli, to the Ain Zara area. We stayed in the home of one of the revolutionaries, Mukhtar Zaid for three days and things kept getting worse. While we were watching mercenaries, battalions and weapons filling up Tripoli, we decided to leave to Misurata. I had called a few friends who were officers at the Air Force Academy in Misurata and they had asked me to come to Misurata quickly because the independence flags had been flying for the past two days and the battles for liberation had begun against Gaddafi's battalions.

On the morning of February 22, Mukhtar Zaid transported us in his private car from Tripoli to Misurata, which was a distance of 200 kilometers. It was the most difficult of all trips because the road had checkpoints manned by revolutionary committees, people's guards and volunteers for Gaddafi. They were carrying light machine guns and they wore green flags on their heads. We destroyed our military IDs and all proof that we were military personnel. We told them that we were civilians returning to our homes in Misurata because the east of Libya had separated from Gaddafi's regime. Being accused of the "crime" of being from the east of Libya would have led to detention or execution. We eventually arrived in Misurata. Colonel Abdul Rahman Al Mengar was waiting at the western gate of Misurata in the area of Al Dafniyah.

The first thing we saw was the new Libyan independence flag which had not been seen for 42 years, that no one had had the courage to raise, to draw or even talk about, although it was engraved in all our hearts and we loved it more than anything else. We stayed in Misurata for 43 days with the revolutionary hero Nuraddin Swahli, the grandson of Ramadan and Saadun Swahli. There we lived the with the pain and heroism Misurata was enduring. Every day and every hour we heard the missiles, shells and gunfire of Gaddafi's army. We kept hearing of martyrs and the injured. We went out with them to their sites to lift the spirits of the fighters. We went to Misurata's radio station and we talked about the tyrant Gaddafi. In Misurata, we lived days in which we counted every minute and every second. In every hour we heard news and we followed everything that happened concerning our country from the first day. We heard about the battalions that invaded Benghazi on March 19 and the coalition that interfered and destroyed the battalions. We heard about and the joy of the people and the attitudes of people and countries over Libya's case.

We were in contact with our friends at the Benina air base, some of whom were Colonel Ali Al Shamekh, Captain Salah Al Faturi and Colonel Mustapha Al Shurksi among others. We provided them with all the news we could get and they tried to get us out of Misurata, once through the Red Cross and another time through Qatar's ferries which were evacuating Egyptian and other foreign workers. Our friends at Benina arranged for us to leave Misurata on a launch. The trip took about 20 hours and we sailed about 85 kilometres from the coast under the protection of NATO. When we arrived in Benghazi, we finally made contact with our families and learned about what had been happening there. The new Libyan navy had provided us with phones and everything we needed. When we saw the revolutionaries it was very emotional. We felt that our families had lost hope and faith because we had been cut off from them for three weeks before we arrived. As soon as I arrived, I made my way to the Benina air base and found my colleagues drowning in work. Some of them had stayed at the air base for the entire revolution without ever leaving. We knew the supreme effort they had made and the aircraft that they had launched to strike the battalions that Gaddafi sent to crush Benghazi. My colleagues were martyred in their planes and on the ground in the face of the tyrant's battalions.

The revolution succeeded by the will of God, and the Libyan heroes and help of friendly countries — those who followed their consciences and not the possibility of benefits.

They helped Libyans and their help was crucial for saving the Libyan people from the crazy tyrannical dictator.

Dictators Behaving Badly

Colin Thompson, UK

I am 38 years old, English. I remember very clearly when the unrest began to happen in Libya. I had been following closely what has become known as the Arab Spring and, on the TV, I saw the protests start to break out. It became apparent immediately that Gaddafi would not allow any concessions, but the level of violence he used on unarmed civilians truly shocked me. I was absolutely certain Gaddafi would show no mercy to the Libyan people if he won. The Western media was only mildly interested, and I felt that, somehow, the Libyan protestors needed to know they had support.

I am ashamed of the way governments in the West have cosied up to these horrible regimes and I knew then that if we didn't help in some way, the Arab nations would never forgive us and those rulers that hate and resent us and do not wish freedoms for their own people would be emboldened to act more repressively.

I knew that millions of pounds had been spent on softening up western opinion and buying influence to support or show indifference to Gaddafi and I hated that with a passion. In my eyes the Libyan leader was a criminal terrorist and despot and I knew that the regime would mobilise its support over the internet to quell dissent and try to make us in the West look away.

So I started to follow AJE, knowing of its reputation for very good journalism. I was delighted to find a blog where you could put comments, so I started posting what snippets I could, challenging the falsehoods and vile hatred of Gaddafi's PR machine whenever I could. I was pleasantly surprised to find many people who felt the same passion and indignation at this man's cruel acts.

It became so easy to counter the lies that were spread – the internet is great for quickly finding information. We were people from many diverse backgrounds with a lot of aggregated knowledge, and many of us had at some stage received a level of military training so we were able to interpret the news we were seeing and give opinions on it to inform others who asked questions.

I also set up a twitter account to gather any scraps of information on Libya and posted as much evidence as I could. The one thing I hoped I could achieve was to say proudly that I supported the Libyan people in their struggle for freedom, and any relatives or Libyan expats would then maybe see that there was real support and goodwill towards the Libyan people – not for money or any reward, but because people should be free and be able to live without fear.

At some point I was approached by a fellow blogger on AJE who had set up a website with a private secure chat room where we could discuss more confidential information and opinions – some of the bloggers were from Libya or had family in Tripoli or Benghazi, and so, knowing Gaddafi monitored AJE, we discussed things privately. It was nicknamed "Bubbles".

This meant that we had a really good level of co-ordination and information sharing, which certainly helped project positive messages. I particularly liked to ridicule the more outlandish Gaddafi supporters' claims (and they were out there!!): "A million tribesmen on the march", "So and so is dead" and the usual "Gaddafi was great, look at how he built the nation."

We also wrote to embassies (e.g. South Africa) to demand action/express disapproval and raided pro-Gaddafi websites such as Mathaba.

Do I think I had any impact or effect? I think the Libyan people won their freedom and showed great courage and bravery. All I did was annoy the hell out of a few Gaddafi supporters. I did tell my friends and my family what was going on and maybe that changed other people's views slightly to become more favourable towards the Libyan people.

In the end, I hope that I have helped break through the cultural and religious barriers between Muslim and non-Muslim and endorsed the views that what we all have in common as human beings is far more important than our differences and that we all should be free. So onwards to a brighter and better future! I look forward to visiting Libya in 2012.

As a last word to Libya – tell anyone from the West who thinks they deserve payment or thanks for NATO's help – businesses and oil companies/politicians and others – to get lost. By all means, trade and foster friendships but don't sell yourselves short to anyone. Your nation was exploited for too long and your resources are precious and scarce. It's the one chance you have to control your destiny and future.

July 15, 2011: Freedom Fighters approaching July's eastern front line near Brega. Some AJE bloggers had military backgrounds and/or specialist knowledge and kept their fellow bloggers informed about the manufacture and capabilities of military equipment shown on television or mentioned in news obtained from various sources.

I Was a Very Lucky Person!!!

Mohamed Saleh Hussein Alshelmani, Benghazi, Libya

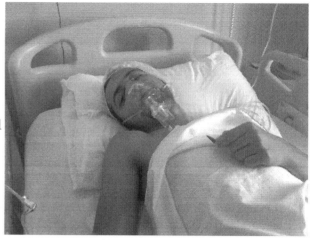

I was born in Benghazi, Libya, on the 14th September, 1992. When I was three years old I went to Bonn, Germany, with my parents. I went to nursery school for two years, and then I entered a joint Arabic-German school at the age of five. By the time I reached 11 years of age, I spoke three languages – English, German and Arabic. I returned to Libya in 2005 where I started secondary school. I finished my study of the Qur'an during this time. I am a good Muslim and a very quiet person. I was not happy with Gaddafi's regime.

On the 16th February, 2011, my friends and I went to the centre of Benghazi and we were involved in the first demonstrations against Gaddafi. The next day one of my friends was killed in front of me on a bridge called the Jauliana Bridge. I was so angry and frustrated with the way the regime was killing its own people that my friends and I went off to Brega and then to Ras Lanuf and later to Bin Jawad, but I did not tell my parents. I sent my car back with one of my friends to tell them that I had joined the Thuwar, Libya's rag tag army at the beginning of the war. In these places, most of my friends were killed by Gaddafi's army.

Ten days later I returned home and joined the Katiba Omar Al Mukhtar where I was trained in all aspects of war, from how to use different types of weapons to how to maneuver in open fields. Two months later, I was sent to Al Zweitina and then to Brega where I was always on the frontline. I participated in 90% of the liberation of Brega.

However, on Tuesday, the 20th July, 2011, I was injured in my back and chest. I was so full of adrenalin that I did not notice that I had been injured. One of my friends saw blood coming out of my back and then I was taken by ambulance to Ajdabiyah hospital. There, I became dizzy and short of breath, so they took an x-ray and a CT scan. These investigations showed that I had a bullet lodged in my chest cavity as well as air, which indicated a serious problem. I was diagnosed with a pneumothorax and transferred to the Benghazi Medical Centre where I stayed for 10 days.

Then I was taken to a hospital in Istanbul, Turkey, where I was operated on and my life was saved. I was very lucky because so many of my friends died, and this bullet entered my chest and lodged itself between my heart and my spinal cord. Remembering how my friends died was horrific and these memories will never leave me until the day I die.

I returned home to Libya in good health, thank God, and when I arrived I found that Libya had been liberated. I surrendered my weapon to the Katiba, and I took up my studies at the Dental Faculty again.

Now I am very happy and I feel as if I have been reborn. Above everything I am so grateful to God that I am alive. I am so lucky because that bullet entered my body at a very critical place – just a few millimeters between my heart and my spinal cord – and yet neither of them was damaged.

23 October, 2011: Thoughts at the End of the Week Gaddafi Died

45south45, New Zealand

In 1986, Ronald Reagan had had enough of Gaddafi and ordered the bombing of the tyrant's compound in Libya; but it did not help the Libyan people to free themselves from the oppression they had experienced for almost 20 years. At about the same time, in my own country, the closest friend I have ever had told me a story of domestic control and abuse spanning almost 20 years, too. I was desperate to find a way to help him, but my efforts were all in vain. He could not break out of the prison his life had become. I tried to speak up but it was not a story anyone wanted to hear. Quietly but surely, I was made an outcast in every way, and finally I became fearful of ever speaking openly again.

In 2011, I read stories of people punished by Gaddafi and silenced for speaking of those punishments. In New Zealand, my friend was still unable to tell anyone but me the truth about his situation and I was still fearful of speaking of his punishments. I could not stand by and simply read when the Libyan people asked for help in their struggle to overcome the control, abuse and enforced silence inflicted upon them for over 40 years! I signed up to blog on AJE.

It was the first time in my life that I had blogged. It was a lucky chance that I happened to discover such a wonderful blog. We followed the actions in Libya through stories told by those on the inside as well as by those on the outside. We scrutinised details to try to ascertain truths. We realised many bloggers were blogging because they knew in some personal way that control, abuse and silencing must be challenged and, if need be, attacked, not only in the big wide world, but also in the small daily lives of ordinary people.

When Gaddafi's personality was declared to be crazy and abnormal and discussed as if unique, I joined those on the blog who said: "Beware of thinking like this. Of course he is crazy, but understand the craziness. If we don't, people just as crazy will trick the world and the communities in which they live just as surely as Gaddafi and his originally smooth-tongued son Saif-al-Islam tricked not only the world but also the groups of people around them." When we laughed at Moussa Ibrahim's blatant lies and historical fantasies, I joined those on the blog who said: "The world has listened to lies and accepted them on a daily basis. As a consequence, truth and falsehood no longer connect in any way within the mind of a liar. For a liar, the truth is one side of a story and the falsehood is simply another side of the same story." When Gaddafi died, I joined those on the blog who said: "I do not care how it happened but I will speak forever about why it happened."

During the months of the Libyan uprising, I had my birthday. Six red roses were sent to me by the closest friend I have ever had. Today, there is a message on my screen from a new friend in Benghazi. It says: "Young girls in Benghazi gave flowers to the Freedom Fighters returning from Sirte and Bani Walid and they put them in their guns."

> "Think not of those who are slain in Allah's way as dead.
> Indeed they are living in the presence of their Lord and are provided for."
> The Holy Qur'an

Mohammed Ambarak Ali Al Ageeli
born in 1960 and martyred on March 19, 2011

This story is written by Tariq Mustapha Ali Al Ageeli, cousin of the martyr pilot Mohammed Al Ageeli.

Mohammed Ambarak Ali Al Ageeli was born in 1960. He was born and grew up near the Benina airbase. He finished most of his studies in Benghazi then studied Military Aviation in Poland, obtaining his pilot license in 1984.

He returned to Libya and married. He and his wife had two boys and two girls: Ali, Fatma, Ahmed, and Aya. He was a kind, friendly person, and appreciated family bonds. He was a moderately conservative Muslim, doing good deeds and avoiding sins. He lived in the municipality of Benina where the airport is.

During the 17th February Revolution, he was among the first who defected from the now-dead regime. He and all his colleagues joined the Revolution.

His specialty was flying interceptor aircraft. During the events of the Revolution, he and his comrade (his plane) once took off and were spotted by the radar of the enemy's plane – that is, the now-dead regime's plane – which was on a mission to bomb Benghazi. When the enemy pilot realized that the interceptor aircraft was that of Mohammed Ageeli, he turned back.

In this period, Mohammed Ageeli and his plane were always ready. Whenever he took off he always put his trust in God; in every raid, in every bombing, he said a statement from the Qur'an: "What I threw I did not throw, Allah threw ... the great truth of Allah". He carried out 17 sorties, most of them combat sorties, before the 19th of March, 2011, the day when he was martyred.

He and his plane left us physically, but his spirit will stay always with us as God wishes. He left to us an honorable history, giving pride and glory to all free Libyans. He also left to us the quote which he was always repeating to everybody including Fathi Alkelani, the commandant of the airbase: "I swear with God, I am ready to give my life to stop him (Gaddafi) from entering Benghazi."

It was true: Gaddafi died and did not enter Benghazi.

God bless Mohammed Ambarak Ali Al Ageeli. We ask God to accept him as a martyr to be with Him in Heaven.

Long live free and independent Libya.

When his plane was shot down defending Benghazi, Mohammed Ageeli piloted it away from the residential areas, minimizing civilian collateral damage, thus paying with his own life by ejecting too late. In these amazing photos, we see just how late he tried to parachute out.

A Time For Change

My name is Del, and I am from the UK.

Like everyone else back in February 2011 I knew Libya was a country in North Africa, which was ruled by a guy called Gaddafi with a questionable past, but who for all intents and purposes "seemed" to be coming in from the cold — how little I obviously knew. I've always followed the news, felt like I've been waiting for the "big one" all my life, and have always been a bit of a rebel, a supporter of the underdog, so when the shooting in Libya started happening in February it grabbed my attention right from the beginning. When the slaughter started I considered my eyes somewhat rudely ripped open.

Back then we had the slaughter on our TV screens every day, very nasty and very graphic, starting with thugs in yellow hardhats filmed on shaky mobile phone footage shooting at crowds of protesters, quickly followed by the full might of a country's armed forces being used. At the same time people started asking for something to be done. At first no one seemed to know what to do, but something needed doing. Over the next few weeks a no-fly zone was discussed, and discussed and discussed. It seemed like so much talk with absolutely nothing being said or done in the face of the rising slaughter, and a rage in me grew with each day. I was watching a civilian population go up against the full might of a ruthless dictator and his armed forces (and mercenaries as it turned out later).

I remember walking to work one day, feeling somehow guilty, dirty, that no one was doing anything. In the hunt for news I had found Al Jazeera Libya live blog and had been reading it a while, and during that week, finally it seemed the politicians woke up and accepted something had to be done. A no-fly zone was announced, but still nothing was done immediately. Then Gaddafi made his famous "Zenga Zenga" speech announcing to the people of eastern Libya, starting with Benghazi that his forces were coming, and were basically going to kill everyone they found in the now Gaddafi-free eastern Libya. He had just announced a ceasefire, announced only to the international audience.

So, with his supposed ceasefire, the no-fly zone in place but not enacted, and his forces advancing on Benghazi to kill everyone, hope started to give way to despair. My patience crumbled along with my belief in humanity as a whole, and I made my first very angry (at the UN and the West) frustrated post on AJE blog, in short: "WTF world? Why are we letting this happen?" Then I started reading the other posts, and was surprised to see many posts similar to mine, but also disappointed to see posts from trolls, either cheerleading the murderer or hating the West so badly that they would freely consign the whole nation of Libya to untold horrors rather than see the right thing done (by the West). It was at that point I knew what I was going to be doing for the foreseeable future, fighting these trolls who were trying to stop the West's involvement by any means necessary, and yes, I do mean by any means necessary.

At this point I was invited to join the www.koussa.info website where I found like-minded people, people from all walks of life and from all over the world, people I would never have come across if it wasn't for their caring and compassion and hatred of the injustice unfolding These were complete strangers, who over seven months became a close knit, extended, if not ever so slightly dysfunctional but amazing family. Basically we have spent from then until now fighting this dribbling mix of West-hating cheerleaders for a mass murderer and his thugs with the keyboard. Luckily I met a lot of good people on the blog who felt the same as I did, and together we started shedding light onto this "by any means necessary" propaganda machine of Gaddafi's, showing their ridiculous claims for exactly what they were, garbage in all its forms.

At some point I also found Twitter. I never would have thought of using it since I thought it was a completely useless social medium used by idiots. I was so wrong about that. I quickly ran into the same propaganda machine on Twitter, only it was much bigger, huge in fact, and for me it was the birth of ByeByeDaffy: This was the name I chose to use on AJE and Twitter and later on YouTube where I put together a little number illustrating with humor the people on the other side of the wall from us so to speak.

During the months that followed we grew as a group, eventually including Libyan people themselves, normal every day Libyan people, Libyans in exile, or who had grown up abroad, and even some of the brave Freedom Fighters on the ground fighting for their freedom. We learned that our efforts were often met with wonder, thanks and tears. We also learned the truth of the ground situation from people there, not just from the international press. We watched an advance while the international press said "stalemate" for months and months, the endgame of the stalemate scenario was truly terrifying — NATO, possibly scaling back ops and the possibility of the thugs coming back.

The Trolls knew it too and ramped up their operations in the continuing psyops being waged all over the Internet. The most ridiculous claims were pouring forth: NATO troops were raping women in Misrata; NATO used cluster bombs in Misrata; NATO was/is using depleted uranium armaments; NATO is carpet bombing Libyan cities; NATO peacekeepers on the ground (Danish no less) beheading captured Gaddafi troops, the list of ridiculous claims went on, day in day out..

Of course none of it happened, and at best it was Gaddafi's horrific crimes turned around and pointed at the NTC fighters and at worst, the next bit of endless garbage from people either too dumb to differentiate right from wrong, or people being well paid for their efforts, saying whatever it took to get the intervention by the West stopped. Luckily they failed. They ran into people like us, and many others who weren't swayed by small-minded political viewpoints, who saw the horror for what it was when it was unfolding on their TV screens, and who also stood their ground against this formidable propaganda machine.

Did we make a difference? who knows, but I'm glad I and others did what we did. The people of Libya deserved better than living life being brutalized by this dictator, the "poor man who only wanted to live in a tent", until the world press saw the truth of just how much he and his family had robbed from the Libyan people. Now he is dead. There aren't many people in Libya mourning him and they as a nation now have a chance of a fresh start.

I for one wish them all the best.

Misurata, May 12, 2011: a Freedom Fighter burns a captured green flag, symbol of Gaddafi's Libya.

The February 17 Revolution Is a True People's Revolution

Al Haj Mohamed Omar Al Mukhtar, a son of Omar Al Mukhtar, the Sheikh of the Martyrs, Benghazi

I was born in the area of Al Ouwila, 16km east of Al Marj, in Al Jabal Akhdar (the Green Mountains) in 1921. I was ten years old when my father, Omar Al Mukhtar, was hung by the Italians.

In 1911, the Italian Army landed on the Libyan coasts and invaded the country. At that time Omar Al Mukhtar was in Jalo Oasis teaching students the Holy Qur'an in one of the centers built all over Libya by the finest Al Snoussi, Mohamed Ali Al Snoussi the Great, the grandfather of King Idris. They were called zawaya (singular – zawiya). When Omar Al Mukhtar heard that the Italians had invaded the country he returned quickly to the zawiya of Al Qusur, near Al Marj, and started to recruit fighters for freedom from different tribes. In 1923 he went to Egypt asking for aid, military supplies and food. During his stay in Egypt one Italian agent tried to bribe him to surrender but he refused, preferring to return to Libya to fight.

When the Italians occupied most of the oases – Jagboub, Jalo, Oujela and Fazan – Omar Al Mukhtar was isolated in Al Jabal Akhdar and surrounded by the Italians. But he was not captured, his hands were never tied, so he started attacking the Italian army present in Derna and the surrounding area. The Italian army came out from Derna and there was a big battle that lasted for two days. The victory went to Omar Al Mukhtar's side and the Italian army was defeated, leaving behind its destroyed cannons, cars, boxes of ammunition and animals as it retreated. 1924 and 1925 were very important years in the life of Omar Al Mukhtar, often called Sheikh Lion in those times, because he was the commander of all the fighters for freedom, and he united all the tribes. The name of Omar Al Mukhtar became famous as a masterful leader. But on September 11, 1931, the Sheikh of the Martyrs was arrested by the Italians while he was fighting on his horse. They brought him to Benghazi, with chained hands and legs, to meet the Italian commander General Rodolfo Graziani.

The General asked Omar Al Mukhtar: "Are you fighting for Al Snouism?" Al Snouism was a religious movement known throughout the Arab world. Omar Al Mukhtar answered: "I am fighting you because of my country and my religion". Then the General asked another question: "You have authority for most of the Libyans and you can order the rebels to surrender and to finish the war?" Omar Al Mukhtar answered with a statement that is very famous even till this day: "We do not surrender. We win or we die."

The Italians decided to try him in a military court but the decision to hang him was made before the court met. On September 16, 1931, in the town of Sloug, they put the rope around the neck of Sheikh Omar Al Mukhtar and hung him until he was dead. But even a dead Omar Al Mukhtar was respected by his enemy: the officer in charge of the hanging saluted his lifeless body. In his book "Cyrenaica Pacified" (published in Italy in 1932 as "Cirenaica pacificata", and in Libya in 1998 as "Barqah al-ha di'ah"), General Graziani wrote that the Sheikh of the Martyrs was confident, intelligent, educated, a true believer, and a man whom he admired.

At that time I was with my family in Egypt where we went in 1927. My father took us there so that he could dedicate himself fully to fighting for the freedom of Libya. I was ten years old when we, and all the European and Arabic countries, received the news about the execution of my father. We returned home in 1945. I joined the Libyan Army because there was no other job apart from those in the army; but as soon as I got a chance I left the army. I worked as a mayor of the Jardas area, 30km from Al Marj, from 1949 to 1951 and as a mayor of the area of Al Marj from 1952 to 1955. After that I was wrongfully fired so I started a business of my own through rising cattle and farming. I was married to Al Haja Fatma Gheryani Muftah and my second wife was Al Haja Azza Feyumi Abdelgader. Both of them are from the Al Mukhtar family. I have no children and this is God's will. My mother, Wanisa Abdalla Al Jeylani, was from the Al Jeylani tribe from Misurata and my father Omar Al Mukhtar was from the Al Mnafa tribe living near Tobruk and his family was the family Breidan Al Farhat.

I was among the first supporters of the February 17 Revolution. I went to the Courthouse, the symbol of the revolution in Benghazi, on February 19, 2011. I went twice to the front lines to support the Freedom Fighters and to raise their morale. When they saw me they remembered my father, Omar Al Mukhtar, and his heroism, so they were very happy to see me among them. They asked me to read with them Sura-Al Fatiha (the Holy Qur'an), and the takbir was heard more and more among them.

I supported the revolution because the tyrant was unjust to our people and he put down Libyans and their symbols of the struggle for freedom, such as Omar Al Mukhtar. He tried to erase the knowledge of Omar Al Mukhtar from Libyan history by removing his grave from the center of Benghazi. It was a great pleasure for me when they brought back the remains of the hero Omar Al Mukhtar to the same place to be one of the symbols of the February 17 Revolution.

I hope that the Libyan people will be united and that this revolution will be successful. I was satisfied with NATO for the support they gave the Freedom Fighters. I offer special acknowledgments to all the friendly Western and Arabic countries that helped the Libyan people, especially Qatar.

I confirm that the February 17 Revolution is a true people's revolution, an uprising against injustice and dictatorship. It is a revolution blessed by God and carried out with God's will.

Al Haj Mohamed Omar Al Mukhtar visiting Freedom Fighters in the front lines at Ajdabiyah and Brega

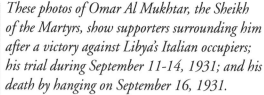

These photos of Omar Al Mukhtar, the Sheikh of the Martyrs, show supporters surrounding him after a victory against Libya's Italian occupiers; his trial during September 11-14, 1931; and his death by hanging on September 16, 1931.

They are reproduced by courtesy of his nephew Mukhtar Ahmed Al Mukhtar who was with the 2011 protestors from the first day of the uprising in Benghazi

By Saturday, February 19, 2011, fear and uncertainty about how the uprising was going to end were great among the protestors in Benghazi

in spite of their determination not to give up. Abdalla Al Senussi was still inside the katiba which had not yet fallen, and the lijan tawriya had done their utmost to try to demoralize protestors. Omar Al Mukhtar has remained a hero and a symbol of the fight for freedom in Libya, so Al Haj Mohamed joined the protestors at the Benghazi Courthouse as a reminder of his father's ideals and determination not to give up. He stayed with the protestors from 11am to 5pm.

The clock shown below is typical of items available in the new Libya now free of the tyrannies of the ousted regime. It features the Libyan flag, Omar Al Mukhtar's photo and his words: "We do not surrender. We win or we die".

A Passion For Libya

KJ, USA

I have never physically been to Libya and I do not know anyone from Libya personally, but I have come to care deeply about the people of this country.

While searching the internet for news of the demonstrations in Libya in February 2011, I found myself on the Al Jazeera website. It was there that I discovered the Libya Live Blog. I had never visited a blog before and I was not sure how to participate, but I kept coming back to the site because it seemed to provide the most up to date news regarding the turmoil in Libya. The bloggers shared my passion for the uprising and supported those Libyans who were fighting for change. In time, I learned how to interject my opinions and how to approve ("like") comments that were posted. I also did daily searches of media sources throughout the world, in an attempt to keep up with the rapidly changing events and to gain insight into different points of view. As this process of exploration unfolded, I developed a sense of intimacy with a country on the other side of the world.

Before the uprising, I had assumed that the people were content with their leader; but Gaddafi seemed a strange character to me, and I wondered if he was really working in the best interest of the Libyan people. When the uprising started, the reality of his insanity became clear. He had become a dangerous, egomaniacal tyrant, who had cleverly built a system that precluded any hope of a fair and inclusive society. I worried about the people who opposed him. It seemed that it would be impossible to overcome him and his sons. Prior to the uprising, the Middle East and North Africa had been of interest to me primarily because of my concern for a peaceful coexistence between the three monotheistic faiths, Judaism, Christianity and Islam. Through my quest to know more about faith interactions, I fell in love with the Libyan people.

I also built camaraderie with my fellow bloggers. It was particularly enlightening to hear from Libyan bloggers. Their shared stories brought Libya closer to me. I could sense their fears and their hopes for a country free of tyrants and I could see an amazing transformation taking place. From my safe, sheltered life in the USA, I could praise them when there were successes and encourage them when there were setbacks. I could cheer the freedom fighters and scold any blogger who did not support the effort to free them from oppression. At times, I felt like a mamma bear, protecting her loved ones. The more I learned about the atrocities of Gaddafi and his family, the more I came to respect these brave and passionate people. The threat to Benghazi shocked me, the siege in Misurata was heart wrenching and the liberation of Tripoli was frightening.

My daily visits to the blog became a bit of an obsession. My family had to endure my constant explanations and justifications for NATO and USA military involvement and my attempts to draw them into my passion for Libya annoyed some of them. Many times, I had to sneak a peek at the unfolding news on my phone in a bathroom or take breaks from my work to check the blog while I gobbled down a quick meal. I got into more than one shouting match with friends or family who took an opposing position on the matter. I was grateful that my husband would say, every evening, "How are things in Libya, dear?" He was supportive of my passion if a little concerned about the amount of time I spent on the blog. I was grateful, also, for any USA government official who supported the NTC but I came to loath any who stood against them. I sent letters to my local congressman, explaining our need for support. In many ways, I came to appreciate my own freedoms as I watched the Libyans struggle for theirs.

As a nurse, I became concerned about the lack of medical services and supplies the Libyans were receiving and I heard the call for more medical staff. I applied to Doctors Without Borders, in the hope of getting an assignment in Libya. I am a seasoned traveling hospital nurse, so picking up and working in a new environment is standard for me. Even so, I have never worked outside North America and my plan caused quite an upheaval in my family. My husband and children did not want me to go to a conflict zone, especially one so far from home. After much discussion on the matter, and some pouting on my part, I agreed to stay in the USA ... for now.

I felt guilty that I was not in Libya to help. I have started to set a plan in motion to travel to Libya when it is a safe and free country. I will take my family with me. I saved maps of Libya on my computer and I keep the current time of Tripoli on my clock. I look forward to walking in the streets and eating in the cafes of Misurata and Benghazi; I hope to meet some of the beautiful people that I have come to know on the blog; I plan to hug Azizor and thank her for her service to humanity; and I want to tell a young freedom fighter that he is my hero.

August 20, 2011: a permanent billboard outside the Benghazi Court House remembers, through flags and photographs, the help given to Libya by France, the United Kingdom and the United States of America.

> "Think not of those who are slain in Allah's way as dead.
> Indeed they are living in the presence of their Lord and are provided for."
> The Holy Qur'an

Ahmad Mohammed Ahmad Al Sharef
born in 1985 and martyred July 19, 2011

Profession: Student at the Higher Institute for Oil and Engineering, Benghazi, Libya
The story is told by the martyr's sister, Saliha Mohammed Ahmed Al Sharef, Benghazi, Libya

On February 15, 2011, the peaceful demonstrations emerged on the streets of Benghazi. The next day, Ahmed joined the protesters on Omar Ben Aaas Street. That day people wearing yellow hats roamed the streets. After the confrontation with those men in the yellow hats, the protestors aided each other. Those scenes were recorded by mobile phones and later we saw them in the media. The third day Ahmed participated in clashes that took place at Al Fadeel Bu Omar katiba. After the fall of the katiba into the hands of the protestors and the discovery of underground tunnels, he found a very old man in a jail. He was still alive but his health was very poor and he was unable to stand on his feet. Ahmed carried him out in his arms. Afterwards he said: "Long life is in God's hands. But I do not think that this man will live long because of his poor health."

Later, Ahmed went to the February 17 camp for military training and then joined the Katiba "The Fight Against Terrorism". He participated in many battles as well as in repelling the attack on the city of Benghazi on March 19. He was in the battles which took place in the vicinity of the city of Ajdabiyah and in the city itself. It was noticed that Ahmed had high combat efficiency, so he was transferred to Special Forces Katiba 21. Later he joined the National Liberation Army and the Katiba "The Martyrs of Za-wiyah". The Freedom Fighters decided to make their way to liberate Brega from the hands of Gaddafi's forces. Brega is an important oil producing area but the residents liv¬ing in the area were experiencing poor living conditions for they had been stranded under siege by Gaddafi's forces. The National Libera-tion Army moved towards Brega on more than one axis. The martyr Ahmed was among those advancing from the southern axis. On July 19, while the Freedom Fighters were trying to advance, Gaddafi's forces tried to get around them and attack them. The Freedom Fighters decided to withdraw, trying to mini-mize casualties in their ranks. But some of them, including the martyr Ahmed decided to face Gaddafi's forces and try to provide cover as the rest of the Freedom Fighters withdrew for they were prepared to die, they were willing to become martyrs.

The martyr Ahmed, God willing, was driving a car in the midst of the battle when one of his friends was wounded. Their friend, the machine gunner, got out of the car to give first aid to the injured friend. Ahmed took his place and, while he was shooting at Gaddafi's forces, he was mar-tyred on the spot when a shell hit the car. He was wounded in the head and received lacera¬tions to his rib cage. The way to Brega was opened up through the southern axis and the city of Brega was then liberated by Freedom Fighters and the brave National Liberation Army.

Ahmed loved swimming and sports in general. Even as a child, he loved to help people. He bred birds, especially doves, as a hobby.

148

A Letter to My Friends

Awaken!Mom! USA

I blundered down this path in search of information; it was I assure you quite by accident that I ended up here. Thank goodness for blunders. All I had in my mind was to fill in the blanks that the mass media has seemed to black out after Egypt had been reclaimed by her people in only eighteen days. I had watched day and night and when the Libyans began to reclaim themselves and their country I just had to follow these people who had faced the deaths and torture of their loved ones. They had let their paralyzing fear melt away and now were of a common heart and mind. They knew there are worse things than death on this planet.

I came to be informed, that is all, and I fell in love with a people, with a country, with a region, with the world and finally with my own country again. I have given nothing more than my thoughts and prayers. I finally worked out what a blog was and joined and felt compelled to join Twitter the same day. The word was out about what a difference the social media had made in Tunisia's and Egypt's fights for freedom and I had to be part of that for Libya.

To my surprise I met hundreds of people from all over the world. Brilliant people. I am just a house mother who has raised my children and being in such gifted company was a bit intimidating to say the least. I found not just intellectuals but a brilliance of humanity gathered together. Their caring and contributions will not all be known to the world but these people are the life-giving force that actually gives this world hope of dispelling the notions many have that we human beings will end in mass destruction of ourselves.

We are all so very different and sometimes misinterpret each others' words but we are all the same in what makes a human being a humane, caring creature of the earth. I am awake after trying to fall into a deep sleep to turn myself off to many of the inhumanities that exist. For some odd reason the media seems not to realize it is the stories of these inhumanities blasting through their airwaves that make us sicker and numb to others.

I am awake and I want to thank you brilliant shining hearts that I call my friends. I am not skilful at writing but I love very deeply and feel even more deeply. There have been multiple days I have not participated and I have had my days of tears for the pain of others. I have had the opportunity to express my pride and love for the brave and wonderful people of Libya in the sacrifices they are making with their lives and the lives of their loved ones.

I want all to know how much I appreciate having been able to express my gratitude for what Libya and her brave free citizens have meant to me. I want the friends I have made here on the blog and its extensions to know how much I appreciate and love them for letting me be part of such an indescribable group of people that will always make a difference for good in any corner of the globe.

How I Saw It

Dr. Anas Toweir, MBChB, Resident Radiologist, Benghazi Medical Centre, Benghazi, Libya

The 15th of February was the night that came earlier to the outcast city of Benghazi, as it was two days before the expected date. We had been waiting for our turn to revolt as our neighboring countries were celebrating the victory of overthrowing their dictatorships. It was the topic of discussion on Facebook but the question that was on everybody's mind was, "Is it possible in real life?" Well, what you must know is that no one ever thought it was. In fact, it was an impossible scenario because, as everyone knew, you wouldn't want to mess with the Gaddafi regime for it was just as ruthless as could be.

Dr. Anas Toweir (left) and Dr. Ahmed Elhasham (right) at the Misurata port, May 2011

It all started at sunset when families of the victims of the Abu Salim massacre – a mass murder of 1200 untried prisoners that occurred in one of the largest Tripoli prisons – started gathering in front of the central security compound aka Almodiria. Their demand was the release of the attorney who was an activist and the spokesman for the families of the Abu Salim case who was being detained for no good reason. It was a peaceful protest, but what must be known is that people were not allowed to protest at all under the Gaddafi regime. Fury made the protesters shout for the undermining of the regime and I was told that it was the women who started it by shouting "Wake up, wake up, Benghazi! This is the day that you have been waiting for!" Soon the crowd increased in number but anyone could tell that they were still afraid and that the consequence of what they were doing was still blurry.

I wasn't far from the scene. I was on a night shift at my workplace in Al-Hawari Hospital, where I was a Senior Medical House Officer at that time. The hospital is on the same street as the central security compound and just a few hundred meters from it. I had people coming in shocked from what they had seen on their way, and certainly not optimistic about the consequences. Word spread all around the city and the reaction was revolution fever. No one knew what to expect in the end, but everyone knew it wasn't going to end quickly.

While the city was asleep a few hundred people, who obviously had a lot of courage, gathered. They marched downtown, getting angrier all the time. What started the bloodshed was the central security officers blocking the march along Jamal Abdelnasser Street, a long street leading downtown. They were smart too, because all they did was stand back and let hired gangs do the dirty work. They had had their reaction planned days before the revolution. The gangs attacked the protesters with swords, machetes, knives and sticks. That didn't scare the protesters at all. If anything, it made them fight in fury. It was a bloody night that ended in a number being injured.

The next day was just the same as the night before, except the march was even bigger and more organized, and was the sign that the revolution was about to ride a higher wave. Whilst a group of lawyers were protesting in front of the North Benghazi Courthouse, another group of people went to the central security compound Almodiria and were fired on, and whoever didn't run away was taken to jail. Another group of protesters on Tree Square, which is also downtown, were once again attacked by the pro-Gaddafi gangs who had started wearing yellow safety helmets so that they would recognize each other. It was getting dark as protesters reached the Juliana Bridge en route towards the Courthouse which was the main protest site. They were fired at with hand-held firearms and it was the fall of the first martyrs. I witnessed the firing as I stood a kilometer away on the Juliana roundabout with my friends. What was odd about it was people started running towards the gunfire and not away from it. That night the city was in a state of confusion.

The day of the 17th of February, the anticipated day, finally arrived and although the outcome was still uncertain, that day it became very clear that there was no going back. The protest continued in front of the Courthouse. Protestors had gathered and had begun walking towards Jamal Abdelnasser Street when they were attacked by security officers and the gangs. Unexpectedly, people fought back with stones. This marked the beginning of a bloody fight.

When I heard the news I went straight to Al Jala, the main trauma hospital in Benghazi, to assist in the Emergency Room (ER). It was one of the most horrific days of my life. Youngsters, as young as 13 years old, were brought in with bullet wounds to the head. About 20 died that night and there were more than a hundred injured. It was a scene I never expected to see in my life, even as a doctor; but what I saw that night in the hospital was just a glimpse of what was to come in the next few days.

The next day I headed to the Courthouse where people were protesting just after the Friday prayer. I saw the fury of the crowds there as they set fire to the internal security building which was just beside the Courthouse. Meanwhile the mourners travelling back from the cemetery after burying the martyrs passed the central security compound Almodiria where the central security opened fire on them. This triggered more fighting that day. I was already in Al Jala that evening, but as the hospital was already full with doctors and volunteers, I headed to my place of work, which was also set up for receiving trauma cases. We had to bring the stabilized cases from Al Jala Hospital to Al Hawari Hospital by ambulance as it was getting full. The drive to and fro was full of danger, and it was the same story the next day. We soon received news that the central security building was taken over. I had to see for myself so I drove there alone and I have to tell you that it was a sight I will never forget: the building that had always brought terror to people was on fire.

On that next day, whilst crowds of people and cars were driving past the Al Fadeel Katiba (the biggest battalion in Benghazi) going towards the cemetery on the way to bury victims, they got fired at as well. The soldiers in the building thought that the crowd was coming for them and opened fire. The fight was now turned towards the katiba. It was certainly a day to remember. We were in the ambulances driving in the areas around the katiba picking up victims and taking them to the hospital. We got stopped by civilians all the time as ambulances had been used by Gaddafi's mercenaries to drive around the city without getting caught.

After heavy fighting and numerous attempts to open the katiba doors, an attempt was made by a brave man named Mahdi Zew, who filled his car with dynamite and gas cylinders and drove it straight into the doors blowing them up and greatly helping the crowd's progress in entering the katiba. Once in the katiba, the young men used dynamite to take it down. The special army forces defected and took sides with the people. This was a big win for the people and it marked the end of what remained of the regime in the rebellious city of Benghazi.

I entered the katiba an hour after it was taken down, riding in the ambulance. It was dark and a lot of its buildings were on fire. We picked up three injured and took them back to the hospital. Two of them had burn injuries and one was unconscious after inhaling a lot of smoke from the fire. I shall always remember, too, a decapitated body I picked up from the ground and took to the hospital morgue.

The days after that were full of joy mixed with wondering what the next step was going to be. There were days of gathering at the Courthouse to protest and pray for peace and prosperity for the country. People were waiting for the United Nations' decision for a no-fly zone, as the regime gave us long nights of terror and numerous threats of airstrikes.

On the 12th of March and on a quiet afternoon as I was on duty in the ER of Al Hawari Hospital, a man was brought in on a wheelchair by one of the reception employees who was out of breath. I jumped out of my seat and was asking what was going on, when I realized that the unconscious man was bleeding heavily from his back. I checked for a pulse; it was faint, so I called for help. Luckily the surgical team was nearby, and we started resuscitating him. To my surprise, an Al Jazeera reporter walked in and I realized that we were resuscitating the Al Jazeera cameraman, Ali Hassan Al Jaber. Unluckily, we were not able to bring him back. His wounds were very serious as there were two bullets in his left lung, and a third fragmented in his liver which was the cause of the heavy bleeding.

The 18th of March seemed to be a quiet Friday evening, when suddenly Al Jazeera announced that a huge army force was 50 kilometers away from the west side of Benghazi. In the streets, people started panicking and running around, some in disbelief and some not really sure what to do. They started gathering and barricading the streets. An hour and a half later there was a continuous call on the radio directing everyone who had a weapon to come to the western gate and fight for their city. That's when the situation felt serious.

I was with my friends at the time, and I went home straight away to see my family. After saying goodbye, which could have been for the last time, I got my belongings and headed to Al Hawari Hospital. Some of my colleagues and I soon left the hospital, and, with several ambulances, headed to the western gate. After spending some time there not knowing what was happening in the front lines, we decided to drive further. Soon, we reached Jaroutha where there were hundreds of men, all getting ready to fight. The chanting of the Takbir (the Islamic calling of "Allahu Akbar", usually translated as "God is Greatest" or "God is Great") was continuous in the background. We decided to drive further but were stopped by the fighters, and when we insisted they threatened to kill us rather than let us cross their line. They were, of course, concerned for our safety. I don't remember who those people were but they saved our lives as we knew later.

After spending an hour or so there, our chief, Dr. Yaser, thought it would be better if we went back to the hospital, so we went back and waited. All I could think about was my family and how I would contact them if something happened, as the mobile phones were hardly getting any connection.

It was quiet at the hospital until about 3 a.m. when the sounds of grad rockets could be heard in the distance. The first case to arrive at the hospital was a man who was injured with shrapnel in his head after a rocket landed in his house. An hour later the sounds were getting louder which meant that the rocket launchers were getting closer; it was as if a huge monster was marching towards the city.

When the sun began to rise, fighter planes began flying over the city. We watched them from the hospital roof but, as we were not really sure if those fighters were friends or foes, we took cover as they flew by.

Soon, the hospital was gushing with injured citizens who had been randomly fired at by pro-Gaddafi forces. Not long after, we received fighters who were in serious conditions from the fighting at the western gate. We also received the corpses of the martyrs found in the areas of fighting, some with bullet wounds that you could put your hands through, some burnt, and some who had suffered other forms of carnage such as the loss of body parts.

I was running between the ER and the rooftop to see if I could figure out what was going on exactly. While I was up there, I witnessed one of the fighter planes light up in flames in the air, and go down to crash somewhere in the Garyounis area. Half an hour later a man came to the ER bringing in an eleven year old boy with first and second degree burns. Their story was that as the plane crashed and seeing that the pilot did not eject, they ran towards the plane to see if he could be saved. As they got close, the plane exploded and caused the brave boy's injury. They brought with them the pilot's helmet, which was blood stained and had brain tissue scattered in it. The forensic pathologist got delayed with work at Al Jala Hospital, so we set up a team and started to identify the victims in the morgue and document everything till the pathologist arrived. At about noon, families started coming in and we had to hand over the victims' bodies for burial.

Hour after hour there was good news coming in, the huge army that was attacking had been depleted by French fighter planes sometime after 4 p.m. and the city looked like it would live to see another day; but I have to say that it was the longest day ever to pass.

On the 12th of April, when Misurata city was in the peak of its fighting days, I set off with two colleagues, Dr. Ayman Swalem and Dr. Ahmed Elhasham, as part of a rescue mission of migrants from Misurata with the International Organization for Migration. We were appointed to take care of the migrants' health on the way back to Benghazi. It was a very dangerous mission, as it was the first ship to enter Misurata; before that only small fishing boats had been going in and out of Misurata.

The Misurata port had been bombarded with grad rockets a few minutes before we arrived at the port, after the 20 hour trip from Benghazi. We were not certain whether it was safe or not, but as we got closer and closer to the docking area we could see people arriving to welcome us, which was a huge relief.

The cargo space of the ship was full of humanitarian aid, some donated by the citizens of Benghazi and some from humanitarian organizations from all over the world. After emptying the cargo, the Libyan Red Crescent brought in migrants from different nationalities, mainly sub-Saharan Africans. Their papers were sorted out, and they were listed and brought on to the ship. This process took quite a few hours. After that was over we were approached by a few Libyan families and a number of injured ambulatory patients asking to be taken to Benghazi. We then realized that the health situation was worse than we thought in Misurata and after we had had a long talk to the chief of mission, he decided to take them onboard on condition that my team and I would take good care of them and be responsible for them. That trip was a challenge for us.

After managing the trip very well, we were anxious to do this again. This time we were determined to be better prepared, so we got permission from the organization and prepared ourselves to accommodate injured people. By the third trip our volunteer team had more staff and we were able to transport intensive care patients onboard the ship. We made more than ten trips. We were always facing trouble but with the help of the chiefs of the missions and the people from Benghazi we were able to help hundreds of injured people.

The spirit that I saw from the young doctors, especially those who participated in these rescue missions, really intrigued me as they were willing to risk their lives to save others. It was certainly something that you don't see every day and I'm lucky to have met and worked with such people.

In answer to the numerous calls for medical aid made through the media, I travelled to Tripoli a few days after it was liberated to help in the crisis in their hospitals. After getting there I realized that the situation in Tripoli was horrific, especially after the discovery of over a hundred dead bodies of patients who had been neglected in the Abusleem trauma hospital; still to this day I don't know the reason for this. As things settled in Tripoli, the city's doctors gradually returned to their positions in the hospitals. I then returned home to Benghazi for I felt my part was done and I was finally not needed in Tripoli anymore. This revolution has taught me that if there is a will there is a way. Despite all I have gone through, I feel that I have woken up from a deep sleep and I thank Allah for letting me see this day where freedom is not a fantasy anymore.

Dr. Anas Toweir sorting out patients to be sent to hospitals after arriving in Benghazi from Misurata, © *Nicole Tung 2011*

One Love

Mohammad Bughrara, Seattle, Washington, USA

In the face of every defining moment in my life I knew that someday I would change the world. I had no knowledge where I would impact it, but somehow I knew I was going to. At first I thought that sports was where I would shine. Then, in January 2011, I severely injured my left shoulder.

Welcome, my name is Mohamed Bughrara, and I am 19 years old and for weeks my only friends were the comfort of the couch and medication to ease the pain. As that medicated life was developing, I heard Tunisia's president had fled the country. Then the voice people of the largest African country proclaimed freedom. However, I hardly understood protesting, so it was shocking to hear of people dying because of peaceful protesting. Nevertheless, the fact is, the people like those of Egypt rose to proclaim that enough is enough. People were in the streets camping all day and night to make a statement for the world to see.

On the 25th of January, Egypt was liberated, and because of my surgery, I was home every day to watch history unfold in front of my eyes. As I was learning more about the movement of these revolutions, I learned that in Libya, my own country, they were scheduling to protest, demanding the very same thing. When family and friends came over to visit and empathize with me while my shoulder healed, I saw that they were all overwhelmed by the news. I did not understand why.

For instance, in the past my dad always joked around when going to work telling me, "If Gaddafi dies, make sure to call me!" I would chuckle and sigh, slightly confused about such hate. I knew Gaddafi as a hated man, one who usurped the top office in Libya. I later learned that the character of this man was unbearable as well. He killed tens of thousands of people in the past, most of them Libyans. I saw Gaddafi in the past as a coward, one who would only spill the blood of his own people.

So, I was surprised in the bombing of Pan Am, at least 270 passengers murdered, mostly Americans. I never thought Gaddafi's evil would extend overseas. I knew then that he would escalate his tyranny. Before the protests, Gaddafi offered about a 24 billion dollar reform to the people. Libyans thought that the revolution would stop there.

I would learn more about Gaddafi every day. I studied every inch of his life since he took Libya by an "iron fist". The more I read about his actions, the more I realized how completely he affected my life here in the States. If it weren't for this hatred of Gaddafi, I know for a fact I would not be writing about this experience right now. I was enraged and inspired. I had full intentions to go to Libya and make a difference. But my physical injuries, parents, and my education made this initial trip impossible.

On the 15th of February, we heard that my hometown of Benghazi had started protesting. Almost immediately, we heard people were getting shot. Days rolled by as I was stuck on my homely couch. I had to do something. I couldn't just sit there knowing people were dying over a freedom we take for granted! A cry for a better life, freedom, which we take totally for granted! I wasn't going to let such a massacre occur in front of my eyes and not do anything about it!

I looked online to see how I could help, and found that organizations were emerging from all over aiding the Libyan cause. I wanted to help, but even more, I wanted to personally touch people's hearts for this revolution. I had family and friends all over Libya with whom we were in close contact. With the information I was receiving, and people in Libya and abroad desperate to know what was going on, I had to try to inform people about what was taking place at the protests.

My goal was to reach as many people as possible and spread the voice of freedom around the world in the quickest and most efficient way possible. Facebook, the biggest social data website that reaches almost everyone, would act as the perfect tool. I had to pick a name for the media buzz I hoped to create. I did not want to pick any names that organizations already claimed. I wanted to do something different; I needed a name with pre-Gaddafi and post-Gaddafi significance, so that after the revolution has ended and Libya has been freed we would continue helping this newly freed country. So I chose "Save Libya".

With the contact of family and friends in the country I was able to deliver updated news feeds to the followers. Each hour of the revolution was a new story, another chapter of freedom, and another page of history turned every second right in front of my eyes.

Friends and family and the innocents killed at the hand of the bloody Gaddafi regime will never be forgotten. I lost many new friends and many old friends. One of them is Mo Nabbous. Mo helped me to stay in contact with those innocent civilians through his network. Mothers, fathers, sisters, and brothers would contact me from Libya begging for the world's help. Day by day, blood was being spilled throughout the country, yet, with each body slain, more people would rise up to claim what was rightfully theirs.

I remember contacting my uncle, and not being able to hear a thing for 30 minutes over the non-stop gunfire of the mercenaries. The only thing I heard was a cry for help, asking America and other countries to support the protests taking place. I shall never forget that moment, nor how much stronger was my need to get to Libya because of it.

But instead, my dad went to visit his family. My father had not been back to Libya in over 30 years. Because of that, I wanted him to go first. I continued my work with Save Libya through donations, dinners, and charity events. As the organization dramatically grew, so did my impatience. Upon hearing the freedom fighters were inching towards Tripoli, the capital, my heart dropped, so badly I needed to be with them. I knew then I had to go to Libya.

What feels like a few heartbeats later, I opened my eyes to Libya. Over the next few months I was on a mission. Despite the fighting, I had to learn more about the revolution firsthand, to hear the people's stories that came with it. I met with my dad briefly in Libya when he visited Benghazi. Then we both went our separate ways to do what we could for our country.

As I traveled from city to newly freed city, I learned more about the stories from eye witnesses who watched history unfold through their windows. I met people from different parts of the country who invited me with open arms into their lives. That gave me a different view of how the country deserved to be free because of how united its people were. It made me feel thankful for how my life is. It made me thankful for my opportunity to practice my daily new right of a free voice, a right for which Libyan people were getting slaughtered left and right for decades.

That wasn't life. No one in this world ever deserves such treatment.

I was at the front lines for much of the trip, and during those days I witnessed more blood than water. It's not the fact that civilians and freedom fighters were dying; it was more how they died. Gaddafi tortured innocent civilians, as if they didn't deserve to live. He would use the most absurd and brutal tactics against his own people to show Libyans and the world what would happen if someone dared speak against him.

Many of his hired mercenaries were caught or killed with hundreds of thousands of U.S dollars in their pockets, their pay for murder of innocent civilians. Gaddafi had paid his expert killers thousands of dollars per day. A sniper claimed to receive ten thousand dollars on a day he killed people. This corruption, this hate, this deadly evil that spread throughout the country from Gaddafi's bloody regime was like a mental disease.

Yet, the people were (and still are!) determined to rise for freedom even if it means going to their certain death. Even when family members and friends die every day, the people's spirits still soar high; it's the knowledge that one will die a free man. Every second of my trip I felt more and more proud of being a Libyan.

It was literally two choices that the Libyan people had; to stand up for their freedom and fight for what's right or to die at the hands of Gaddafi's destruction. It was as Omar Mukhtar said 80 years ago: "We win or we die".

Now we have what is rightfully ours, freedom. Till this day, it still has not sunk in all the way that Gaddafi is gone and Libya is free. So much sweat and blood has been consumed by this struggle that this day still seemed impossible. Nonetheless, the future is now as bright as ever for Libya and its people. It's time for the youth of this revolution to grow as one. As a country that will be our initial goal. For the peace of the people, and not just in Libya, but the rest of the world.

One love.

Wazin Boarder Crossing in the Nafusa Mountains: Welcome to Libya

Allahu Akbar Allahu Akbar

Mohammad Ali Mohammad Al Ayan, Born1993
Student in the last year of secondary school, Zlieten, the Kadoosh area, Libya

On Sunday February 20, 2011, I went out with the rest of the youths of Zlieten to the demonstrations. These demonstrations had begun in the eastern cities of Libya and we went out to support them. The people in the east were demanding the downfall of the tyrant as well as demanding their freedoms and rights. We had burnt centers belonging to the oppressive regime such as Internal Security, Baraem (pioneers of Gaddafi), and what are known as revolutionary committees.

During the last few days we tried to keep the city of Zlieten safe and clean until the tyrant came out and gave his cursed speech demanding his supporters to crush, kill and throw out on the streets people who were against him and those who went out to demand justice and freedoms. We could stand in front of his supporters for only a few hours because they were armed with a lot of weapons and they controlled all parts of the city.

Beginning the next day, all rebels gathered to prepare to get back our freedoms — the freedoms we realized we had the first minute we went out to protest.

And then began a campaign by the katiba to arrest all rebels, however their injustices and tyranny increased our determination and resolution to achieve our goal. Although all our actions and communications were limited by the presence of the katiba, we did not stand idly by. We moved in secrecy. We closed the road to prevent the movement of the tyrant's vehicles during the night and wrote slogans on the walls against the miserable regime.

After the noose was tightened around us, I thought about moving to Tripoli to stay with my relative to avoid being arrested.

On Wednesday May 25, 2011, I went to Tripoli and passed several checkpoints until I reached the checkpoint in the Karaboli area. They searched me personally and it was similar to the previous inspections. But this time they found in my pocket the memory card from my cell phone. There were the pictures and video clips that showed all we had done: the writings and demonstrations that show all the knights and lions of February 17.

It was their joy to torture me. They took me inside the place for detainees within the checkpoint where they kept me for one day. And then they took me to Abu Salim Prison. I was tortured by all the disgusting methods they had. During the interrogation they brought me a list of those who they called "wanted", but whom I call the heroes of freedom. There were names of each person who came out calling for freedom and justice, and they asked me how I knew them. The names I knew were either my cousins or friends, and the others I knew from their bravery on that memorable day of freedom.

The more I answered that I didn't know, they increased torturing me to force me to tell them what these people did or the whereabouts of others. They kept me in this prison for almost a month. Then I was taken to the Ain Zara Prison. It was the same ill-treatment and torture for long periods and deprivation of food and drink for days. And even when they gave us something to eat or drink, it was often dry bread and contaminated water.

They demanded that I repeat their slogans of infidelity and tyranny. Whenever I refused, the torturing was increased and some of them were saying I should be killed. They said they would stop torturing me if I confessed on television that I killed, looted, and carried out acts of sabotage — things I never did.

There was nothing left for them to do except torture me as they used to. Whenever I refused, they put me in solitary confinement for days.

This situation continued in this prison for approximately forty days. Then they took me to Al Jadayda Prison, a new place for me but which was no different from the previous two. This continued until August 19, 2011 — that unforgettable day. They decided to execute all prisoners. We did not know whether to rejoice at the thought of being free of the punishment of the tyrant and his followers, or grieve because our end would come by their hands.

This situation continued until August 21, 2011, the date of freedom and end of slavery. The Freedom Fighters of Libya freed all the prisoners from the hands of tyrants. And this was the end of the tyrannical era in which many free Libyans have suffered.

Allahu Akbar (God is great) Allahu Akbar(God is great), praise to God.

"Beginning the next day, all rebels gathered to prepare to get back our freedoms - the freedoms we realized we had the first minute we went out to protest." Only a year later, on February 17, 2012, many groups of people gather in Libya to enjoy freedoms gained.

A Chance Remark

Jane Massey/Wosson, Cornwall, UK

A chance remark by a friend at a birthday party sent me to Al Jazeera English a few months before the Arab Spring began. As I watched Tunisians and Egyptians oust their dictators and people in Yemen and Bahrain protest, I never imagined it would be possible for the Libyans to rise up against Gaddafi. I can't remember exactly what I knew about Gaddafi at that time but I knew he wasn't going to give up easily.

Soon AJE was on in the background all day, every day. I watched the Libyans start to demonstrate and at first we all laughed at Gaddafi's rambling, lunatic speeches. The man was clearly insane, on drugs or both. Then he started shooting the demonstrators and somehow he wasn't funny any longer. How could this man be fit to run a country?

The most compelling thing was watching live coverage and listening to Libyan people being interviewed. They were intelligent, articulate, reasonable and, above all, likeable. In fact, they were nothing like Gaddafi who was the face of Libya to the world.

The contrast between my life and the lives of the Libyans was striking. My sons live, quite by chance, in a country where they can say and do more or less as they please. The young men we were seeing risking their lives in Libya didn't seem so very different but their courage and determination was breathtaking.

The Libya Live Blog on the AJE website quickly became an addiction providing the latest news, background information and different opinions. For a few weeks I just read the comments but I soon had an account and had started posting. Having never joined any kind of internet discussion before I had nothing to compare the AJE blogs with but it seemed as if this was quite a special group of people.

A sense of community grew fast as we got to know each other and realised that we didn't want to lose touch. Our 'Moussa Koussa' and a few of the other bloggers made the koussa.info site where some of us could discuss what was happening, get to know each other and talk about food a lot!

On the AJE blogs I was Wosson, the ginger cat with the hat but away from the internet I am a 55 year old woman and home is a smallholding in Cornwall where I live with my husband, two sons aged 22 and 24, my mother aged 88, two cats and a dog. Although I trained as a teacher I don't work and my time is mostly spent trying to maintain some semblance of order in a fairly chaotic household and fighting Mother Nature in the 'garden' as we laughingly call it.

Although I've never been to Libya or (to my knowledge) known any Libyans until recently, I've been aware of Libya since I was quite young.

My father hardly ever spoke about his war experiences but he went to Libya on leave in 1943 and spoke about Tripoli with some enthusiasm. He was interested when Gaddafi took over and quite optimistic when he nationalised the oil. Gradually, it became apparent what Gaddafi was really like and while we would laugh at his outlandish fashion sense, Dad's disappointment was evident as the situation deteriorated. Dad died in 1984 but I know he would be very happy to see Libya as it is today, a free country.

Watching the unfolding revolution without the support and friendship of the other bloggers would have been impossible. The stories, pictures and videos were often unimaginably horrific and maybe it was our sense of helplessness that made us type on and try to collect news to inform each other and anyone who might be reading. Gaddafi seemed to have an inexhaustible supply of weapons and absolutely no regard for the suffering he was inflicting on 'his people'. Thank God he had been persuaded to get rid of his WMD, for there is no doubt in my mind that he would have used any weapons at his disposal.

So for eight months the housework, the garden and just about everything else was pushed aside while I was glued to the computer screen. Now, the man who was ultimately responsible for affecting every Libyan's life has gone. Libya is a free country where the people can decide how they want to run things.

My hopes for the new Libya are that they don't dwell on the past. Many questions need answers but I sincerely hope they can focus on rebuilding rather than revenge. I hope that people will try to understand and maybe, in time, forgive. I hope that no more Libyans will lose those dearest to them because of Gaddafi. Last but not least I hope that I will be able to watch a new democracy grow and maybe help in some way.

"My sons live, quite by chance, in a country where they can say and do more or less as they please. The young men we were seeing risking their lives in Libya didn't seem so very different but their courage and determination was breathtaking."

Above: April 28, 2011: young men help load a Benghazi fishing boat with food, medicine and weapons bound for Misurata, a city under siege by Gaddafi's forces.

Below: May 9, 2011: part of Tripoli Street, Misurata, where young men from many backgrounds fought tirelessly with family and neighbours to free their city from the tyrant's siege.

Liberating Zlieten

Muhammad Atiyah Qasim Al Fitouri, born February 23, 1981; citizen of Benghazi, Libya

When the revolution started I was in the city of Zlieten and went out in the peaceful demonstration on February 18, 2011 with some young men until February 21.

We donated blood for our brothers in Misurata and we were filmed by the mobile phone cameras of the Revolutionary Committees, "the fifth column" on February 19, 2011. Then we were chased and attacked on February 21 by the brigades of the tyrant. In this attack there were a number of wounded, including two protesters who were seriously injured.

We ran to the area of Al Boujaza in Zlieten where we were pursued by the Revolutionary Committees on February 23, 2011. We ran back into the area called the "Tuesday Market", where we had relatives.

On March 3, our people were told by the tribal elders to not go out in demonstrations again. They forced us to sign agreements that we wouldn't take part in the next protest. They threatened to jail us and threatened our families.

In April, a local committee was formed in the city of Zliten made up of lawyers, judges and doctors. This committee, with God's help, smuggled 60 people, including me, out of Zlieten to Misurata. In Misurata groups of revolutionaries were formed and trained in a military camp for a week. We trained on RPGs, FN-FAL rifles and heavy weapons.

A week later we were sent to the front in the area called "Abdel Raouf", located in the south of Misurata and we stayed there for four or five days and it was quiet. After that, they called us to the front in the area of Al Dafniya, located between the city of Zlieten and Misurata, to support the Freedom Fighters there. We stayed on the defensive line in the Al Dafniya area.

In the month of May, a specialized committee of several people, including myself, smuggled arms to Zlieten; these were FNs for civil defense. There were clashes with Gaddafi forces and we were making progress toward the city of Zliten of about a half a kilometer to a kilometer, each day until July 6. We progressed to the area of Naima in Zlieten, about 30 kilometers from Misurata.

On this day, violent clashes occurred between us and Gaddafi's battalion. Some elements of the battalion, including mercenaries and three female Ukrainian snipers, who were on a mission to hunt the Freedom Fighters, were arrested by the revolutionaries. On this day, exactly at 8:00am, I was wounded by a rockets launcher as was my cousin. Three revolutionaries of the Badr Battalion were martyred as well as the field commander of the Free People of Al Dafniya Battalion. They took us to Al Hikma Hospital in Misurata where there wasn't sufficient equipment and supplies to treat the wounded. I stayed in hospital until July 24, and after that, I was transferred to the city of Benghazi for treatment there. On August 17, I returned to the city of Misurata, and we liberated Zlieten fully, capturing a number of Gaddafi soldiers. 33 of the revolutionaries of Zlieten and Misurata were martyred. The field commander of the Abdul Gadar Dalf Battalion was also martyred. Then we progressed and liberated the other cities – Al Khoms, Al Nagaza and Gout Al Roman and we joined the revolutionaries of Tripoli.

Band of Bloggers

Suzanne, Australia

This has been the most extraordinary experience.

For over half a year I have sat at this screen and pored over news sites, transfixed by a tidal wave of passion, anger and despair as the citizens of Libya fought to oust a despotic regime.

Initially drawn to the seemingly quick toppling of Mubarak in Egypt and riding on the hope it promised, I was then attracted to its neighbour Libya.

The local parochial press offered snippets of information, but breaking news was hard to find. I turned to Al Jazeera. And it was there that I found the blogs. At last here was a forum to ask questions and express opinions to a worldwide audience. An amazing array of people were chatting, dissecting, fighting and disseminating news and opinions hours, often days, ahead of mainstream media. It was like Pandora's Box to a news junkie like me.

I admit I was naive to begin with. I took some of the disruptive posters comments at face value and argued on a personal level. But it has been a steep learning curve. Through the blogs I have found firm friendships and a deep respect for the wishes of oppressed citizens fighting for democracy. Corresponding with a worldwide community has allowed most of us posters to see beyond preconceived stereotypes and recognise that we all share similar aspirations on this, the Home Planet.

Sitting in front of this screen is a middle aged inner suburban mum, living in a country that a delightfully irreverent Prime Minister once called "the arse end of the world" (Australia).

Australians are used to the "tyranny of distance". We seldom feature on the world stage. But our isolation has been a source of solace to thousands of refugees from worldwide turmoil for over two centuries. Most of us embrace the cultural diversity that new citizens bring and we love travelling to discover those cultures.

An older relative of mine has strong ties to the Middle East through various shipping ventures. One of those ventures was as owner with a "particular friend" of ships taking pilgrims to Mecca. It was on one of those voyages that his ship and hundreds of pilgrims were delayed in berthing at Jeddah whilst Gaddafi's vessel and entourage, including the ubiquitous Amazon Guard and several white Arabian Horses, tried to pull rank. Gaddafi didn't get his way. My relative also travelled widely in the region on other adventures. There are a number of authorities who would still like to know a few more details about some of his adventures. I think that some of those family genes have allowed me not only to be an outspoken and avowed supporter of freedom fighters but also to be a poster using my real name.

The fight for democracy in Libya has been a long and exciting battle. At times I felt so helpless that all I could offer were words. Words of encouragement, humour, sympathy, disgust, anger. But most of all, I've offered support.

I wasn't cowering in a house whilst it was being shelled mercilessly. I wasn't standing in a hospital crying at the broken and bloodied bodies of freedom fighters as they were admitted for urgent care. I didn't cry out in anguish to the world because a close relative of mine was missing in battle. But some of my friends on the blog were doing these things. It was distressing and frustrating. But we did assist in a variety of ways, all through social media. Calls of help bounced across the planet and were answered in kind. The networking was amazing.

Instant communication in the middle of a war zone has been astounding. We were able to converse in real time with freedom fighters as they dashed across the mountains collecting supplies, shelling enemy positions and even as they came under fire. I remember this particular chap typing on his laptop, feet on the dash board, saying words to the effect of "Hang on, we're under fire." Jokingly I replied "Well, get behind a sand dune quickly! Get off the computer." He said he'd have to "deal with it" and would be back in half an hour. Well he was a bit late coming back, but he did. It was like something out of a Monty Python script.

Months of typing into cyberspace on AJE blogs, and subsequent connections on social media, coalesced when news started breaking regarding the rumoured capture of Gaddafi senior. Old "frizzhead" **himself.** I was wide awake at midnight, furiously trawling Twitter, Facebook, AJE, friends' websites, anything, to find credible confirmation. In the back of my mind was the thought that Benghazi and Tripoli would erupt, so I kept multiple tabs open to monitor the slightest whisper. We were so successful at gathering the news, that we broke the news about Gaddafi 20 minutes ahead of AJE.

The only cloud on that news was that Gaddafi's death nearly got me sacked at work the next day when my boss ventured an opinion that the more sensational media were touting. I have become very adept at keeping my mouth shut in public. But not on this occasion! My personal view is that it was "death by cop", and not before time, too.

Reflecting like this has firmed up my resolve to continue this extraordinary journey. I already am following other countries' turmoils in the Arab Spring. My overwhelming impression is that people power and the desire for freedom, democracy and basic human rights is unstoppable. One day I shall travel to the new fledgling democratic Libya. I think that I shall be amazed.

February 17, 2012: Two little girls welcome freedom in their own unique way; and, after years of control and restriction, visitors to an art museum delight in walking right across the mat on the floor in the entry.

Sixteen Years in Hiding: Amro Alsnowsi Aldarrat, Benghazi

The story was written by Amro's brother-in-law with Amro's approval.

In 1995, Amro Alsnowsi Aldarrat was accused of joining a plot against the Gaddafi government. He felt forced to go underground so he hid in his own family home for 16 years.

From 1995 to 2011, his family home was subjected to numerous break-ins and unannounced inspections by officials. For five of those years, these visits resulted repeatedly in broken doors, the demolition of the kitchen and the smashing of its cabinets and cupboards in random violence. The regime confiscated Amro's car and money, and frequently arrested, interrogated and tormented his father and brothers. His brothers were forbidden to travel abroad.

Yet Amro's relatives still managed to secret him away from the authorities in a concealed room of the Aldarrat's apartment. For 16 years they lived in fear. His mother, especially, constantly worried about her son's fate and wondered how long it would be until the secret police found Amro's hiding place. Afraid of being overheard, she avoided addressing him by name and used imperatives like: "Take", "Give me", "Listen"… and when the family moved from the apartment to a new house, Amro was transferred crated in a big box along with the furniture.

To complicate matters, after 12 years confinement Amro developed a chronic illness indicated by intense hemorrhaging. Fearing colon cancer, the family admitted him to hospital under a fake name. The family's fear was true, and the colon was removed surgically. The surgeons gave him 48 hours to live. But Amro beat those odds, spending a month in Intensive Care recuperating. While he was in hospital a doctor wondered why Amro's skin was pale to that degree!

His surgeon had wished to refer him to Oncology to receive chemotherapy, but he refused the treatment fearing he would be recognized and expose his family to further dangers. After his discharge from hospital, Amro was supposed to return in two weeks to have the temporary drain removed but, fearing he would be found out, he didn't return. Instead, he kept the drain and relied on colostomy bags for his natural biological function despite their inconvenience.

During the 16 years of his concealment inside the house and his family's repeated subjection by the authorities to random arrests, interrogations and visits, Amro suffered from a lengthy list of diseases including ulcers, vomiting, bone pain due to confinement in a small space and lack of sunlight, and colon cancer. His mother was stricken with many diseases, also. These included diabetes and hypertension due to her constant worrying about her son.

On 20 February 2011, after the fall of the katiba in Benghazi, Amro went out to the street for the first time in 16 years. His mother was worried about him and tried to stop him, but he refused to stop and went out even though the yellow helmeted Gaddafi mercenaries flooded the streets of Benghazi. His mother suffered a blood clot and there was no medical aid available for her because of the violence being created on the streets by Gaddafi's mercenaries. The blood clot proved to be fatal and she died after three days.

The 17 February Revolution freed the Aldarrat family from the constant fear and worry about their son Amro. The Revolution also brought much needed remedial care for Amro. In April 2011, he was able to travel to Egypt, where he underwent additional surgery. Later, he went to Tunisia for further surgery. In January 2012, Amro fell ill again. His doctor, suspecting the metastasis of the cancer to the liver, sent Amro abroad for further diagnosis and treatment.

I Supported the February 17 Revolution Anywhere In Libya: It Is All Our Country

Wael Al Taher Al Mahdi Areefa, Sebha, Libya

I was born on November 5, 1974, in Switzerland but I am a citizen of the neighborhood of Al Gardah in Sebha. I graduated from the Military College in 1996 with a Bachelor of Military Sciences, having specialized in the engineering field. When the Revolution of February 17 began, I held the rank of captain in the national army and specialized in the management of military engineering.

At the beginning of the events of the February 17 Revolution in 2011, I was in Sebha and, together with Colonel Ali Mehrez, was assigned by the tyrant's regime to secure the neighborhood of Al Gardah. We were also assigned to the task of preparing the youths of this neighborhood to help secure the area, and 200 Kalashnikov were given for distribution to them. We supervised the arming of the youths and allocated them to checkpoints within the neighborhood. On March 1, 2011, I talked with Colonel Ali Mehrez about what was happening in Misurata and Zawiyah and the events and crimes that were being committed by the tyrant's kataib (battalions). There were no barriers, cautions or fears between us because Colonel Ali Mehrez was my relative (my mother's nephew), so we talked openly and we decided to join the February 17 Revolution and prepare the youth of our area to join it, too. We gathered them together and told them that we were going to protect the neighborhood but that it had nothing to do with protecting the regime. In April 2011, one of those young men from our neighborhood, Ismail Abu Sbeeha, was engaged by the tyrant's kataib and was martyred. During the funeral of the martyr, the inhabitants of the neighborhood demonstrated and demanded the fall of the regime.

We joined this demonstration, which was the first one against the regime in the town of Sebha. To my surprise I met my father in the midst of the demonstration. He was one of the protestors strongly and enthusiastically chanting for the overthrow of the regime right there in Sebha's Al Gardah Square! My father's name is Al Tahir Al Mahdi Areefa. He was born in Sebha in 1944. He graduated from Benghazi University in 1969, with a Masters degree in Islamic Philosophy, and began to work in embassies in 1972. He is the author of several books, the most well-known of which is titled "A Trip and Alienation". His presence at the demonstration made me even more enthusiastic and determined to support this glorious revolution of February 17, and it encouraged the rest of my brothers to join the revolution, too.

Immediately after the demonstration, clashes with Gaddafi's Kataib began in Al Gardah Square and lasted for four hours. The next day Gaddafi's Kataib began to search for, and arrest, people who had participated in the demonstration, searching especially for military personnel. Gaddafi's internal security began massive invasions of the farms in the area of Al Gardah Square carrying out arrests and kidnappings. This encouraged us to resume the fight against these unjust Kataib. Among those whom they arrested was Colonel Ali Mehrez. So the Al Gardah thuwar [freedom fighters] formed a sariya [a company] and started to buy medium arms to face the tyrant's regime, which was facing us with medium and heavy weaponry.

On June 6, 2011, I heard on the news that Gaddafi was planting mines in the area of Brega. Because mines are one of my specialty fields, I felt the eastern thuwar desperately needed specialist officers to help with the removal of these mines, so I decided to go to Brega. I gathered my brothers and told them that I had decided to go to the eastern region and that all of us must support the February 17 Revolution until the end anywhere in Libya because all of it is our country, especially as our father had gone out to demonstrate in support of this revolution and the overthrow of the tyrant's regime. Then I went to my father and told him that I was going. He said to me: "God is with you".

We had to go to eastern Libya via a long southern route through the desert to avoid the areas held by the Gaddafi regime. The journey took us from Sebha to the area of Um Al Araneb, a distance of 200 kilometers, where we coordinated with the thuwar of Al Tabu tribes, before going on to Al Kufra, because they are people who know those who are familiar with the Libyan-Chadian Sahara. We travelled with them from Um Al Araneb to Hmaira and then to Al Kufra which is 800 kilometers far into the heart of the desert. The journey took over three days in a row, and we travelled continuously except for a few hours in the nights. After our departure from Hmaira on the first night, we faced the tyrant's Katiba, but fortunately they could not catch up with us because the commander of the journey was an expert person called Mali who was a thuwar from the city of Murzuq. The chase continued for half an hour in the desert. After one full day of travel, we met some Al Tabu thuwar on the desert road. They were transporting supplies to the thuwar of katiba "Desert Shield", which was close to Al Qatrun and, at that time, under the command of Baraka Wardko. At the end of the third day we reached the Rebyana oasis. There we rested until morning and then set off to Al Kufra. We entered Al Kufra at 11am and were welcomed by the commander of the Al Tabu thuwar, Issa Abdul Majeed.

We stayed in Al Kufra for a few days and then we were sent to Benghazi where I went to the National Army Headquarters and was directed to the Department of Engineering. They sent me to the Administration of Engineering for the Eastern Front which was part of Operation No.1 under the commander of Engineering Operations, Colonel Saleh Faraj Alagouri. I was appointed to command the detachment responsible for the reconnaissance of the mine fields and the opening up of safe passages through which the thuwar could move forward safely. When I came to the front it was the beginning of the battle to move from Brega to Sirte. At the start of the offensive battles of the move, all the detachments were assigned to clean mine fields in the Brega area. Then an Engineering reconnaissance detachment was formed to advance with the attacking forces. It was the Engineering reconnaissance detachment's job to explore the mine fields in front of the fighters so that they did not stray into areas that had not been cleared of mines.

While I was at the front – to be exact, in the Um Alhunfus area near Ben Jawad, which is part way between Ras Lanuf and Sirte – we received news from Sebha that the worst fighting yet had taken place in Al Gardah between thuwar and Gaddafi's Kataib. Colonel Mehrez had been martyred in the battle and his body had been mutilated as revenge for joining the thuwar again after his release from prison. Two of my brothers had been wounded: Faisal Al Taher was wounded by a shot in the chest and Mahdi Al Taher was wounded by shrapnel from a grenade launched by a RPG [a Russian rocket-propelled grenade launcher] and they had both been taken to Tunisia. I arranged to join the companies that were going to Sebha after the liberation of Sirte. A few days before the liberation of Sirte we received news that Sebha had been completely liberated and that the thuwar from Jadu, in the Nafusa Mountains, had come to support their brothers, the thuwar of Sebha, in liberating the entire area.

Lies in the Sand

Marevostrum, London

The Arab Spring swept away long-standing dictatorships in Tunisia and Egypt and held out hope for the rest of the region, yet one country seemed likely to resist the trend. In Libya, the quixotic autocrat Gaddafi had deftly alternated the anaesthesia of oil wealth with a sharper edge of brutal repression. His will-o'-the-wisp diplomacy, skidding between pan-Arabism, pan-Africanism, anti-colonialism and expedient engagement with the West was always tinged with the implied threat of a terrible revenge on anyone who dared oppose him.

Over the years I have seen the grieving faces of the Lockerbie bombing victims' families, I have sat beneath the tree planted in memory of WPC Yvonne Fletcher, murdered by a gunman shooting from within the Libyan embassy in London, and I have witnessed how Gaddafi was welcomed back into the world community, the blackmail payment for his renunciation of nuclear weapons. Seven years ago I visited Libya, a land rich in oil, history and open-armed welcomes, but, beneath the surface, a country smothered in fear, where every careless reference to Gaddafi by an ignorant foreigner provoked terror lest one of the omnipresent secret police should overhear. The opulent wealth of Gaddafi's set-piece projects, such as the Green Book Centre in Sirte, sat uneasily with the crumbling infrastructure of Benghazi, while the Libyan leader's funding of (often highly violent) revolutionary movements made a puzzling contrast to his own suppression of minority rights within Libya, where even to utter a few words in Tamazight (the Berber language) could earn a jail sentence.

The unimaginable lives of the Libyans, caught between the rock of their own regime's brutality and the hard place of the outside world's seeming indifference (and the active connivance of those African countries that took the dictator's dole), seemed likely to persist indefinitely. And yet they rose up, lawyers, students, cooks and housewives, in what to everyone – and above all to Gaddafi himself – must surely have seemed a doomed enterprise. As the brave Libyans protested and died, as their movement seemed to flare, flicker and falter in a ferocious burst of long-suppressed fury, I came in search of news.

It was perhaps an act of sorrow, a desire to be present at the funeral of Libya's freedom, to be a witness to the dignity and bravery with which the protestors faced death. But when I came, I found not only news, but a community of people from all around the world, dedicated to the belief that Libya's day of freedom would truly come. Day and night we held our breath as the plight of the Freedom Fighters grew ever worse, and cheered when the international community finally – at the eleventh hour – stepped in to prevent a humanitarian catastrophe. Through the long months of the war, we found ourselves with access to expert views and news from the ground which would have rendered any news editor green with envy. This was the positive side of the information revolution and the thought that even a few in Libya might become aware of the tremendous groundswell of support for them, that they might somehow know that they had a legion of supporters abroad, was deeply comforting.

There was a negative side, too. Having never posted on a blog before, and certainly not one connected to international politics, I had never encountered the online communities of people deeply entrenched in a loathing of western democratic values and humanitarian idealism. For them Colonel Gaddafi was a convenient tool with which to beat the "West". I found myself in long online arguments with a West African who felt that outside support for defence against Gaddafi was immoral because it involved Europeans and that a more principled stand would have been to let every last revolutionary die on the streets of Benghazi, and yet, in contrast, he thought Gaddafi's sale of high explosives to the IRA was the moral act of a man supporting "freedom".

Now that Gaddafi is dead, there is a hope that Libyans can move forward into a free and democratic society, a prize they have earned with their own blood. This isn't a Revolution imposed by a small ideologically driven coterie of army officers, as was the 1969 coup that brought Gaddafi to power, but a genuinely mass movement of a people fed up with 42 years of lies and suffering. I was honoured to be a witness to their struggle, to come to know Libyans (albeit second-hand through their words on a blog) and to understand many of the things that they could never have told me in person when I visited the country seven years ago.

I hope one day to visit Libya again. I hope to see a country where the veil of dictatorship has been drawn aside, and where never again will one man hold the lives (and deaths) of six million people hostage to his personal whims and idiosyncratic philosophy. The history will be just as rich, and the welcomes, I am sure, will be just as warm. But this time I will understand a little more and, in gazing at the crowds in the souks or at Martyrs' Square in Tripoli, I will know that in some small way I have been a friend to Libya. While Libyans were shedding their blood for freedom, I was just spilling a few words. The waiter at the restaurant in Libya will not even know it, but it will make the couscous taste just that little bit more delicious.

February 17, 2012: On the day of remembrance in Benghazi, a group of women pass the burnt-out Mathaba building and a memorial board naming the members of the Alhilal sports club martyred during the revolution.

I was a Member of the National Front for the Salvation of Libya

Maajeda Ali Al-Sahli, Born in December, 1955, Libya

In April, 1976 I was expelled from the University of Libya, Tripoli when I was studying in my third year at the faculty of science – department of mathematics. I had only one year left till my graduation. In January, most of the students of the same year from different faculties of the university went out in protest against the intervention of the Qaddafi regime in the university who wanted to impose certain people in the university's student union by force. Some of the students were wounded and others were arrested.

On April 6, 1976, Abdul Salam Jaloud gave a speech in the yard of the university and said: "Tomorrow, the blood will reach the knees, run over the traitors and agents of America."

The next day, April 7, groups of high school students from different camps were brought in by buses and they attacked us. We were beaten with sticks and stones, and they did even more. They arrested some of us and put us in jail.

After that, unfair decisions were issued against 70 male and female students from different cities, to be expelled from the University of Tripoli, and I was among them. This was in addition to the expelled students from Benghazi University. They deprived us of all our civil rights; we were not able to work, nor to travel.

In 1984 I was jailed for four years because I joined the Libyan opposition – the National Front for the Salvation of Libya - and I had two girls 6 years old. My husband, Faraj Saleh Al Amam was imprisoned for one year. 10 women were jailed with me: two from Benghazi – Fatima Tayib who had a daughter two years old – the other woman Eman Fitouri, newly married, only 6 months back – and an old lady from Tripoli and her daughter – she had four children (who were with relatives), and four brothers who were also in prison. Also four girls aged 17, were imprisoned with us and confined for two years.

We had not seen anyone from our families, did not know anything about them, and they knew nothing about us as visits were not allowed. We all stayed in one room throughout this period and there were no comforts nor sanitary conditions; the toilet was inside that little room. We stayed in Gaddafi's prison for four years and were denied the simplest rights.

During the first few days they led us around blindfolded and handcuffed. We were beaten and threatened with dogs and they put us in rooms filled with the blood of the prisoners, men, who were suffering from the cruelest torture, dog attacks which bit and tore them.

After four years of prison we were freed as kind of political show and fake drama directed and led by Gaddafi and his thugs.

After Libya became free, thanks to God, we are now trying to complete our studies and participate in building our beloved country. We pray to God for Libya to be a sovereign and free nation enjoying a free democratic system.

Free at Last - Free at Last - Free at Last

Heckyes/Michael, USA

I am an American and live in Vancouver, Washington. Like many others I was attracted to Al Jazeera English for news of the Arab Spring. I expected distorted news reporting, but I found it was fair and unbiased. I watched as Egypt freed itself from Mubarak and I wondered how this would play out with the military still in control.

Then Libyans were standing up against their dictator. After the no-fly zone was created by NATO, I started watching the Al Jazeera "Libya Live Blog". The major news agencies of CNN, BBC and Fox were way behind the news we were getting on the blog. AJE English was way ahead of all of them with fresh and timely news. The major news agencies kept saying there was a stalemate. We knew that was not true. On the blog we heard that Gaddafi's forces were being given Viagra and told to rape women. This was verified by reporters months after we knew about it.

The blog had someone in Malta who would report on planes going tactical, that is, being armed with weapons and heading to a target in Libya. There was also a "tourist" on the blog who helped the un-trained Freedom Fighters become a cohesive army. "Tourists" were experienced military men from many countries that volunteered to help and train the inexperienced Freedom Fighters. Many other "tourists" were helping, too, and the helter-skelter fighters were transformed into a cohesive fighting force that ultimately won out over the dictator's forces. Some posts on the blog came from other Libyans who were in-country. I believe NATO also watched the blog. There was a man on the blog who did assessments based on the surveillance satellites. He would let us know what was coming up. He was mostly right on his assessments.

I noticed there was an inner group of bloggers. I was invited to join them and, on their private blog, I found a group of dedicated supporters of the Libyan cause. They countered untruths and confronted Gaddafi supporters. Many of them have written stories for this book.

One of our group's members got us invited to join the Libyan community in Seattle to celebrate the end of the month of Ramadan. Three of us went to the celebration. It was wonderful to see all the joyous faces. The children had the Libyan flag painted on their faces. All the women were beautiful and had such smiling faces that my heart was truly warmed. The men and women we talked to were very happy to know that Libya had support on the internet. We were treated with a lot of kindness and respect. Until then, they had had no idea that we waged cyber war with Gaddafi's paid bloggers and other malcontents on the internet. We met a young Freedom Fighter just back from Libya. He had driven Toyota trucks and supplies into Libya. He told us every load of supplies had toys for the children so they wouldn't be too distracted by the war.

I still get a warm feeling when I recall my time spent with the 300 people who were at the celebration. At the celebration we learned that before the revolt the young men used to hang out and not be very productive. They were called "saggy jeans". Now it is a term of endearment as the "saggy jeans" guys became Freedom Fighters.

I have a great respect and love for the Libyan people. I was most fortunate to spend an evening with the most joyous group of people I have ever encountered. Freedom means more to me than ever, now.

I am very optimistic the people of Libya will form a government that is inclusive and supports equality and human rights. They have earned their FREEDOM.

The Story of a Hero

Abdul Salam Abdul Nabi, age: 37
Freelancer, Tobruk, Libya

My story with the tyrant began during my childhood. Since I was 11 years old, I used to spend a lot of time by myself on the beach imagining myself living in some other country where I could play on the playground with my friends like every normal child in this world should.

I used to hear stories told by the adults of how wonderful and progressive this country was before it fell into the hands of the tyrant and how it had descended to the lowest possible level.

I was always ahead of my generation and my friends who were older than me, in terms of awareness and thinking and there was always one question that kept troubling my mind. Why? Why do we live like this? Why are we marginalized? Why do we lack the most basic human rights? Whenever I traveled abroad, why was Gaddafi the first thing that came into people's minds when I said that I was from Libya? Why was education and healthcare in Libya at such a low level?

The feeling of injustice and oppression had always been present with us, but given the circumstances in the country that rose from the constant tyranny and bullying of the people, it was very difficult to talk and discuss in depth about the matters and things that we were unsatisfied with. I had a close friend, who was so upset and afraid of talking about these matters, that we started using symbols and codes, fearing for our lives and the lives of our families because of that tyrant Gaddafi, who had been feeding on our souls for the past 42 years.

When the revolutions in our two neighboring countries, Tunisia and Egypt, were over, I was yearning and hoping that my country would awaken from the lethargic hibernation that had lasted for decades, and finally begin to feel the sun of freedom, because life with Gaddafi is no life at all and a life which I could not accept because he killed all of my friends.

Gaddafi tried to bribe the Libyan people by inducing and promising cheap and false improvements in life, forgetting the fact that the lions had awakened and would not rest until the whole country was cleansed from his impurity.

On February 17, during our lunch, at my home on Palestine Street, where I live with my mother, my father, my brothers, my wife and my four children, we heard voices coming from outside.

When we went out, internal security men had surrounded a house in which some young people lived. The youths who came out to join the peaceful demonstration demanding their basic human rights and freedoms, managed to force the internal security men to lay down their weapons and thus made all of the youths gather and take to the streets in order to cleanse the city of Tobruk. Thank God – we were able to liberate the city within 24 hours!

During the liberation of Tobruk, more battles for liberation and struggles were taking place in several other Libyan cities, and with the help of God several more eastern cities were liberated. My comrades and I, along with many freedom fighters from the eastern cities, began to march towards the capital Tripoli.

We participated in the liberation of areas beyond Ajdabiyeh, specifically Ras Lanuf, and there we lost one of our dearest comrades, Naji Zayed, after whom a freedom square in the city of Tobruk on Palestine Street has been named.

After we entered Bin Jawad and liberated it, we had to pull a tactical withdrawal to the city of Ras Lanuf. The next day we entered the city, assured that it was liberated, but we were surprised by mortars and rockets that were launched and fired by the tyrant's soldiers. Several of Gaddafi's brigades and volunteers launched a counter-offensive against us and as a result we were surrounded and separated from our comrades. There were many wounded and martyred. I had been shot in the leg and after a piece of shrapnel pierced my back, my comrade Khaled and I were captured by Gaddafi's forces. After tying us up by barbed wire and giving us severe beatings, they took us to the city of Sirte. While we were on the road to Sirte, they tortured us in the cruelest possible manner. Apart from cursing, insulting, spitting and other degrading methods of torture, I was beaten by one of those criminals with the handle of his rifle so hard and frequently that my head started to bleed profusely and it seemed as if the bleeding would never stop.

Later, when we arrived in the city of Sirte where the internal security facility is located, I was thrown out of the car in a such violent manner; the fall was so severe that I lost consciousness and was lying there on the ground for about 10 minutes. Gaddafi soldiers, these criminals, began to compete for whose insults and torture methods were the more efficient and degrading. But then I stood up and asked them: "If you have the slightest decency to treat me as a human being, and to stop torturing me, it is better that you empty your gun magazines into my head… for I am Libyan and I am free and proud and I will not be humiliated."

After that, they took my friend Khaled and me into the interrogation room, and while we were walking towards the room, we heard loud voices and screams from people being tortured. The screams were so loud that it felt as if the whole building was shaking. We weren't able to see anything, because they had put cloths over our heads which they removed once we entered the interrogation room.

They began with the interrogation and asked me what my name was, where I was from, and they also asked me if I had any personal documents. I told them that my documents were lost during the fighting and I told them that I was coming from the city of Bani Walid where my sister was living with her husband. I talked very loudly on purpose so Khaled, who was outside the room at the time, could hear me. While I was being interrogated I hoped to God that Khaled could clearly hear all the things I said, so that later, when they interrogated him, there would be no inconsistencies in our stories. After I finished telling them my story, the questioning about the people of eastern cities of Libya began. They called my people names such as traitors, dogs and rats, and I, on the other hand, with my whole heart, defended my people by saying that they were free and brave Libyans and suddenly somehow I felt that I had gained the upper hand in this situation.

When the interrogation ended, they threw us into a cell and the soldiers began to exchange insults and cursing until a soldier, who in my opinion had been sent by God, appeared. That soldier asked us if we needed anything, and I replied that I needed a phone to talk to my wife, because she hadn't heard from me since I had left the house. He then told me to wait and came back after 15 minutes carrying a phone and told me to make this phone call as short as possible because I had very little time before the other soldiers came back from torturing other prisoners.

In that moment, I was very confused, and I couldn't clearly recall all the things that happened, but fortunately God helped me to remember my wife's phone number. I called her and the only word I heard from her was "Hello". I told her that I was being held captive at an internal security facility in Sirte and that she should inform my sister's husband who lives in the city of Bani Walid because we were arrested not far from their home, and then I hung up. The call didn't even last a minute. During this call I tried to send a message to my sister's husband through my wife, and I tried to reveal as little as possible even if the message was not be conveyed at all.

And indeed, the message did reach my sister's husband, who, thanks to God, had a friend who was in charge of internal security in the city of Sirte. He called one of his contacts in Sirte who was from the Gaddafi tribe and when he entered my cell I was stunned. He grabbed me by my arms and asked the guards "Have you finished interrogating him? Do you need anything else from him?" Then he took me outside the building, and just before the exit there was a hall in which I witnessed a horrendous scene that will never be able to forget. Approximately 30 prisoners were kneeling on the ground and were being tortured in the most appalling manner possible. At that moment I felt a strong urge to grab a gun off one of those soldiers and kill them all so that they themselves would become the victims of their own torture.

When we approached the outer gate, I asked the man who helped where we were going. He told me that we were going to his house and at that moment I asked him about my friend Khaled. He told me that he would look into it later but I wouldn't take a no for an answer and insisted that we go back for him because when we left our homes we had sworn to each other that nothing would separate us except martyrdom. He went back and tried to free him and thank God, succeeded. We all went back to his house where we stayed for three months. During these three months I was literally boiling inside, listening to the news from the front and feeling sad and depressed for being away from my family for so long and for not being able to participate in the ongoing battles for the liberation of Libya.

We came up with a plan to go home by leaving the country through Tunisia and reentering again through Egypt. But the problem was that Khaled had previously been employed in the security sector which prevented him from leaving the country without permission. So he asked me to go by myself and I rejected his proposal and told him not to bring up anything like that ever again.

We continued to work on our plan of returning home. We met one of the elders from the city of Bishr, a pious and virtuous man who welcomed us warmly. I asked him if he could help me return home, because the city of Bishr was the only city at the time from which Gaddafi brigades entrenched in the city of Brega, could be circumvented. He immediately asked his nephew to take us to his home where we stayed for four days. We then began our journey through the desert towards the city of Ajdabiyeh.

Once I laid my eyes on the freedom fighters' checkpoint, I got out of the car and rushed towards our freedom flag and embraced it with all my strength. I told the freedom fighters at the checkpoint that I had been dreaming of this moment for three long months and that I thought I would not live long enough to experience it. Then I knelt to the ground and kissed it and started thanking God for giving me the strength to endure and survive the horrors I had been through, but God's mercy upon his believers is endless.

The day when I finally was able to speak to my father for the first time in several months was a Friday. At the beginning of our conversation I asked him how he was, and how our family was and how all of my friends back in Tobruk were. Then I made a joke by asking him if my mother had made couscous for lunch, and he replied with a laugh that she had – then I asked him if he would like me to have lunch with them. This last question obviously upset my father and he kept asking me again and again where I was. I told him that I was in Ajdabiyeh on my way back to my beloved Tobruk. Suddenly my father started to cry and then he started to praise the name of God again and again.

On my way back to Tobruk, I had a lot of mixed feelings that were tearing me apart. On one hand I was extremely happy because I would return to my house and see my family and my friends; on the other hand I was sad because I was returning home without my closest friends. I knew that they were beneath the earth resting in peace and I knew that I would never see them again in this life, but I was, in a way, happy for them because they are now residing in the house of God as martyrs.

It was a day that I will never forget. There was this feeling of joy and happiness among my family, my friends and the whole neighborhood. A lot of people came to ask about me and to see me and to make sure that I didn't need anything.

A lot of people, such as my relatives, friends and neighbors, were beginning to gather at my house along with the media who wanted to interview me and to write a story about my experiences in the war, but I refused to do so fearing that this could bring harm to the people who were still imprisoned in various camps and facilities, at the time.

I stayed in Tobruk for a while, and later on, I went to Benghazi in search of the relatives of people who had helped me during my imprisonment so I could express my endless gratitude and thank them for doing right by me.

One had been a volunteer with one of Gaddafi's brigades and he was imprisoned by the freedom fighters and there were rumors that he had been transferred to the city of Benghazi. I searched for him here and there but I wasn't able to find him. I went to the doctor to have various tests performed. I was told that I must have back surgery because my spinal cord was slightly injured and affected. The doctor told me that the recovery from this surgery would be no less than six months. So I rejected that option because the situation in the country wasn't stable yet and I wasn't ready for such a risky operation especially with this tyrant still in power.

I was advised by my doctor to start treatment on my back which would last for about a month in order to alleviate the damage that had occurred after the injury. This kept me away from the battle front. However, I insisted on providing as much help as I could and I was frequently in contact with the local council of the city of Tobruk to provide assistance to the freedom fighters on the fighting fronts.

After the completion of my treatment I went to my parents and told them that it was of utmost importance that I go back to the front. So along with many volunteers from our battalion, which was called the Ali Hassan Al Jaber Brigade, under the command of Muftah Amr Al Shahny – who was like a father and a friend to us – we united with freedom fighters from the eastern front and after achieving numerous victories we headed towards Sirte. I was one of the first who joined up with the freedom fighters from the western front. Later on I headed to the city of Misurata in order to fulfil the dream of martyr Muhammad Al Misrati, who dreamed of entering Misurata overland. His comrades suggested that we enter Misurata by sea, but he refused and insisted that he wanted to enter the city overland on foot along with his children who were freedom fighters. Thank God, I was able to fulfill his dream and I entered the city of Misurata overland in his memory. Over a certain period of time I met a lot of freedom fighters from all across Libya and I became friends with many of them. Today, with the revolution over, I consider them to be my brothers. The most important thing in this noble revolution of ours, is the fact that Libya gathered all of its children and united them and thus killed all the seeds of evil which had been planted among us by this tyrant.

I went back to Sirte and was injured by two bullet wounds to my back after which I was transferred to Benghazi for treatment. It was in Benghazi that I had received the news of the liberation of Libya and elimination of the tyrant. The dream of all Libyans came true.

I thanked God that the blood of our martyrs wasn't shed in vain and for everything we were able to do for our precious land. Now I have finally achieved peace of mind regarding my children's future in this country, for I am now sure that they will have free will and a decent life thanks to our martyrs who sacrificed their lives so that we could enjoy this moment of freedom.

Live Free Libya… God is Great, God is Great, God is Great.

Freedom Fighters in Sirte on October 17, 2011

Throughout the World, People Deserve to be Free

AmericaGrl, USA

I fell in love with Libya quite by accident. It was April of 2010, and I was on an Irish football league website. A curious comment caught my attention, and I "clicked" it to learn more about its author. The next thing I knew, I was looking at a young man's Facebook profile page. I almost reflexively clicked the "back" button on my internet browser, but something stopped me. Before I could reason it through, I typed a quick greeting to the young man and went back to reading football statistics. What ensued from that innocuous little "hello," was an enduring friendship between a young Libyan man and me. Throughout the months that followed, I exchanged e-mails and phone calls with my new friend Ahmed. He knew little of the United States, and I knew even less of Libya. Ahmed told me about his country, and I told him about mine. I learned of his family; of his brothers and sisters. I learned about Islam and Ramadan. And finally, I learned about Gaddafi, and the monstrous crimes he had committed against his own people.

I'll never forget the night of 19 February 2011. My telephone rang a little after midnight. I could tell from the number on the Caller ID that the call had originated from Libya. Instantly, I knew something was horribly wrong. Ahmed would never call me at that hour unless he was desperate. Feeling sick to my stomach, I answered the phone. I could barely make out what Ahmed was saying. After a few minutes I pieced together what had happened. My friend's father had been killed by Gaddafi mercenaries in Benghazi.

It was at that moment that the war became very real to me. Ahmed told me of his plans to join the Freedom Fighters and we said our goodbyes. Weeks dragged by. During that time, I scoured the internet looking for any news of the war I could find. As luck would have it, I happened upon the AJE English website and the AJE Libyan Blog.

And so began a journey that has lasted six months and introduced me to some of the finest people in the world. It was there, on AJE's blog pages, that I poured out my anger and frustration, where I shed many tears, where I was able to follow the war almost as if I was on the ground with the Freedom Fighters themselves. It was the only place where I felt like I could fight, and fight I did. At times, the blog was crawling with Gaddafi supporters and anti-NATO sentiment. Many of the "Freedom Writers" took shifts, actually working nine, 10 hours at a time sitting in front of their computers refuting the vitriolic Gaddafi propaganda smeared across the blog's pages.

After several months I heard from Ahmed. He was on his way to Ajdabiya, where a large group of Freedom Fighters were congregating to launch an offensive against Gaddafi forces holding the town. It was then that I also discovered that my friend's little brother, Ayman, was now a Freedom Fighter as well. Ayman was not yet 20 years old. Days of uncertainty followed. I did not know whether my friends were safe, or even where they were. Finally, I received a message from Ahmed. He was safe for the time-being. Ayman, however, was missing.

The next few days were horrendous. All of us knew that if Gaddafi forces had captured Ayman, there was little chance of his surviving. Reports of Freedom Fighters dying at the hands of Gaddafi's men were heard daily and we all feared the worst. I remained on the blog throughout the gut-wrenching experience until the news came. It was the best news anyone could have hoped for. Ayman, and 20 other Freedom Fighters, had been found. They had been separated from their battalion and had gotten lost in the desert. Ayman was alive!

With the exuberance expressed on the blog at this news, one might have thought that we were all related somehow. Perhaps, indeed, we are related. This small group of people, these "Freedom Writers," are related in that we share the same belief that no man, woman, or child should live under an oppressive, cruel dictatorship, and that all people, throughout the world, deserve at the very least, to be free.

Libya is free.

September, 2011: the Free Libyan National Team celebrate victory after their first game played as a free team of the new Libya. They played Mozambique, winning 1 – 0, in Cairo. In October, the team qualified for the 2012 African Cup of Nations, the football championship organised by the Confederation of African Football.

I returned home full of pride

Jalal Al Sharif, Benghazi, Libya

My name is Jalal Al Sharif. I am a Libyan citizen, born in 1970. I am married with two children. I am an auto parts dealer and I had had no military or weapons training up until the time of the Tunisian revolution, which ousted Zine El Abidine Ben Ali, and the Egyptian revolution, which brought down Hosni Mubarak. The Libyan people finally had a chance to breathe freely after the suffering and tyranny of 42 years, after the state of fear and panic caused by officers of internal security and the battalion in the city of Benghazi when the officers were ordered to declare a state of emergency. I joined the revolution on February 20, 2001, the day of the liberation of Benghazi.

I joined the Camp 21 special forces – artillery branch – where I trained on rocket launchers and then joined the anti-aircraft group and trained on maintenance, disassembly and installation of weapons. Then we mounted these weapons onto freedom fighters' vehicles up until February 25. We then transferred to Camp 2nd of March in Slimani where we established an anti-aircraft battalion; we stayed in this camp till March 17 when Gaddafi aircraft targeted this camp; we shot one of them down. The following Friday we received orders from the commander of the battalion to go out and help defend the city of Benghazi from Gaddafi's invasion and strike a defensive line in an area called Tika. Most of our battalion did not have any weapons except anti-aircraft guns and we stayed in Tika from 6:00pm Friday night until the morning of the next day. We were surprised by the approaching enemy and the powerful weapons they had along with a lethal column of tanks and armored vehicles. One of the officers ordered us to withdraw and prepare for guerrilla warfare to cut off the road in front of this army and prevent them from entering Benghazi.

Then I joined the February 17 Battalion and worked with their units processing weapons until the end of April. Following this, I joined the Jawara Brigade at the western gate of the city of Ajdabiyeh and was made field commander. Then, on May 20, we entered into clashes with Gaddafi forces at Forty, 40 kilometers from Brega. Before zero hour, one revolutionary was martyred and I was injured by shrapnel in the leg following the explosion of a rocket mortar. On June 13, one day before my injury, we had rescued a full medical crew consisting of a driver, two doctors and a nurse, including an ambulance, from a very severe Gaddafi bombardment. We saw the medical crew lying on the ground and hurried to get them into the ambulance. Then I and a driver took the ambulance away; thank God there were no injuries.

I received treatment for my injury and I returned to the front after 27 days of recuperation. I joined Ali Nuri Asbag Battalion, and we entered the city of Brega. The resistance was very strong at the beginning of the month of Ramadan and our cars were struck by Milan missiles twice on August 8, but I was not injured. I then went to the front on August 15, and the temperature was very high. We were being bombed from inside Brega and there were strong clashes between Gaddafi forces and us. I was injured again by shrapnel from a rocket. The injury was severe as the main artery in my left thigh was damaged, so the field hospital evacuated me to Benghazi where I had emergency surgery to transplant the artery. I was in hospital for 15 days and then transferred to Tunisia for physiotherapy. Thank God that I was able to walk again, so on October 12, I decided to return to the front in Sirte and arrived on a stretcher so that I could provide assistance with my experience in the maintenance of weapons. I stayed in Sirte until

October 20, the day Gaddafi fell and was killed and Sirte fell to the revolutionaries. I stayed two more days helping comb the area and then returned home full of pride that I had been part of the defense of my nation.

October 22, 2011 The freedom fighters returning from the Sirte front lines to Benghazi

A Wish for the New Libya

Vaska Tumir, Canada

My connection to Libya goes back to 1971 when, just a teenager, I arrived in Tripoli with the rest of my family who would live there, on and off, for the following couple of decades. We were part of that international expatriate community made up of professionals in various fields who'd come to Libya either through various technical-aid programs – as did my family, my father being a medical doctor – or were working for one of the oil companies there.

For the first several years, I spent only my school holidays in Tripoli, visiting my family there, and was only vaguely aware of the political repression in the country. My recollections of that time are of the immense, dry heat of the Libyan summers, of the best bread I've ever had, of teenage parties I was always being driven to and back from by my long-suffering father, of the huge night skies of Tripoli, black as the proverbial ink and studded with more stars than one could credit there were in the entire Milky Way (Tripoli was a poorly lit city at the time, and the view of its night skies was one of the benefits of Gaddafi's stinginess about things public), and of sporadic, sotto-voce discussions of his rule and his growing megalomania, his thirst for absolute power, that took place in my parents' living room.

While all the Libyans I met were invariably friendly and welcoming, no one dared to speak about politics openly: the only "conversations" they allowed themselves were obviously fake, forced expressions of love for the "Great Brother Leader." All of the grumbling, and there definitely was some, was restricted to one's immediate circle of friends, however – any open criticism of the regime was simply unthinkable.

I came to know Libya a little better only at the end of the 1970s, when, freshly graduated from university, I visited again to see my folks there – and stayed a whole year, getting my first-ever job in Tripoli, cutting my teeth as a teacher of English. By that time, my father had taken up a position in one of the few privately-owned hospitals in the capital, and since he had a close relationship with the owners of the clinic, I was asked to give private lessons to the young woman married to the son of the family, who was studying English at the university.

I'll call her Aisha: my private student. She was a member of a prominent Tripoli family, married into another prominent family, several of whom were lawyers and legal scholars. I saw Aisha regularly, but it was months before she and her husband finally felt "safe" enough with me to start to open up about what was going on in the country. It was from them that I learned of the fate of the university students in Benghazi and Tripoli who had dared demand a free student union, the fate they shared with the group of Libyan army officers who had declared themselves against the Gaddafi regime. Everyone in Libya knows about that black April of 1977.

The events Aisha and her husband told me about had taken place two years before, but they were as fresh in their memories as if they'd happened the day before. By then, in early 1979, Al-Fateh University in Tripoli was a "dead" campus, with students utterly cowed and traumatized by the sight of their peers hanged in public on the very campus where they all went to school, their deaths televised to the whole country. Aisha's husband had worked on the defence committee for the military officers who met the same fate, and was himself, as a result, under constant, close surveillance by the regime. Aisha rarely went to university lectures and was trying to cover the syllabus by herself, studying at home, taking private lessons, hoping that she could finish her program and graduate despite the black mark on her family name. I don't know what eventually happened to this young couple, both of whom would have been such assets to the Libyan society if allowed to lead normal lives.

To this day, my sister also remembers driving in a car with my parents and my mother turning to the back seat to cover her eyes so she, still a child, would not see the corpses hanging from the public lights in Tripoli.

What I remember most poignantly, however, were my girl students at the teachers' training college: their eagerness to learn, their high good spirits, their immense curiosity about the world, their palpable longing for a freedom they imagined me having and knew I would enjoy fully once I left Libya. It was of them, first, primarily, that I kept thinking of as the real Libyan Revolution began: they would be middle-aged women now, most of them mothers of the young fighters we were seeing on the videos pouring out of Libya, sisters and wives of the older men who also stood up with the youth of Benghazi, of Zawiya, of Misurata, and all the other cities and towns, until Tripoli, too, began to stir. Some might have turned Gaddafi supporters in the years gone by, but knowing Tripoli and its people, I expect only a few would have chosen that route into full adulthood. And even though it was the young men of Libya who were fighting and dying for the freedom their neighbours also longed for, it was still my students that I kept thinking of: hoping they and their daughters would also get to taste the sweetness of freedom they had yearned for and could only imagine – never for themselves – in the late 1970s, in those Tripoli class-rooms, in which one or another would tell me, or write me a little note, smuggling it inside her home-work, about how they feared their future husbands would not allow them to continue to study or work after marriage, how they wished they could fly away, like birds, somewhere where they would be free.

The image itself comes from one of those smuggled notes a student had written me, not daring to con-fess and entrust her deepest hopes to anyone else but this foreigner, barely a year or two older than her, who would leave Tripoli in the summer of 1979, would a year later meet, entirely by chance, a Libyan Jewish friend in Milan, Italy, and reminisce with him about the mutual friends they'd left there, and who would, decades later and thousands of miles away in Canada, stand with so many others on that electronic "Tahrir Square of the World," – as I once called the AJE Libya Live Blog – day after day and week after week, to give some support and aid, however small, however slight, to the new Libya being born from the suffering, the courage, and the heart of its people.

Now, that the birth-pangs are over and the new Libya begins to breathe more freely, my prayers go out for those girls-become-women of Tripoli, of Misurata, of Zintan and Benghazi, of every Libyan town and city I have seen and have yet to see: May my former students and their daughters never again have to dream and long for a freedom elsewhere. May this new Libya be spacious enough for that freedom to reach its daughters in as full a generosity of spirit as it greets all of its sons.

October 23, 2011: the liberation of all of Libya is celebrated in the city of Benghazi. Canada is among the countries remembered as one that helped protect Libya's people from Gaddafi's indis-criminate use of violence against civilians.

Story of a Rebel
Hosam Al-Din Saleh Faraj Muhammad Alagouri
Student, Benghazi

By Hawa Al Masdour, Hosam's mother

It was late in the afternoon when we were sitting for afternoon tea when my fourth son rushed in exclaiming: "He has lost it all!!!" It was always our wish to get rid of the tyrant. My son said loudly: "Down with the tyrant!" I put my cup of tea on the table nearby and raised my hands begging God to support us. Very quickly all the young people gathered and sat around an olive tree, as we live on a farm inside Hawari village. Everybody heard the news and came to be a part of this big event. I encouraged my son to go out and say "No" for the first time, as we could never say it before. It was kept silently in our hearts. So Hosam went off saying: "The tyrant prevented me and others from achieving our goals and always caused us a heartache."

Hosam was born on May 9, 1990. He was a very polite, calm and clever boy. He finished his primary school in Sloug, in the village of Omar Mukhtar. Hosam grew up in Benghazi and finished his schooling at Abdelrazeq Shekhi Secondary School. He became a student of the Faculty of Economy and from that moment, he hated the tyrant and his system.

Hosam always admired uniforms due to the fact that his father is a colonel in the army in the mines division. He secretly wore his father's hat and insignia. He graduated from high school and tried to join the army as well, along with his best friends. But because his cousin was killed by Gaddafi, Hosam's application was rejected, and during the interview he was asked silly questions, such as if he prays and what he thinks about religious people. His answers were honest. He said what he felt, so the army committee rejected him, but accepted his friends. Later, a letter was sent to his father saying: "Your son is an extremist." The boy was hurt badly.

When the February 17 revolution erupted, Hosam joined the peaceful demonstrations asking for freedom for the people. The tyrant let his dogs on them, geared up with yellow helmets, knives, guns and clubs. At first, the most of protesters were family members of victims of the Abu Salim Prison. Hosam kissed me on the head and said: "Forgive me mother, but it is time for jihad." It was a very difficult moment but without hesitation, he went out, accompanied by his four brothers, Salahdeen, Emad, Faraj and Mahmoud.

During the demonstrations, Hosam was shot in the hand. His shirt was completely stained with blood. His brother tried to get him to the hospital but there was no ambulance around so they decided to carry on until Hosam fainted because he lost a lot of blood. Hosam was taken to the hospital, and was unconscious till February 20, 2011 when he woke up surrounded by doctors, heroes and two of my other sons.

Then everyone decided on the second day after the burial of the martyrs who fell on that day, not to give up (to remove the regime) and joined together to continue with the revolution. The protesters secured the entrance to the Hawari Hospital, which is also the entrance to our neighborhood, to protect the families. My sons were among them. I and other women prepared food for the protesters. During the holy month of Ramadan we made food for thuwar on the front line.

After his recovery Hosam was very active till the liberation. He went several times to Sloug and asked the members of our family to come to Benghazi to donate blood for the hospitals in Benghazi. We own a bakery in Sloug (80km from Benghazi). The foreigners left the country and there were no workers in the bakeries, but Hosam, with the help of his friends, decided to bake bread for the refugees in Al Bidan area, near Ajdabiyeh. For two months, every day they baked bread and transported it to Al Bidan to distribute among the displaced families. Also he used to bring bread to Benghazi for the displaced families from Ajdabiyeh. Hosam and my son Emad repaired our old truck and went to Tobruk, Derna and Beida to collect weapons which they brought to Benghazi to send to Misurata. Our old truck full of the weapons was sent by ship to Misurata. Hosam was among the youngsters who were guarding Hawari Hospital and helped organize traffic in the city. All members of my family took part in the revolution and we supported it to succeed with all that we had: our effort, our money and our lives. We did it for a free Libya.

On March 19, 2011, one of the freedom fighters, Ashraf Asadig phoned to tell us that a very long convoy of army trucks equipped with heavy guns, tanks, Grad rockets and anti-aircraft missiles, Gaddafi's loyalists and his private army were in the city of Gamines. One of my sons went to check this information and then all of them went, like eagles, to resist this convoy. They did their best with the help of God. Gaddafi's forces were tremendous and if NATO had not intervened at that time, Benghazi would have been history. Gaddafi's forces retreated to Ajdabiyeh and started planting mines, but Hosam's father, as a specialist in mines, left to defuse them. He was accompanied by his other son. During the fighting in Brega, Hosam's uncle Idris Mohamad Abdalla Al Masdour was martyred and his brother had to have his right leg amputated after he was wounded by 23 caliber anti–aircraft missile.

Gaddafi's forces were later surrounded in Sirte and he was caught with his son and killed. This was the happiest moment in our lives.

It remains that our only demand is freedom and long live Libya and her brave men.

February 19, 2011: protestors surround Al Fadeel Katiba in Benghazi

The Fighter
Ehsan Abdallah Ben Ali, Benghazi

Narrates her story of her struggle and fight with Gaddafi tyrant regime

My story with the tyrant Gaddafi's regime started when I was a child in the sixth year of primary school, when the husband of my eldest sister was imprisoned. I was very close to her and her husband and we also had very strong ties because the husband of my sister, Professor Abdelaati Khanfar, taught me Arabic language in school at that time.

He was arrested and imprisoned in 1970 one year after Gaddafi led a coup against King Idris and he was sentenced to life imprisonment. He had four sons and one daughter. With the mercy of God, he came out of prison in 1988 on an occasion called "Dawn began". My sister died of cancer three years before he was released. I watched my sister melt in front of me from sorrow, sadness and the disease. Her small children were deprived, first from their father, and when he came back, they were deprived of their mother. My sister's tragedy left in me a hatred for this inhuman regime, in addition to the hatred which was planted during my childhood when the money and property of my father was confiscated as he was one of the wealthiest merchants in the eastern area. Negative feelings accumulated inside me as the days passed; injustices and tyranny were obvious in the country and people.

The husband of my sister smuggled recorded tapes when he was in the prison and I saved all of them. All my uncles were in the opposition and they left the country due to the pressure of the Gaddafi regime on them.

In the 1980s I traveled to Switzerland several times for medical treatment. Because of the situation of my family and because some relatives in my uncle's family were members of the Libyan opposition abroad, I met prominent figures in the Libyan opposition, members of the Libyan Front for the Salvation of Libya. Since then, I have been in touch with them. During one of these travels abroad I was in a hospital outside Geneva receiving treatment. During my stay there I met a Libyan woman. She was in a car accident and was hurt badly, requiring a long stay in the hospital. Naturally, I was drawn to my countrywoman: we were both far from home. Her name was Aalia Akoub Al Barasi, and there was nobody with her to help her and stand by her side. Because I was accustomed to moving freely inside and outside Geneva because of my wide ties with the opposition there, I started to help her in her affairs, having sympathy for her. I stood with her as I felt it was my duty as a human being towards a sick woman from my country.

I found out that this woman was being treated outside Libya, not with her own money, but because she was a member of Gaddafi's personal revolutionary guard, as well as her husband, who died in an accident when he was with Gaddafi.

I didn't have any suspicion of her – on the contrary, I did my best to help her and stood by her especially when I learned she had a problem with the People's Office (Libyan embassy). We were close and our relation became stronger even after my return to Libya, as she visited me at my home several times.

She had no evidence against me except a few words against Gaddafi which I spoke in front of her during telephone calls with some members from the opposition.

Afterwards, it became clear that this woman was reporting on me during that period. Once she called me to her house pretending that she was sick and needed medicine. I went to her and found a person who she introduced as an engineer working for a Swedish company who was affected by the Gaddafi regime. The man started to talk about the situation of the country grudgingly, showing his displeasure with the system.

We talked about the execution of dissidents, at that time, in the 1980s, and went on with the talk... I remember before I left he said a phrase I did not understand then. He said, addressing Aalia: "Mouse is in the kitchen."

When my husband came to pick me up from Aalia's house, he saw the man coming out, asked me about him, and told me that his face was familiar.

My husband was working in a building opposite the internal security building, and remembered later that he had seen that person coming often to internal security. The next day, before sunset, I was out of the house driving my car, picking up things for my small daughter Maram who was three years old and was with me in the car. When I entered the street in front of my house, there was a large number of cars and strange people; my neighbors were confused and wondered what was happening.

These people prevented me from entering my house; my daughter was screaming in my hands and repeatedly shouted "Mama, Mama is taken by soldiers."

The rest of my children, Marwan, Maher and Mayson were in the apartment above when the soldiers entered the apartment with their horrific faces and searched the entire house.

I was arrested that day (November 18, 1986) and I was put in a car. On my right and left side were armed men and the car headed for the building of internal security.

In one of the offices a person entered. I learned later that his name was Salem Al Magrous. He started interrogating me, and cursed my family which he said was against the tyrant's regime. He tried to provoke me by talking about my father, who had recently passed away, and I was still affected by my loss. I said, nervously: "Do not speak about my father who lived and died as an honorable and honest man."

Still I didn't speak my thoughts out loud, and his hand slapped my face hard and which felt as if electricity shocked my head. All of the questions directed to me indicate that Aalia was behind all this. I said to him: "I know that Aalia is the reason for my arrest." He turned toward the man who was taking notes during the investigation and said to him: "Tell her where Aalia is now." The man said: "Aalia was beaten and she is in Jala Hospital."

This was to delude me that Aalia did not report me and that she was accused like me. I was expecting that it was just an interrogation, and after this I would return to the house. But Al Magrous gave me paper and told me to write about my activities in opposition to the regime or any other information, and locked me in the office for three days.

In these three days I did not see anyone from my family. On the fourth day Al Magrous came after midnight and said: "Let's go." I asked him: "Where to?" He said: "To your home." I believed him then. They put me inside a car parked amidst many cars with suspicious people. I suspected that they were not going to drop me at my house. First, the late hour aroused my suspicions, and secondly, the number of vehicles and suspicious persons inside. We set off and went through Al Dollar neighborhood where my parents lived. I remembered my father and was overwhelmed by his memory and started to cry. Al Magrous was in the car with me and asked: "What is the matter with you?" When I told him that I was thinking about my father he said to me: "Forget thinking about anything outside of this car."

I knew that we were heading to the airport, and when we came close to it they covered my face and did not uncover it until we were in a lounge furnished with sofas. Then we boarded a plane in which there were a small number of passengers. I did not know whether they were prisoners like me or internal security like them.

I put everything in God's hands and relaxed. The plane took off and I felt that it would be the longest flight in my life. When we arrived at Tripoli airport, they took me by car to a location unknown to me. After they covered my face and I heard the gates open and then close, I knew that it was Abu Salim Prison.

They put me in a small room called shaylla (metal container for isolation): 1.5m x 1.5m with a toilet inside.

I felt sorry for myself — that I had wound up in a dirty place like this and for being humiliated in such a way: me, who was spoiled and had a comfortable life. I started to cry. It was the most difficult night of my life. I remembered my children and Maram's cry when I was arrested.

I sobbed bitterly till the next day. They came and took me for interrogation. My statements were the same and did not change under pressure. I didn't mention any name of the opposition members that I met. They returned me to the "shaylla". Nobody visited me or talked to me. They brought me very poor food. I needed clothes to change, as I was in the same clothes I was wearing when I was arrested. After some time they brought me a sports suit. I hadn't seen anyone except prison guards, who were scary by sight, provocative and talking loud.

With God's mercy there was one guard who helped me by bringing me a bucket of hot water when he was on duty. I was waiting for his shift, especially for his usual question "How are you?" This question took me out of my loneliness and terrible solitude.

He asked me once, saying: "What is the matter with you easterners?! Politics is too difficult even for men, let alone for women!"

I turned to the Lord of the worlds. I prayed and called to Him, and embarked on daily fasting and they started to think that I was on a hunger strike. I did not know anything about my family, nor did I see any of them.

Information had been leaked regarding my transfer to Tripoli and that I was in Abu Salim. It leaked to my family through prisoners from the same family of the opposition member (Dr. Mohammed Al Maqrif) who was with me in the same prison. They knew that there was a prisoner from Benghazi and knew my name. They sent information through their neighbors and this is how my family knew that I was in Abu Salim Prison in Tripoli. My brother immediately started to write letters in order to meet any responsible person. But to no avail.

The status quo lasted days and months, broken up only by investigations in which humiliation and beatings took place – that, only God knows about. Then I was summoned to an interrogation by a large group of new investigators. They pressed me greatly in this investigation and threatened to take off my clothes until I was naked and take pictures and send them to the opposition.

I replied nervously: "If you cut me piece by piece you will not be able to take my clothes off." One of them was behind me and beat me constantly with a stick on my shoulders; I was secretly terrified. What if they did what they threatened to do? I couldn't fight all of them. "Oh God, I have only you on my side."

One of them (I learned later that he was Abdul Salam Al Zadma) said to me: "It's better for you if you are comfortable in your home with your children, isn't it?" I said to him: "It's God's will, but imagine that your mother or your sister was in this situation!" He took an ashtray and threw it at me and start to shout to the men with him: "Where is her little girl Maram?? Did you bring her in?" I jumped out of my seat and lost my balance and asked: "Maram, my little baby?" One of them responded: "We threw her in another cell".

I knew he was provoking me to psychologically defeat me. Then my hair was pulled and I was continuously slapped on my face from all directions. This investigation was difficult both mentally and physically. I had been weakened significantly as a result of the continued fasting, and they tried various ways to manipulate my morale by inhumane ways that no human being could possibly imagine.

They closed the investigation after they lost hope that I would change my words. They threatened that they would bring people who had recordings that contradicted my statements. Then they asked me to sign the papers where the sentence of the death penalty was written and one of them said to me: "We will hang you in Al Berka Square in Benghazi to give all women of Benghazi a lesson. I signed the paper, shaking in horror.

They left, and the guards came and took me. I didn't feel my legs carrying me due to fear, weakness and fatigue. It seems that when they put me in the cell I fainted. I wasn't aware that I was moved to another room. It looked like a clinic and I was lying on the bed and receiving an intravenous infusion. I recovered a little bit and when I was leaving the clinic, I saw one of the men who was present during the last interrogation, and with him was Salem Al Magrous, who brought me from Benghazi. He told me to prepare myself to return to Benghazi.

I looked at him bitterly and I couldn't believe what he said after that unjust sentence of death without a trial. I was taken directly from the clinic to the car. My eyes were covered when I was leaving and then the cover was removed. I knew I was in a Peugeot 505 with Salem Al Magrous and a driver heading toward Tripoli airport. Al Magrous turned to me and asked: "I want to know what good you did in your life?" I answered: "By Allah, I do not know and God willing I'll be able to do good always." He said to me: "I swear, that no one I took to Tripoli came back with me." I praised God and gave thanks to Him.

We arrived at the airport late at night – I did not know the exact time. Al Magrous was with me and talked to me in a normal manner, opposite to what I had previously experienced. He asked me to welcome Aalia when she came to me. I said to him: "It's not possible. If she comes I will kick her out." He said to me: "Why would you kick her out? She was imprisoned just like you." However, I was sure day after day from the nature of the questions during investigation that she reported me, and she was the one who gave all the information about me.

We boarded a plane from a door different from the other passengers. I did not know what kind of passengers were on that plane. I could not believe that I was on a flight to Benghazi.

Several months had passed since I left Benghazi, and I felt that I was going to the unknown. I put the matter into the hands of God and would accept whatever happened to me. We arrived in Benghazi, but there was no one to meet us except one car which was waiting. The time was late – nearly dawn, and the stillness and sadness hung over the streets of Benghazi, and it looked like a ghost town. That was in February 1987.

I was overwhelmed by the feeling that I would be taken to another prison in Benghazi to be later executed. Hope began to seep in slowly when the car that was taking me started taking the way which led to my home. I could not believe it and my heart started beating hard: "I'll see my children after all this suffering!"

When we arrived in front of the building, Al Magrous got out of the car and kicked the building's door with his foot and rang the bell. My husband replied: "Who is there?" Al Magrous said to him: "Open!" When my husband opened the door Al Magrous said to him: "Here she is; take her in." I entered and my children were asleep. They woke up crying: "Mama, Mama!!" and I hugged them tightly. By morning the house was overcrowded, to the point there was no foothold, with family, relatives and friends who came to greet and welcome me.

I went back to my house and my children, but my life never went back to normal. The crisis left psychological and social scars and I and my family suffered a lot. I became very nervous and was under severe stress. I became suspicious of all people around me: It seemed to me that the walls were recording every word I said. I no longer called anyone, and lived in isolation, as I was under surveillance by the security apparatus. They started to call me for questioning whenever something happened in the country.

I lived in a big prison; I was prevented from traveling outside of Libya until 1988 when an idea came out of the blue for Gaddafi to tear up the list of names of people banned from travel. The withheld passports were given back to their owners. When I went to pick mine up, I was refused and directed to Tripoli. I traveled to Tripoli and there they offered me to work for security service as a kind of atonement for what I did "against the system", according to them. Of course, I refused and returned without my passport. I made several attempts to get it back and eventually got it from the security apparatus of Benghazi in 1990.

What hurt me the most was my husband's and other people's question about whether I was sexually abused. This tore at me from the inside, especially because of the extreme sensitivity I felt when I came out of prison and the psychological stress I had endured, which now continued in different way, from people I knew and loved.

This added to the previous accumulated problems between me and my husband which reached the point where we had to separate. After the divorce I devoted my life to my children, especially after I was deprived of being able to return to my work at the university. After a period of time I met Aalia by chance in one of the corridors of the Tourist Village. She tried to hold my hand, but I snatched it strongly and she swore: "By God, not me; by God, not me!" I said to her: "Whatever you swear I would not believe, because everything I said to you I heard from security investigators since the first interrogation."

Five years after the divorce, I married again, and gave birth to my son Siraj. In 1995, after about ten years from the date of my arrest, my eldest son Maher was arrested by the security apparatus. He was in the first year of law school. The only thing he was arrested for was praying regularly in the mosque and his religious interests.

I have noticed that Maher took this path since he was in the second year of secondary school. He started to bring cassette tapes home from religious scholars which were forbidden at that time. Fajr (dawn) prayer started to be a "crime" according to the Gaddafi regime, especially as Benghazi was boiling at that time because of the movement of the Islamic group against the tyrant's thugs.

Once I found a video tape of one Islamic scholar that Maher was hiding between the wardrobe and the wall. I was really afraid for my son and sent our neighbor to Maher's father to tell him to watch and take care of his son, but he did not care.

Maher was arrested. I did not know about his whereabouts and condition in spite of my attempts and struggles with the security forces. My real tragedy started with the imprisonment of Maher. I was cut off from society. I didn't go anywhere except to knock on the doors of the security forces in hope of getting some news where my son was. I had no social life. I went only to funerals and I almost went crazy when people began a rumor about the massacre at Abu Salim prison in 1996, which was not clear at the time and just talking about it could lead to one's arrest.

I was torn apart by the news about the number of prisoners killed and how their bodies had been removed by bulldozers and other heavy machinery. I couldn't calm down and could not stop knocking on doors seeking to learn the fate of my son, until 1997, when one day my neighbor came to tell me that she learned from a reliable source that her imprisoned son was brought to Benghazi with a group of prisoners which included Maher, my son.

I went out speeding with car and entered Al Oroba police station's gate with full force. One military officer came to me and said: "What do you want?" I said to him: "I heard that my son was brought here from Tripoli. Is this true?"

He said nervously: "Who told you this?" They had arrived only the night before. I did not want to tell him the source of this information and I told him that we heard from Tripoli. He closed the door in my face and I was begging him: "God bless you, tell me if they brought my son or not." He asked me: "What is the name of your son?" I told him and he assured me that he was with the group, but would be released tomorrow due to procedures.

I left there and headed directly to the security station in Al Hadaeq to meet the head of area security and begged him to let me see my son. They told me that it was impossible today and that he would be released the following morning.

Maher entered our house the next morning. He was very weak and had lost a lot of weight. Days passed and Maher could not return to his studies because he had already been expelled. A year after his release, he was arrested once again, and this time it was the longest. The harsh suffering ruined my health and life completely.

They came to his father's house to arrest him but did not find him and instead they seized my son Marwan, until Maher turned himself in. When they took Marwan at 3:30am, he was wearing only his shorts. They were a group of masked gunmen. They didn't give him time to put on his clothes. Marwan was a year younger than Maher and was studying at the university, department of media, and he was suspended due to security orders.

They came to my house. Those criminals entered and asked for Maher. They searched the house violently, and I did not know that Marwan, my son, was with them in their car in front of the building. They wanted to take my husband with them, but they left him after learning that he was not the biological father. And I told them that Maher was not home and that I would turn him in when he got back.

Marwan stayed with them that night and was beaten and severely humiliated. They didn't even allow him to put clothes on. That night affected Marwan a lot and he still suffers from it to this day. The nature of his personality makes him refuse to talk about what exactly happened. He suffers from mental disorders and even after receiving psychological treatment, he became introverted and wouldn't speak to anyone or even to shake hands.

The next day Maher came to me – he did not know that the security forces took his brother instead of him, and I also did not know it – and Maher told me that when the security men came to the house of his father, he went out through the back door to hide in the garage and he survived miraculously because when they entered the garage and searched it, only a cardboard wall separated him from them. If they had spotted him, they would have shot him, because it was the policy of the security forces to liquidate people found in such a state (hiding).

Maher decided to turn himself in, in order not to expose the family to the risks and subsequent arrests and went with my husband and the husband of his aunt to the internal security headquarters next to the blood bank. We didn't know what happened to Marwan until he returned around 6:00pm. He was in a deplorable state as the result of having been beaten and tortured. Marwan still suffers from depression, especially because he lost his academic future after being suspended from the university. This is how they destroyed the future of my children and, actually, my children committed no crime. I swear to God, that I will never forgive those tyrants for violating the human rights of my children.

Maher was imprisoned and the bitter journey of my torment began. He was transferred to Abu Salim Prison and visits were allowed in 2001. Before that, some scraps of paper (letters) were smuggled from the prison to us to comfort us about his condition.

The prisoner files (cases) were transferred to the People's Court and I hired a lawyer. The first court hearing was on March 12, 2001, the second on March 26, 2001, and the third was on April 16, 2001 when the verdict was delivered. They took me out of the courtroom and I felt something suspicious was happening inside. Maher and I were expecting four or five years of imprisonment which he had already spent in jail, but I was surprised when the lawyer came out of the room looking grief-stricken. I said to him: "What happened?" He said to me: "Say, there is no God worthy of worship except Allah" and then he told me that Maher was sentenced to life imprisonment.

I did not cry but I went down, running to the entrance of the court to see him before they took him away by car with other prisoners. But it was too late. Someone told me: "Madam, he is not here, they took him away." I learned that Maher wanted to see me after the verdict and asked them to allow it, but no one responded. At that moment, my blood pressure was extremely high and I was alone. I don't remember how but I was taken by ambulance to Tripoli Medical Center. There I found out that I had had a stroke as a result of the sudden increase in my blood pressure. I stayed in the hospital about three weeks to receive treatment.

We asked to appeal, but the court was a theater performance and the script had been previously written. The lawyer had no significant role. After the appeal, the verdict of the life sentence was reconfirmed. I had such a feeling of despair which I did not feel before. I went out of the court dragging my legs, not aware of which direction I was going. I did not miss any opportunity to visit and see him or to send a message. Maher's morale was very high and he comforted me and was optimistic that his release was close. I tried to give him and his comrades all their requirements. His room was the best room with its bed, curtains and his library.

In 2002, Libya began to open to the world little by little; human rights organizations started work and questioned the status of prisoners. They started improving the quality of food to some extent and provide them with some of the requirements like cooking stoves for heating water and other things. I did not stop writing letters and complaints about the issue of my son until they started to know me in Tripoli in the offices of internal security, the offices of fighting heresy ("zandaqa" as they call it), and among the prisoners I was known as "Iron Woman". Once they gave me a decorated panel covered with woven strings, and I still keep it.

Maher's case was with a group of 19 prisoners. They did not appeal the ruling after the primary verdict as did Maher and another prisoner named Mohammed Al Saadi. This was due to the fact that the other prisoners didn't have lawyers. But it was an advantage because the verdict was not confirmed as for Maher and Mohammed Al Saadi. At the same time Gaddafi decided to cancel the People's Court and therefore the remaining 17 prisoners appealed in a criminal court to consider their case again.

I was called by the Department of Heresy (Zandaqa) in Tripoli to inform me that the possibility of the release of Maher was 70%. At the same time I booked a plane reservation and flew to Tripoli at 7:00am.

I was surprised after my arrival when I was told that Saif Al Islam Gaddafi wanted to meet me at the National Oil Company building next to the Administration for Fighting Narcotics. I went there but he wasn't in. I said to the secretary: "He asked to meet me." I met him, but in another place, in the offices at the Port of Tripoli. Saif came out, greeted me, and asked: "Are you Maher's mother?"

Saif promised me in a week or 10 days Maher would be released. I went directly to the jail and begged to visit Maher to give him the good news of what Saif promised – that he would be released within days. The days were long like years with no changes. A week passed, then 10 days passed and Maher was not released. I went frequently to the Department of Heresy (Zandaqa) and complained and pursued the case in detail, but to no avail. I went back to Benghazi on Thursday.

Maher called me on Saturday and told me that they released the 17 prisoners who were with him after they were declared not guilty but excluded Maher and his companion from the release. I felt that this was a substantial prejudice against my son and his rights and a flagrant injustice. I returned to the Department of Heresy in Tripoli, and opposed the acquittal which did not include my son as his case number and charge was the same as the others. It was the peak of unfairness and contrary to justice by all means, and represents the mismanagement of the security and juridical systems. They were convinced, but could do nothing, as they considered it a "decision of the court". I placed it in God's hands.

The pain squeezed me and I felt very disappointed, Saif didn't keep his promise – this was August 2005. I often protested and demanded the rights of my son. They promised that my son would be on the top of the list when they issued a pardon.

On Thursday, February 16, 2006 I visited Maher and I found him very reassuring and optimistic, especially after he told me about a vision seen by one of his friends. He saw something that he interpreted as Maher being released in the month of March. I asked God to make this vision true. My daughters and my husband were with me during this visit as we came to Tripoli by car.

We returned to Benghazi the next day, February 17, 2006 and found a very critical situation and the city was very crowded. Security personnel and special forces were everywhere because of the events of the Italian embassy. I was bothered by these events because they were sure to form an obstacle to the release of my son, but again, I put everything in God's hands.

I sat and waited for March 2 to come, hoping the days would bring something new. On March 1, Maher contacted us to tell us the news of the release of 85 prisoners, but that he was not among them. I lost hope for the release of my son.

The next day at 2:30 pm, Maher contacted us to give us the good news of his release. I went to bring him back. I finally was able to return to life after I had reached a state of despair which cannot be described.

Poem dedicated to Ehsan Ben Ali by her son Maher, written in Abu Salim 2005

Present from the prisoners of Abu Slim given to Ehsan Ben Ali on April 17, 2005 (front and back). The words written in Arabic read:

"To the virtuous mother: Mother of Maher. We are delighted with your honorable stand and this modest gift is to appreciate that kind stand. We hope you will accept it from us. April 17, 2005."

My Voice Against Gaddafi Was Heard

Halima Mohamed Saad Trablsi, born in 1959

I heard as well as all Libyans that on February 17 there would be a day of demonstrations in all the cities of our beloved Libya and they were coordinated through Facebook in order to denounce this regime in Libya.

I said: *"God helps"*. The system, as usual, mocked us saying that it would join the demonstrations. On Tuesday, February 15, 2011, late at night, I watched Al Jazeera on television and saw the demonstrations in front of the Internal Security Headquarters in Benghazi. A group of people were screaming loudly: *"Wake up... Wake up, O Benghazi, today is the day you were waiting for!"*

I could not control myself and broke down in tears from the impact of these words on my heart. I felt joy and fear for the people who went out. I started to chant with them at home and then contacted my sons and asked: *"What's going on?"* They told me: *"Oh, mother, the country is waking up!"*

I was overwhelmed and very happy. I prayed and asked God Almighty to protect these people who came out. Then the connection between Al Jazeera and the demonstrators was cut off. After that my children returned and told me it was a demonstration of men and women of families of victims of Abu Salim. It started at Tree Square and youngsters from different areas joined, until they reached the Internal Security Headquarters in Benghazi, which is very close to my home. My children told me people were beaten and arrested and they dispersed the demonstration; after that I did not hear any news.

The next day in the morning, the situation was very normal. I was overwhelmed with a feeling of anger and I said to myself: *"What happened?"* My eldest son said: *"We are preparing ourselves to go out again."* I said to him: *"God is with you."* I was proud of my city and its young men and I started creating enthusiastic chants for the demonstrators to take to the streets. I had never written poetry, but the first words off my tongue at that moment were: *"Tell Muammar and his sons that there are men in Benghazi!!"* (Goulo Le Moamer wa Iyala Benghazi Feeha Rajala) After that, to encourage other cities to come out with us and not to leave Benghazi alone, I started chanting, *"There are men in Libya"*. I started to type slogans and distribute them to young people in response to the thugs of the tyrant such as:
"God, then His Messenger, then Libya only"
"God is the only one and will destroy Muammar completely" and other slogans.

Then I and other women from my neighborhood went out in the street near my home, because my children prevented me from going out in the square fearing the bullets of snipers. Because my house is very close to the Hawari Hospital, Cemetery Hawari, and the Directorate of Security, I saw the wounded and the martyrs. Most of them were unarmed young people who carried the bodies, and then they were hit and also became martyrs.

I went with the youth to Tahreer Square. When the entire eastern cities were liberated, I and my neighbors prepared sandwiches and hot drinks for the freedom fighters. The young people went to the fronts to liberate the rest of the cities of Libya. We had started to gather every day in the court house to support Zawiya, Tripoli, Misurata, the western mountain, and all besieged cities.

The young people were fighting on the fronts because the tyrant turned the peaceful revolution into a war.

All Sorrow Around the Martyr Turned To Joy

Hawa Al Masdour , Benghazi, Libya

Hawa Al Masdour, Benghazi, Libya One day while I was enjoying sitting surrounded by my family, all of a sudden one of my sons came running in and shouting: "Mother, Allah answered your prayers and sent us people who grew up under the tyrant's ruling, to get rid of him!"

I am Hawa Mohammad Abdallah Al Masdour, born in 1963 in Ajdabiyeh where I grew up and went to school till I finished secondary school. I was working during the days and going to "Tahrir" school in the evening. I was the fourth among my sisters, but I was more into the responsibility. My father passed away and left a big family – eleven children – and the youngest was only a year and a half. He is now an engineer working in one of the Arab countries in the oil fields. I was enrolled in law school in Benghazi and at the same time I was working as a teacher at Martyrs Al Damoor School. I was like a father to my siblings and thanks to Allah they were all religious, but this made them a target for the tyrant. They were sent to Abu Salim Prison. One of them became a martyr during the people's uprising of February 17, may Allah accept him with His mercy and grant him a place in His vast heavens.

The years went by and I moved to my husband's house. It was only a brief period of time later that my mother passed away. This increased the ever-growing responsibilities on my shoulders. My family grew up and so did my six boys and three girls and I am very proud of them. Praise be to God they are all well educated, well mannered and gentle people. I was living a relaxing, quiet life, but what made me uncomfortable and unhappy was that my eldest son was prevented from going to military school. Nonetheless, since the dawn of the February 17 revolution, we got rid of that nightmare which caused us insufferable pressure on our chests. Though I paid a high price during the revolution I am happy that it ended in a spectacular way – getting rid of the tyrant and even killing him. This gave me patience and healed me of my agonies.

In addition to the loss of my brother, who was the father and the mother to our family during the past few years, my beloved son Emad Al Din Saleh Faraj lost his right leg. The loss of my son's leg has a story. As God is my witness, this is a true story that happened in Jala Hospital.

Emad had hoped to join the police academy, but he had a terrible accident that left him laid up in bed with nine fractures. A year passed before he had healed completely. He finished his studies and started working, but he was always unhappy because of the favoritism that went on at work. He kept telling me that if he did not fear for our safety he would gather some people and go against this criminal Gaddafi. His greatest fear was for his father's safety because he was a minefield engineer in the army.

After February 17 he urged members of the family to go downtown in Benghazi to join the uprising because he felt badly for the people killed during the events related to the Italian consulate in 2006, and he was full of hatred because his uncles Idris and Mahmoud were jailed and tortured in the tyrant's prison. During the peaceful demonstrations in February 2011, his brother was shot in the hand by Gaddafi's security forces at the Juliana Bridge. This event did not hinder him from demonstrating in front of the security building on Hawari Street, going against the katiba of Gaddafi and the secure places of the tyrant's son and his agent Abdullah Senussi, chasing the rest of the men with yellow hats at Benina airbase, or organizing groups of youngsters to protect the neighbors and thus establish security. The situation in Benghazi became calmer.

Our family was watching Al Jazeera TV channel and we saw a woman from Misurata urging men from Benghazi to save them from becoming victims of rape and killing. She was one among the families from Misurata who had arrived in the Port of Benghazi. Emad jumped up, kissed my hand, took his machine gun and went to Misurata on one of the small fishing boats. He fought there for 50 days till Misurata was liberated and then came back to Benghazi. Afterwards, he joined his father who was removing mines. He was a member of a team which removed 20,000 mines including water mines as he was an excellent diver. His uncle was martyred on July 15, 2011. This was the final push for him that kept him fighting until Sirte was liberated. Emad was a member of the "Dawn of February" Katiba.

They advanced towards the first gate where they fought against the retreating tyrants' forces. That was ended for him when he was shot in the leg by a 23-caliber anti-aircraft shell, but that did not stop him from fighting till the end. Suddenly, there was a pool of blood under his foot. He was taken to the hospital but the attempt to save him was too late. He went into a coma because of the loss of a large amount of blood. His hemoglobin was critically low, his heart almost stopped and everybody thought that he would be martyred before he reached Benghazi as it was 450km away. Nevertheless, they sent him to Benghazi. Thinking that he was going to die, they prepared his death certificate, and wrote his identification on a piece of paper attached to his chest which said, "The martyr Emad Al Din Saleh Faraj". Seven hours went by before his rescuer arrived at his destination. As he was a friend of my eldest son Salah, he called him late at night to tell him about his brother.

All the sisters and brothers and friends of my wounded son were waiting in front of the hospital emergency room. The ambulance entered the hospital without any siren. When they opened the door of the ambulance my son saw his brother lying inside with the piece of paper on his chest. He hugged him tenderly and said: "You lived as a hero and died as a hero." Suddenly, the "martyr" opened his eyes and his brother shouted: "He is alive, he is alive!" All sorrow around him turned to joy. He was sent for resuscitation and from there to surgery. The doctors tried for six hours to implant a vein but they failed and lost hope. We were nervous and tense waiting and watching through the window of ICU. His father was among the group. His face was flushed and he was in agony seeing his son in this condition. My son said to him: "God is great. I and my life are a sacrifice for Libya. Don't be sad. We were made for heroism, not for sitting in a café eating ice cream and sipping a drink." His father told him that he was satisfied with him till the Day of Judgment. This was all witnessed by a member of the NTC who was with them to ensure that any help needed to send Emad overseas for treatment was available. When Emad was stabilized, he was sent to Jordan. His return later was a great happiness for all the family and friends who were waiting for him at the airport. I phoned him and said: "Be strong and brave. You fought Gaddafi's thugs." The wounded hero was dreaming of going back to fight the tyrant's troops. Luckily, before he came back Gaddafi was captured and killed.

Before we could get rid of Gaddafi he managed to destroy everything in Libya. He left behind many badly wounded people; I will neither forget them, nor the Libyan people. He killed, destroyed and burnt everything in Libya but God saved it. I am not sad, not even because my son lost his leg. Rather, I am proud that my sons and my husband were heroes. I always think that if we want to know our place with God, we should see our present life; and, thanks to God, I am the mother of heroes, the wife of a hero and a sister of a martyr. There are many whom we meet during our lifetime, but only a few we remember. I have never understood why, but now I understand that heroes are those who are remembered in the past, present and the future. I am proud because of what I have offered to my country and all of us are ready to sacrifice ourselves for Libya.

The Most Difficult Journey of My Life

Ahmad Saad Al-Shaikhi, Benghazi, Libya

In His name, Glorified and Exalted, we start; to His light and His path, upon which he guides the human and his noble Prophet, we surrender.

Glory to our martyrs and mercy upon them, and we pray to the Almighty for our injured to recover. Also, may Allah extend his blessings to us as we return to our families. We are praying to Him and He is the only one who can bring back to their families all the missing in her land.

She is all names, she is all the scholars, she is all the homelands, she is the sea of seas, and she is the mountains beneath its bases and its peaks. She is the earth with everything upon it. How can I write my story without talking about her? Because she is the story: "She" is Libya.

I came to this world in her. I was breathing her air, but I did not smell it. I lived by her, but not in her. Her true features were replaced by others painted by the green brush of Gaddafi's regime and moved by his black iron fist. We saw her but we did not know her; and we became scared of that fist after we figured it out.

Let me introduce myself.

My name is Ahmad Saad Al-Shaikhi. I am Libyan. I was born in Benghazi in 1982. I have graduated from the Faculty of Industrial Engineering of Garyounis University. I have lived in this pleasant land and have grown up here. I have seen everything around me embodied in one person. When I entered school, he was the first teacher; when I studied history, he was the first hero and thinker. And yet he, himself, was this history. The years passed by and while in high school I started to realize something. Little by little, the cover has lifted from he who was describing himself as a hero. Yes, he was a hero: a hero of some sort of silly theatrical play. He fed upon our minds. Truth is, this pleasant land was controlled by this monster. In order to live in this land, he devoured the damp and the dry in it. This started the conflicts and challenges linked to this criminal. All the time he killed and destroyed, keeping his tight grip on everything.

These challenges for us persisted until this promised day arrived. All the people have revolted against him and this Revolution was started by the will of Allah; it is a Divine Revolution. When all the people went out together, the strong and the weak, the poor and the rich, the old and the young, they said "'No' to injustice, 'Enough' to deception, 'No' to obedience!" They stripped off the cloaks of fear and silence. They went out with open chests, strong and faithful hearts, determined tongues, hands rising ready for victory and martyrdom. The people went out not to come back. By then, it was the beginning of the end.

The beginning took place in Benghazi, on February 16th. It was a scene I cannot describe. I saw people of different ages out in the streets, chanting with one voice. They came like a wave. They spilled onto the streets. Then we saw bullets being fired at them and saw their pure bodies filling up the streets. Following that, moved by passion, more and more people started to gather. From here my story from this Revolution begins. I was not like one of those lions who sacrificed their lives at the forefront, but I was with the crowds in Benghazi's Tahrir Square.

A month later, on March 17th, I was heading towards Ajdabiyah in order to aid our revolutionaries and fighters. I was traveling with my cousin, Muhammad al-Sanussi, and his cousin, Mahi al-Din al-Sanussi, both from the Sanussi family. During our entire long journey, the road was completely empty of the revolutionary forces, which was very unusual. According to our information, the forces of the tyrant were stationed at the Western gates of Ajdabiyah and surrounding the city of Ajdabiyah in its entirety until its Eastern gate at Zweitina. They were attacking by firing Grad rockets from 20 km away, using the coward's weapons with results that were very severe and random. At that moment we felt we were in trouble. The next moment, we found ourselves surrounded by the Gaddafi forces. It was thus the suffering started.

They searched us and stole everything we had. They tied our hands and feet and blindfolded us. They started beating us from all sides. They wanted to terrorize and scare us. Then they put us next to a Grad truck from which they were shelling Ajdabiyah. We were so close that we could hear them laughing and saying, "It's time for dinner in Ajdabiyah". I was repeating the Shahadah and I expected them to kill me at any moment. They were happy and celebrating because they were advancing towards Benghazi. After sunset, around 8 p.m., they started interrogating us. There were around 30 of us; they were taking us one by one and nobody was safe from them, not even elderly people. They found out that my cousin was from the Sanussi family and they were very aggressive with him. They asked him: "Do you want the return of the monarchy?" and they interrogated us in a special manner. They told us: "You are traitors and spies". One of them told the others to take care of us.

In the middle of the night they took us to Sirte. There were checkpoints everywhere throughout the whole journey. We noticed that some of the people at checkpoints were opposed to their colleagues using foul language with us, advising them to just beat us up. They said: "They are Libyans, they are our people". At this time, unfortunately, most of them were saying a lot of profanities. When we entered Sirte, they took us to the Military Police Station; those days were the most difficult. We were put into the 3m x 2m jail cell and there were 11 other people with us with no water or anything at all. In the morning of the following day, some of the soldiers attacked us and beat us all up. After Asr they took us for interrogation. We said, "We were heading to Ajdabiyah to bring back a family with us that was trapped there". Fortunately, when they captured us the soldiers stole our cell phones, as they steal anything that does not belong to them. Thus, they could not prove that we were helping the revolutionaries.

The following day they told us, "We will take you to Community Service and release you to your families". They put us in a big cage in a truck together with 67 other people. That was on March 20th. According to them, we were going to a Community Service Center, but unfortunately it was in the opposite direction. They took us to Tripoli, to Abu Salim prison, for which there is a saying: "Whoever enters it is lost, and whoever exists in it is born again". Upon our arrival, we were, of course, subjected to beatings and there was a lot of foul language. They placed us in a section where luckily there were bathrooms, because most of the sections have no bathrooms. The cell we were put in was 8m x 5m and it was packed with 35 people. The food was scarce, it was bitterly cold, and there were no blankets or beds. After a while they brought us some blankets. We had one blanket for every three people. Some of the guys who were with us were injured and the entire prison was filled with prisoners from every Libyan city. There were two guys with us from Egypt and two guys from Tunisia, and interrogation was very difficult.

There were five torture cells. Praise be to Allah, I have not been inside any of those cells. However, there was a Libyan doctor among us, who also had American citizenship, who was tortured severely. When they brought him back to us into the cell, he was not able to speak or stand on his feet. This affected us deeply and we ourselves were very shocked. We increased our supplications to Allah and prayed for our release.

After approximately 20 days, on April 8th, they called us for interrogation and we trusted the matter to Allah. They took us to the interrogation headquarters and the interrogation lasted from Zhuhr until after the Maghreb prayers. Praise be to Allah, I was not subjected to torture, which was one of my greatest prayers.

The following day, they told the prisoners from the Eastern part of the country to come down to the yard. We came down and they gave us military uniforms. They told us to act out a play. The story was that we have joined the armed resistance and have formed the Omar Al Mukhtar brigade and that we would fight the Crusaders and al-Qaida, and other nonsense and lies and fabrications. Those moments were very silly but they recorded them and aired them later on Gaddafi TV channels in order to deceive the world.

I was really scared that they would use us as human shields and after approximately 10 days, on April 20th, we heard the soldiers calling out names; my name was on the list. They led us out, blindfolded us, and put us in a bus. There were approximately 270 people, the majority of whom were from Misurata. We were clueless what they wanted to do with us and we left this matter to Allah. We were taken to Tajura prison. When they brought us inside the prison, the Assistant Prison Commander welcomed us. He said, "Here there is no torture or humiliation", and praise be to Allah, the words of the Commander were truthful. The treatment here was much better than in Abu Salim prison. Some of the soldiers were not happy about the situation. One of them was Rida al-Tarhuni, who was one of the residents of the city of Tajura. He was always reassuring, telling us that the conditions and circumstances were working in our favor. There was another soldier with him named Lutfi, who brought medication for the sick and injured. They were taking care of us, by the mercy of Allah. On May 12th, they interrogated me and my friend. The interrogation went smoothly and they told us that we would be released.

On May 16th they released 200 prisoners, and my friend who got arrested with me was among them. It was the hardest moment. It was my fate to stay in this prison, me and the rest of the guys. The days and months went by. Soon came the Blessed month of Ramadan. We were very optimistic about this month and we were confident that we would soon get released because Rida was telling us that he wanted us to escape and that when he had a chance, he would act accordingly. One day he let the sheikhs, the elderly and the injured escape. He told us that they would open the prison gates for us. That day came; it was the 20th day of Ramadan. Rida, together with Lutfi, with help from their brothers from among the revolutionaries, opened up the prison gates and told us, "Now you are free".

That day was indeed very strange. We were released and went out from the prison; we found the Tajura houses in front of us open and the women were making the Zagharit. There was Takbir everywhere. I will not forget till the end of my life the kindness of the people of Tajura, who opened up their houses to us, treated us as their own sons, and served us different food and drinks. They celebrated with us and congratulated us; the emotions and feelings we had at that moment are hard to describe.

We had missed our relatives and our cities greatly. The return to our families began and we went from Tajura to Misurata by bus, and stayed in Resilient Misurata for two days. On the 28th day of Ramadan, I boarded a plane which took me to my dear city of Benghazi. Once I saw my family and my people, I forgot all the troubles and the time that I had spent in prisons.

They released us and liberated Tripoli with Allah's help first and foremost, and with the efforts of our revolutionary heros secondarily. Praise be to Allah, we have won and the banner of truth has prevailed.

Allah the Almighty said: 𝔙erily, if 𝔄llah helps you, no one can overcome you: 𝔗he 𝔥oly 𝔔ur'an [3:160], 𝔄nd it was due from 𝔘s to aid those who believed: 𝔗he 𝔥oly 𝔔ur'an [30:47].

I pray to Allah that he protects our country and brings the best of us to serve because we have completed our journey and we have provided for our country, but we are still falling short. May everything expensive become cheap for our land; we give our souls to her. Congratulations to those who have sacrificed their lives to protect her. We have liberated her from that one who tried to make himself into an idol to be worshipped and we have enabled her to breathe freedom. We will live in her with pride and dignity. Whether it takes a long or a short time, there is no truth but truth and there is not righteousness but righteous. This is the Sunna of Allah for his creation to follow; this is the example of life as it should be lived as it was taught and practiced by the Prophet Muhammad (Allah bless him and give him peace).

Long live free and independent Libya! May the dictators die and may the lucky remaining people realize the Sunna and be aware and wise.

Peace and blessings be upon you. Praise be to Allah and His grace; I testify there is no god but Allah; I seek His forgiveness and repent before Him.

A Student's View of the Revolution

Nardeen Ramzi Tatanaki, Benghazi, Libya

It was one of those January winter days when the sun would shine after a day of heavy rain. It was around 12pm, and we were sitting on an old wooden bench in one of the wrecked old hospitals that had been listed on my monthly fourth year medical schedule. It was then he spilled the secret that tore me apart. "We are starting a revolution," he told me. I was speechless. My exact words were, "He'll kill you! He's a butcher!"

There was a sudden silence, a severe chill as if the temperature had just been turned down to zero. Our hearts beat quickly as we realized that someone had just passed by us. "Oh God, do you think he heard us?" I asked. "Are you stupid? You're a girl and Gaddafi won't hesitate to put you I prison. Promise me you will be more careful!" he yelled at me. We never again mentioned that weird discussion that we had had on that old wooden bench.

The evening I can't forget, when I couldn't move, when my heart froze for a second, was the evening that I read about an event on Facebook. The event listed was, "Libyan Revolution – reserved for Thursday the 17th of February". My Facebook account instantly went from being extremely active to being a deactivated account.

The morning of February 15 was an ordinary morning. I woke up late as usual and had to dress and leave in a hurry to go to my lectures. I stood in a small group of five of my best friends in a hall at one of our tutorial hospitals waiting for a lecture to be given by a doctor who never showed up. After an hour of gossip and fooling around, I asked in a very low voice, "Do you think IT will happen on Thursday?" One guy answered in a voice even lower than mine, "IT sure will."

I could see the fear in everybody's eyes, and their hearts were beating so loudly that it sounded like a band of drums. We were all dismissed from lectures and we promised to meet again the next day to see each other before IT started.

I spent that whole day studying. I was planning to get high grades in my midterms. I heard the front door slam so hard. "You won't believe what I just saw," my dad shouted several times. I ran to see what was wrong. "I saw them protest, I saw them scream!" my dad cried. I saw my father's tears of happiness and I can't deny that I shed some too. "I was with them, I heard them," my dad kept repeating. He seemed to be in a state of shock. I called a friend immediately and said, "IT has started" and then hung up fast. Beginning that night, Libyans knew that their dreams of freedom had come true.

February 17 was expected to be the day of the biggest gathering of the youth. My dad had left to see IT with his own eyes and he came back in a hurry with many pictures to show us. We heard the loudest frightening sound. Everyone shouted, "What's that?" We all ran up to the roof. The sound we had heard was that of continuous loud explosions. "He's killing them," my dad said. I started crying and trying to call my friends to check on them. The phone kept ringing, but with no answer. Finally someone picked up, "We are being shot at by real bullets," he cried through a background of gunfire and screams. Then the call ended. Later I learned that no one I knew had been shot and the sound that we had heard was that of anti-aircraft guns being used against unarmed human beings.

Benghazi fell from the grip of Gaddafi in just four days. February 21 was the day I stood in Freedom Square and sang anti-Gaddafi songs. I volunteered in a hospital to help provide care for people in need.

There was an extreme lack of medical supplies and an overflow of injured people with bullet wounds. It was such an inspiring experience but also very scary. Life began getting back to normal somehow. We had a lot of volunteer work to do and everyone was open to doing whatever is necessary to help.

A group of young people gather in Benghazi on March 19, 2012, to remember Black Saturday March 19, 2011, and to honor people who were martyred during the tumultuous days of the intervening year

Our Country and Its Freedom Are the Greatest Treasures We Have

Khadija Ahmed Al Mukhtar, Benghazi, Libya

I am a granddaughter of Mohamed Al Mukhtar, the only brother of the hero of Libya, Omar Al Mukhtar. Omar Al Mukhtar was a symbol for the protesters and Freedom Fighters of the February 17 Revolution, especially for his famous words "We do not give up, we win or die", which he said to the Italian commander in Libya, Rodolfo Graziani, when he was standing before Graziani on trial. Gaddafi's regime had tried to obliterate the history of this hero from the history of Libya by moving his body from Benghazi to Sloug and demolishing the mausoleum which was built in the city of Benghazi during the era of Libya's independence and had become a historic symbol of Libya.

Khadija Al Mukhtar (in the middle) visiting the Libyan refugee camp in Tataween, Tunisia

My husband Sharif Borahil is a grandson of Yusuf Borahil, the deputy of Omar Al Mukhtar and, after Omar Al Mukhtar's execution at the end of 1931, the leader of the Jihad against the obnoxious Italian invaders. After Yusuf Borahil was martyred in the battle Um Rokba near the Egyptian border, his head was cut off and brought to the city of Benghazi to make the rebel fighters extremely scared of fighting the invading Italians. Most of the rebel fighters were in prisons, such as Benina prison, and the Italians told them: "Yusuf Borahil who was your last hope is dead and you now have nothing left but to surrender and submit to Italian rule". Indeed, the Libyan resistance against the Italian invasion ended with the martyrdom of Yusuf Borahil.

His family, also, has not been spared from the tyranny of Gaddafi who tried to obliterate its noble history just as he tried with Omar Al Mukhtar's. The youngest son of Yusuf Borahil was one of the first lawyers who graduated from an Egyptian university in the early days of independence and was among the first opponents of Gaddafi's coup. He was imprisoned for ten years at the beginning of 1970, less than a year after the beginning of Gaddafi's rule. He was released from prison but was infected with tuberculosis and died in 1988. Because he had opposed the Gaddafi regime, his father, Yusuf Borahil, was not mentioned in the film about Omar Al Mukhtar.

The sons and daughters of our families have been taught to walk on the path of our ancestors, to walk in the honorable footsteps our grandfathers put in place during the history of the struggle against the Italian invasion. Since childhood, we have been taught that our country and its freedom are the greatest treasures we have.

My husband graduated from ETSU in the United States of America in 1985. His main specialty is mathematics and his sub-specialties are computer science and physics. He is now a professor of mathematics in the center for outstanding students in Benghazi. I am a teacher and I live with my husband in an apartment in the building behind the katiba in Benghazi.

On February 17, 2011, we saw protesters chanting in front of the katiba: "The people want to overthrow the regime". I had no choice but to come out on my balcony and chant with them. Then my husband went out and joined the protestors to demonstrate. Since that day we went to the court yard daily to demonstrate for Gaddafi's regime to leave. Those were hard and bitter days in which we saw the funerals of the martyrs passing in front of our house from morning till evening.

One day, after things had calmed down in Benghazi, we saw on the Al Jazeera news channel a child of the displaced Libyans in the city of Tataween in Tunisia, crying and saying to Gaddafi: "We have had enough of you. We do not want you to govern us. You must leave our country." The tears of the innocent girl and the sincerity of her words affected us very much. We decided to go to Tunisia to visit the displaced people in Tunisia, to stand with them in their plight and try to provide support and assistance to them.

We had already contacted Mr. Tawfiq Ben Jmayaa who headed one of the charity organizations in Benghazi. It was a civil organization founded after the February 17 Revolution with the aim of taking care of the affairs of refugees from non-liberated cities such as Ajdabiyah, Brega, Ras Lanuf, Zweitina and other non-liberated cities situated to the west of Benghazi. It was also providing meals and other necessities to the thuwar. We told him we wished to go to the displaced people in Tunisia to support and assist them and to establish an administrative department to take care of their affairs in Tunisia. He welcomed our idea and offered us a place with a group he had already selected that was going to Tunisia that weekend. The group was composed of Dr Seham Sergiwa, a psychiatric doctor, Ms Abeer Ben Shatwan, an active lawyer, Mr. Nader Al Jhawi, an engineer, Mr. Khaled Belkhair, a drug company employee, and Mr. Haitham Al Brky, an education employee.

We traveled to Cairo with this group on April 23, 2011, in a small bus. At that time, the road to Cairo was not safe in either Libya or Egypt. We were greeted in Cairo by Khaled Ghouqa, a Libyan who resided in the United Arab Emirates (UAE) and who came specially to arrange our meetings with a coalition group of the Egyptian January 25 Revolution. We stayed in a hotel in Cairo for three days and held several meetings with the coalition group. We asked them to expel the Libyan ambassador in Cairo which was still under the management of Gaddafi's regime and was using Libyan assets in Egypt to bring mercenaries from Africa to join Gaddafi's battalions, to stop the broadcasting of the Gaddafi regime's TV stations on NileSat, and to freeze all Libyan assets in Egypt. We held a number of seminars with the Egyptian people and asked them to stand in support of the Libyan people in their plight. I spoke in the Raabi'a Al Adawiya Hall about the tragedy of the oppression and tyranny suffered by the Libyan people during the forty two years of Gaddafi's rule.

We visited those who had been wounded and injured during the February 17 Revolution who were being treated in hospitals in Cairo. The cost of their medical treatment was being paid by Hassan Tatanaki, a Libyan businessman who lives in Cairo. We saw a lot of young Libyans who had lost limbs during the fighting. The visits were distressing and painful for us, but psychologically the morale of these young men was high in spite of their sad situation. We told them that their blood had not been spilled in vain, and that we would never accept Gaddafi's rule again no matter what price we had to pay. I remember especially a young freedom fighter from Misurata who had many wounds from shrapnel in his leg saying, with tears in his eyes, that as soon as he recovered he was going back to fight till Gaddafi was dead.

We traveled by air to Tunis, in Tunisia, and arrived there at 3am. At the airport in Tunisia we were greeted by Sami Bobtaynah, a Libyan residing in Tunisia, who took us to a hotel and told us that he had booked us for the flight to Djerba which left at 10am. The next morning we went to Djerba and were greeted by Al Sanusi Qwaideer, a Libyan resident in the UAE (who was representing Al Omrani, a Libyan resident in the United Kingdom) and Adel Al Shawesh, a Libyan resident in Canada. All of them had left their jobs and their families and come to Tunisia to provide help and assistance to the Libyan refugees there and supervise the administrative affairs of the displaced. They took us to a hotel in the city of Jarjes and, following lunch, to the Armadah camp which was supervised by the United Nations Mission.

The camp was situated in the south of Tunisia, about 250 km from Jarjes. There were about 500 families and most of them were women, children, and the elderly fleeing from the oppression of Gaddafi. The men and the young people were not among them because they were guarding their homes in Libya and fighting the battalions of the tyrant Gaddafi. We were the first Libyan family, and the first group with women members, to have come from Benghazi to visit the displaced people in order to support and encourage them, and to provide as much assistance as possible. They were very happy to have us visit, especially the women and children, and they were overjoyed to learn that a granddaughter of Omar Al Mukhtar's family and a grandson of Yusuf Borahil were members of the group.

They told us about the things that had happened to them – the tragedies and the rapes of women by the tyrant's battalions acting under Gaddafi's orders – that had forced them to leave their homes and their homeland and flee to Tunisia. They expressed their dissatisfaction with the National Council for not visiting them up until that moment. Dr. Seham examined the psychological condition of the women raped by Gaddafi's battalions and provided them with treatment. Abeer, the lawyer, obtained the power of attorney from the raped women to raise a lawsuit against Gaddafi and his battalions for the rapes. We took several photos and made some videos with them to remember and we marched with them inside the camp in support of the February 17 Revolution.

We offered to move all of the families to the city of Benghazi, or any city of the liberated east, but they refused to leave their sons alone on the front lines. We stayed for several hours and then we returned late to our hotel in the city of Jarjes. When displaced people living outside the camps learned about our presence, they came to visit us in the hotel to thank us for coming from the city of Benghazi. We discussed many things with them, including the payment of salaries for the displaced just like their brothers and sisters in the liberated cities.

The next day we went to a camp in Tataween, far away in the south of Tunisia about 300 km from Jarjes. The camp was supervised by the Tunisian Red Crescent and was better than the Armadah camp as its buildings had been built for the young people of Tunisia. There were 75 displaced families there, and among them we met the girl whom we had heard on the Al Jazeera news channel when we were in Benghazi. We found out that her name is Malak. We took several pictures with her and talked with her. My husband told her: "You're a hero among the heroes of Libya. We saw you on the Al Jazeera channel when you were crying and shouting. Our souls and the souls of everyone who saw you on that channel were so deeply touched that you are the reason for our coming here to show you and all the displaced people how closely we are connected with you. We are one people and the rule of the tyrant cannot divide us whatever he does." Her joy was intense especially when she learned that I am a granddaughter of Omar Al Mukhtar's family. My husband spoke with her uncle, who was blind, and he told us that he was one of the graduates of the Islamic University Mohammed Ben Ali Al Sanusi in Beida. He said he had graduated at the end of the 1960s and that he had been a political prisoner for 10 years during the rule of Gaddafi.

On the third day we went to the Dehiba camp in the south of Tunisia, approximately 400 km away from

Jarjes. Dehiba is a small town at the customs gates on the Tunisian side of the Tunisia-Libya border. The customs gates within the Libyan border are near the city of Wazin. The camp, under the supervision of the Red Crescent of the UAE, was a large camp with a fully equipped mobile hospital. In this camp there were around 400 families: women, children and older men. We filmed inside the camp and talked with people, seeking to comfort them in their ordeal. Again, Dr. Seham examined the psychological conditions of the women who had been raped by Gaddafi's battalions and provided them with treatment, and Abeer obtained power of attorney from the raped women to raise a lawsuit against Gaddafi and his battalions for the rapes. And again, we took several pictures and made some videos with them to remember and marched with them inside the camp in support of the February 17 Revolution.

We did not stay more than two hours in this camp because of heavy shelling by Gaddafi's brigades across in Wazin. The Tunisian Army asked us to go out of the city Dehiba because of the intense bombing and the shelling inside the Tunisian border, which led the army of Tunisia to return fire. They told us that Wazin had been conquered by Gaddafi's brigades and that the Freedom Fighters in Libya would have to go back and liberate it because this border crossing was important for them. And, indeed, even before we arrived back in Jarjes, the Freedom Fighters told us by phone that they had liberated the Wazin crossing and were flying the new flag of independence there.

The next day we visited the injured and wounded Libyans in the town of Tataween in Tunisia. There had been a significant increase in the number of displaced people, even during the period we were in Tunisia. The existing camps could not accommodate such large numbers of displaced people so the people of the cities and villages in the south of Tunisia opened their homes to accommodate, free of charge, the Libyan families that could not find a place to stay in the camps. The brotherly Tunisian people played a great role in providing aid to Libyans even before their displacement in Tunisia. In addition, the brotherly State of Qatar had established a large camp under the supervision of the Qatari Red Crescent in Tataween. Two Tunisian people were in charge: Asaad Assowiei, a supervisor from the Armadah camp, and a young woman named Sabrine from Tataween. They were working as hard as they would have worked if they had been helping their own people. Libyans will never forget that Tunisians stood with us during this revolution and that many brothers from the UAE and Qatar gave considerable amounts of aid and humanitarian assistance to the Libyan people.

My husband would have liked to stay in Tunisia with the displaced people to support and care for them, but Al Sanusi Qwaideer suggested that our group should return to Benghazi and arrange seminars in the eastern regions to describe the situation of the displaced people and to urge those who attended the seminars to provide material assistance and moral support to the displaced people. After four days in Tunisia we returned to Cairo by air via Rome. When we arrived in Cairo we again attended seminars at the Al Azhar University's halls and the Teachers Association's halls.

We returned to Benghazi by car on May 4, 2011. We and the members of the group with whom we had traveled held several seminars in Benghazi and urged people to raise money and donate supplies and clothing for the displaced people. As a result of the seminars, several charities were founded to collect donations for the displaced. These charities played a significant role in fundraising and in establishing sites in the south of Tunisia for the distribution of donations to both displaced people and the poor in the south of Tunisia. We made a request to the National Council to open up the air and sea lines from Benghazi to Tunis to facilitate the tasks of these charities.

At the end of June, my husband traveled by plane with a group of people from these charities after four containers loaded with food, milk, dates, clothes, shoes and nappies for babies had been sent by sea to the city of Jarjes. The Association of Religious Endowments in Benghazi paid all the costs. My husband and those who went with him visited wounded and injured Libyan Freedom Fighters in Tunisian cities, and distributed food and supplies to displaced people in the south of Tunisia. Then they went into Libya to distribute the remaining food to the population in the liberated cities in the Nafusa Mountains and Zintan. They persuaded young Libyan men who were presently in Tunisia to join the fronts for the liberation of Libya rather than stay in Tunisia.

We supported this revolution as much as we could, all the time looking forward to the liberation of all of Libya. We did this because we love our country and we wish to see our people living in a free, safe and prosperous country. Our last activity was greeting the Freedom Fighters of the eastern region when they returned to the city of Benghazi on October 22, 2011, after Gaddafi had been killed and the liberation of Libya from his oppression was complete. We raised banners and greeted them in front of the Garyounis University. That was an historic day in the history of Libya!

*Visiting wounded FFs in a
Cairo hospital, April 2011*

*Visiting the Libyan refugee camp in
Tataween, Tunisia, April 2011*

*Malak, the girl whose words on the Al
Jazeera news channel prompted the visit
to Tataween. The Arabic printed on her
T shirt is a quote from her words to Al
Jazeera: "We are fed up with you. What
do you want from us?"*

I Have Now Two Fatherlands

Zorica Pejak,
Born in Belgrade and raised in the city of Sid, Serbia
Living now in Benghazi, Libya

I have lived in Benghazi, Libya, for the last 28 years of my life, a period that now slightly exceeds that which I had lived in my native country, Serbia. In Benghazi, I have lived with the best man in the world, my husband. He is Libyan. All these years we have had only one problem: the country we lived in. The problem was not the people, not the land; the problem was Gaddafi's regime. My husband's family was on the regime's blacklist. I knew this when I agreed to marry him, and during our marriage he has tried to spare me from experiencing the nightmare he, his family and his people have been living through.

I came to Libya in October, 1984. I liked the sunny days, Libyan bread, and golden sandy beaches. But there were many strange things that I could not understand. Benghazi looked as though it was recently bombed. In many houses people lived in the ground floor but the iron bars coming out from the concrete walls showed that they planned to extend it by adding more floors. The facades of the old buildings were neglected. Only the main city streets were paved, although full of holes, while secondary streets were not paved at all. The city was littered with rubbish and trash cans were rarely seen. Instead, old rusty drums were placed around the streets for the collection of rubbish. I, and my fellow foreigners, had salaries two or three times higher than Libyan employees, but I never heard them complain or become angry or rude. It seemed as though the country belonged to us, the foreign workers, not to the Libyans. We had our parties, enjoyed the warm, crystal Mediterranean Sea and looked forward to returning to our countries with our savings.

Libyans were so quiet, almost invisible. It was very rare that foreigners had family friends among Libyans. I tried to get answers from foreigners who had worked in Libya for a long time and this is what they told me: "Do not ask much, do not mention Gaddafi's name, never criticize publicly what you see and you will not be in trouble. Keep in your mind that logic ceases from the moment you step on the land of this country." There was a very popular joke among us: "When one enters Libya, they say: 'Do not breathe. Hold your breath as if they are going to make an x-ray.' Then they forget to tell you that you can breathe freely again."

Even when I was married to my husband it took a long time to get all the answers to my numerous questions, to understand what lay behind the slow, emotionless life Libyans lived. Finally, though, I understood: they were not satisfied with their lives; they were an unhappy nation, scared to talk or complain; their enthusiasm and hope had been broken; they were in deep depression. The most common sentence I heard was this: "I am not a Libyan. What you are talking about and seeing in Libya has nothing to do with me." They were ashamed of everything that was going on in the country, from the lack of infrastructure to the corruption and ignorance of the people in charge. Life was difficult and many were struggling to feed their families.

From 1985 to 1990, the shops were almost empty. Libyans had money but there was nothing to buy. After 1990/1991, the shops were full but many had no money to buy. I cannot decide which period was worse. When the wealth of the country was taken into account, the Libyans' salaries were shamefully small. But the people could do nothing to change it. Gaddafi had no mercy for anyone who dared to say that Libya was a rich country, that its people are extremely smart, that Gaddafi should build first his own country then help others. Some people tried to change it, but they were cruelly punished: imprisoned for years, killed, exiled. Their family members suffered also for their actions, because if one member of a family was Gaddafi's enemy, the whole family was on the regime's blacklist.

Every year, I hated the 1st of September, the day of the celebration of Gaddafi's "revolution". First, it was announced that the celebration party would be in one of the Libyan cities and preparations were started. Then, the people would find out that he had gone to another city to give his nonsense speech full of empty promises. It was always a big insult to Libyan people. Every year, I was sad when at the end of the Holy month of Ramadan the other Arab nations were looking forward to Eid but Libyans had to wait for Gaddafi to decide and announce on television when the first day of Eid would be. Libya was a big workshop for foreigners but a big circus for the Libyan people. It was not a circus for entertainment to make them laugh; it was a circus with one cruel, merciless, tyrannical, lunatic clown who for 42 years kept their attention by force.

Even after the uprisings in Tunis and Egypt, I did not think that Libyans will dare to do the same. Libya is a huge country and its cities are far away from each other. But it was not only geographical distance between them. Gaddafi did everything to keep them apart and people from Benghazi , Beida, Tobruk, Derna, Al Marj, Ajdabiyah, Al Qubah, Sebha, Tokra, Jalu, Al Kufra knew little or nothing about the cities of the western part of the country; and the cities of the west knew little about the eastern cities. Every city lived in a kind of isolation and was aware that if anything happened it would be on its own; no other city would be able to help them fight Gaddafi.

I was wrong and the 17th of February happened and succeeded. It was not a war, it was not a civil war, it was not an outside intelligence conspiracy, it was pure revolution. Libyans had had enough. This revolution was a matter of life or death.

From the 16th to the 20th of February, 300 unarmed protestors in Benghazi were killed by Gaddafi's forces. People were in a state of shock, but the young people did not give up. There was no going back. Gaddafi hated Libyans and told them: "Whoever does not love Muammar Gaddafi should die". I could hardly believe my ears when I heard this! In Arabic "Muammar" means "a builder", but people called Muammar Gaddafi, "Mudammar" which means "a destroyer". He had been destroying Libyans for a long time but in 2011 he showed that he was ready to kill them all if this was the only way for him to continue to keep Libya as his own property.

The net connection was cut off and I spent almost 24 hours a day in front of television or listening to Radio Benghazi. I was terribly afraid of chaos in Benghazi, knowing that there was no police and no law, but there were many young people armed and without any control. But Libyan's love for their country, for their city, and for their people emerged with its full strength. They did their best to support each other and the success of the Revolution, but they realized that Gaddafi was going to crush the uprising if they did not get help from the outside world. Gaddafi had enormous amounts of weapons and forces, and many of his forces were mercenaries from African countries. The knowledge that he paid foreigners and brought them into the country to kill his own people made Libyans even more determined to fight. I will never forget the days from mid-February until the 19th of March when the no-fly zone was established by the UN. These were the longest days in my life. The supportive words of the leaders of the most powerful countries of the world were our safety belt. We knew that if those countries did not help us Benghazi would not exist anymore.

For the first time I realized how much I love these people and this country. I felt that if I left the country I might never come back. My husband did not understand my decision to stay as he wanted our daughter and me to be safe and far away from Libya. I was scared and worried and I had no one with whom to share my fear and horror. For the first time I could not lean on my husband as, at that moment, his heart belonged only to his country, to his people. I could not cry in front of Libyans as I knew my pain, as a foreigner, did not match the pain they felt as they saw what Gaddafi was doing to the young men and the best men of their nation.

The only way to live through all these terrible days and months and stay sane was to do my best to help Libyans as much as I could. In February, I made food for the protestors as soon as I was told that women from my neighborhood were doing this. My husband worked long hours and shouldered many responsibilities at the hospital. Finally, one day, he needed to rest – to rest from the stress of the work at the hospital as he and his colleagues tried to save young protesters' lives, and to rest from his anxieties about our daughter and me in light of the stories he was hearing about the orders and behavior of the forces whom Gaddafi employed. As the eastern front was quiet and no wounded thuwar were being brought to the hospital, he could leave his job for a little while. So, we travelled to Serbia and rested there as best we could for almost six weeks.

When we returned to Benghazi, I became one of those making food for the thuwar at the front line. I stuck small messages on the packages of food: "God protect you, thuwar, our heroes". In June I suggested to the ladies in our neighborhood that we clean it and fix whatever we could. We replaced broken lights, we planted flowers, and we painted new beautiful Libyan flags wherever we could. We made boards asking people to keep our neighborhood clean, with words such as: "I have nobody to love me and care about me, except You – Your city, Benghazi". Being busy helped to make bearable the deep sorrow we all felt that so many were killed, injured or missing because of the fight for freedom.

During the fight for Sirte, the hospital was overcrowded with wounded Freedom Fighters. Daily, I could hear in my house the noise of helicopters landing in front of the hospital bringing wounded from the front line. The emergency and ambulance sirens pierced my already-bleeding heart every few hours. I worked in the hospital as a non-medical staff member and one day a young doctor called me to come with her to ICU to see a wounded Freedom Fighter who had just been brought into the hospital from the front in Sirte. A surgeon was tending a wound on his head. I was paralyzed looking at the surgical needle going in and out of his wound. The Freedom Fighter, now a patient, was sitting in the bed, looking at me. His eyes were filled with pain but he raised his hand and made the victory sign. I will never forget the expression of his young face and his eyes. I burst into tears and left ICU. Next day he was operated on and very soon sent abroad. How brave these young men were! They deserved to be called heroes, Libyan lions. From that day Dr. Khalid Barakat and I visited wounded Freedom Fighters in the morning and afternoon every day. We talked to them, and wrote down their requests and complaints so that the management of the hospital could take action.

The doctors, nurses and auxiliary staff of Hawari General Hospital in Benghazi did their best to serve the heroes fighting for the liberation of their country. It was not easy as there were shortages of nurses, medicines and other medical needs, but they did their best. The wounded Freedom Fighters were grateful and they did not ask for much. My neighbors and the ladies of my husband's family also went several times to visit them with me. Each time, we made a nice meal and took our children with us to see the brave thuwar, to offer a kind word and a smile to the young men who were fighting for their better future. Each visit was very emotional but the wounded thuwar deserved to know that people appreciated what they had done.

During all these months I was supported by the bloggers from Al Jazeera English blogs. I shared with them my fear, sorrow and hopes. They became my friends. They were fighting for Libya on another front. They fought pro-Gaddafi trolls and encouraged the Freedom Fighters with their keyboards. They sent warm, supportive messages to the wounded Freedom Fighters which a group of doctors translated into Arabic and printed in a small booklet. When we handed the booklets to the wounded thuwar they were all surprised. It was hard for them to understand that there were people all over the world who understand what was happening in Libya and cared about them. These messages were precious medals for them: the world cares and supports Freedom Fighters. They felt that Libya was finally recognized because of its good, intelligent, honest, brave people, not because of its lunatic leader.

For 28 years I had felt sorry for Libyan people but after the 17th of February Revolution I admired them. I finally realized how deeply they hated Gaddafi's regime. There was an indescribable mix of sorrow for lost lives and joy for breathing the air of freedom, for Libyans felt free after 42 years of living in one big prison called Libya. When the katiba in Benghazi fell, it was as though I could touch the freedom with my hands. It was a newly born nation. The people's faces were radiant and their eyes were shining. Neighbors started to sit together in front of their houses talking freely, the doors of their homes were opened widely and in every heart there was concern for each Freedom Fighter. The people of Benghazi shed tears for wounded Zawiya; they risked their lives to take help to heroic Misurata; they were proud of brave Zintan and Nalut; and they prayed to God to give the strength to endure to Tripoli and Zuwara.

I have faith in Libyans based on all that I have witnessed since the 17th of February. I believe they can and will make a country of which they will be very proud. I hope that many readers of this book will come to visit the new free Libya. Dear reader, if you decide to come, you will be warmly welcomed – Libyans are good people! They have become one body, one soul, and in my heart I have now two fatherlands: Serbia where I was born and Libya where I live.

Photographs of victims of the 1996 Abu Salim massacre outside Benghazi Courthouse, October 30, 2011

> "Think not of those who are slain in Allah's way as dead.
> Indeed they are living in the presence of their Lord and are provided for."
> The Holy Qur'an

Mahdi Mohamed Zew
born in 1962 and martyred on February 20, 2011

Mohamed Hussein Zew, Prof. of Internal Medicine, Hawari General Hospital, Benghazi, Libya

I knew Mahdi Zew since he was a child. He was my close cousin and we lived in the same street but, most importantly, we were friends.

He was a decent person. He was married and had two daughters, Zuhur and Sajeeda, and he loved them very much. He was not interested in politics. Instead, he loved life and enjoyed it.

On 15th February, the great events started when tens of people took to the streets of Benghazi. On the second day, hundreds followed by thousands joined them. They went out to demonstrate peacefully, asking for freedom and justice, but Gaddafi's battalions faced them head-on and, without any warning, began shooting at them with heavy weapons which are normally used only in the war battles. There were tens of martyrs and hundreds of wounded protesters. In the beginning the protestors faced the battalions with bare chests. Then, they armed themselves with poles and stones and Molotov cocktails.

The regime mobilized for attack, arming hundreds of their mercenaries, snipers and special forces with heavy weapons. The fight was not equal but the strong will and determination of the freedom fighters, which always win, won from the beginning. They forced soldiers to enter inside the military camp, the "katiba", and then they surrounded it. The katiba was the symbol of Gaddafi's tyrannical system in Benghazi and was fortified by high walls and heavy weapons. For decades, nobody would dare to walk near its door and walls.

Mahdi lived not far from the katiba. He went out to join peaceful protesters from the first day. He saw boys in their blossom age falling down on the streets of the neighborhoods of Berka, Keesh and Assaballa. He watched how they were brutally massacred and their bodies shattered into pieces. He helped the wounded and provided bottles of water to protestors. On the second day, he found himself more and more actively involved. He bought TNT bombs for 3000LD and gave them to protestors to fight the battalions in this unequal battle. In the evening of the same day, he found himself close to the walls of the katiba. There he saw the youngsters advancing towards the gates with fury but without result because the shooting was fierce whenever they came closer. He took shelter with a friend at the entry to a building nearby. A young lad, not older than 17 years, fell down dead near them, just a few meters away. The lad had been hit in the head. When the shooting calmed, he and his friend crawled to the martyr to take his body away. They called for an ambulance and put the body inside. Then he said to his friend, "Something must be done to stop this slaughter. The gates must be opened at any price."

On the decisive day, the day of the fall of the katiba, another friend saw Mahdi sitting in a car in the street leading to the katiba. He came closer to see what was going on. He saw that Mahdi was reading a pocket edition of the Qur'an. His friend asked him what he was doing in this dangerous place. He answered, "Whatever happens to us, it's written by God."

Earlier that day, Mahdi loaded his car with two cylinders of cooking gas and a huge TNT bomb. Before sunset, shortly after his friend had left, he put the Qur'an beside him, started the car engine and drove slowly towards the doors of the katiba. When he was near the katiba's main gate, he lowered his seat down to a lying position. The next moment everybody saw a black car running as fast as a rocket in a straight line towards the main gate. Fire was opened from all sides but the car continued with increasing speed. When the car hit the first gate, the strike was so strong that the gate was forced widely open. Then it hit the second gate less forcibly and stopped. Many soldiers raced towards the car and, as they approached, the car suddenly blasted in a huge explosion, killing and wounding most of them. The second gate was smashed. The crowds hailed "Allahu Akbar… Allahu Akbar…" and hundreds of them pushed towards the opened gate like a rumbling wave. Half an hour later, the katiba was under full control of the protesters. They used the weapons and ammunitions obtained in the katiba to fight Gaddafi's soldiers in the remaining army camps in the city. It took them a few hours to free the whole city.

On the next day, as the freedom fighters started to march west towards Ajdabiyah, we gathered for Mahdi's funeral. We could collect for burial only a few burnt bones in a small wooden coffin.

That day, as I stood at his grave, I saw his face in the sky, above the clouds. He was smiling and waved his right hand with the sign of the victory.

Translation of Arabic text: *Martyr Mahdi Mohamed Zew broke through the main gate of the Al Fadeel Katiba in Al Berka in his private car on Sunday 20/02/2011. He was shot by 14.5 mm caliber rounds, and his car exploded after he broke down the gate. May Allah have mercy upon him and take him into Heaven.*

الشهيد
المهدي محمد زيو
الذي اقتحم بسيارته الخاصة البوابة الرئيسية لكتيبة الفضيل بالبركة
يوم الاحد الموافق 20 \ 2 \ 2011 وتم رميه بـ " 14.5 " وتفجير سيارته بعد
أقتحامه للبوابه .. رحم الله الشهيد و أسكنه فسيح جناته

213

Glossary

<u>**Religious Entries**</u>

Mus'haf – The volume of the Holy Qur'an

Allahu Akbar – "God is Great" or "God is the Greatest".

Takbir (takbeer) – the chanting "Allahu Akbar" three times to raise the morale of the freedom fighters during battle or to welcome each item of good news during the revolution.

Shahada – the Muslim declaration of belief in the oneness of God and acceptance of Muhammad as God's prophet: "There is no god but God, and Muhammad is the messenger of God." Sometimes it can mean martyrdom, as demonstrating the ultimate expression of faith.

Al Haj (m) or *Al Haja (f)* – the title given to anyone who has performed the Islamic pilgrimage to Mecca and Medina, the Hajj. The Hajj is one of the five pillars of Islam and should be performed by any devout Moslem who is able at least once in his/her lifetime. The five pillars are profession of belief in Allah, the one and only true God; prayers five times a day; zakat, or giving a percentage of earnings to the poor; fasting during Ramadan; and the Hajj.

Zamzam – the name of a famous water well in Masjid al Haram in Mecca, 20 meters east of the Kaaba. It is the well from which Allah quenched the thirst of Ishmael the son of Ibraahim when he was an infant. One version of the story says that his mother was desperately seeking water for her infant son, but could find none, but her son, Ishmael, anxiously scraped the land with his feet, and suddenly water sprang out. Those who make the Hajj, the annual pilgrimage to Mecca and Medina, will carry back large containers of Zamzam water to their home countries, usually to share with selected friends.

Sunna – a way of life

Sunna of Muhammad – Sunna is the practice of the Prophet Muhammad, the best example of life as it should be lived, that he taught and instituted as a teacher of the shar 'ah.

shar 'ah – Islamic law.

Sheikh (pl. shuyukh) – a religious man who teaches Islam, preaches in the mosque, performs religious marriages and gives advice to the people and explanations of the Qur'an. The same word also means the chief of a tribe (and in the plural, the elders of the tribe), and an old man.

(Salaat) Al Zhuhr – the prayer time just after noon

(Salaat) Al Asr – the afternoon prayer time

(Salaat) Al Maghreb – the prayer time just after sunset

<u>**Cultural Entries**</u>

Yellow Helmets – At the outset of 17 February Revolution, February 17th through February 20th, Gaddafi freed violent criminals and recruited thugs and sub-Saharan mercenaries to join Lijan Tawriya and others of Gaddafi's inner groups of supporters. These men were issued public works uniforms (yellow helmets) to blend in with the utility (sewer, telephone, electrical, etc.) workers. These Yellow Helmets were armed and told to fire randomly on unsuspecting civilians to instil fear and confusion. In the ensuing days, unarmed protesters were brutally murdered and the entire Libyan civilian population suffered losses at the hands of Yellow Helmets.

Lijan Tawriya – the most powerful of Gaddafi's supporters. During the tyrant's regime, members held the high ranking positions in Libya's institutions, being the managers of factories and commercial enterprises; the deans of universities and their faculties, and health facilities; the ambassadors, consuls and staff of embassies. They were followers of "The Green Book" and their principal functions were those of protecting the interests of Gaddafi and his sons, spying on people, and reporting any who spoke or wrote against Gaddafi either inside or outside the country. Most members were wealthy, sent their children abroad for study, and owned villas and good cars. The most loyal received military training, were armed and had the functions of investigating, arresting, terrorizing or killing people inside Libya or in the countries to which they had fled. These members were known as haras tawri. In some stories Lijan Tawriya has been translated as "Revolutionary Committees" and haras tawri as "Revolutionary Guards". The term "Revolutionary" is used in reference to the period of Jamahiriya established by Gaddafi's 1969 coup and not in reference to the 17 February Revolution of 2011.

Katiba – the name for both a military regiment and the fortified barracks housing it. It literally means "battalion" or "phalanx"(*plural kataib*) in Arabic. In this book, we have followed the pattern of using an upper case "K" to denote the battalion and a lower case "k" to denote the fortified barracks.

Thuwar (singular thaer) – freedom fighters

RPG – Russian rocket-propelled grenade launcher

Al Hisan Al Aswad -- lit. "A black horse", a prison in Tripoli

"Asbaha Al Subhu"- "Dawn Began" – March 3, 1988, when some political prisoners were granted amnesty.

Tahrir Square – Liberation Square

Al mahkamah – a court

Zagharit – the ululation commonly used by women to express celebration

Culinary Entries

Tanur - the homemade bread which is made in a pot made of clay. At the bottom of the pot there are live coals (embers). Thin oval layers of dough are stuck on the side walls of the hot pot.

Ruz blau – traditional Libyan dish consisting of rice, nuts, raisins and chicken (or other meat)

Asban – traditional Libyan dish of sheep intestines filled with a mixture of small cubes of meat, heart, liver, lungs, rice, parsley, green onion and tomato

Asida – flour combined with boiled water cooked on the stove until it forms a dough; served with hot melted butter and date syrup

Geographic Entries

The Arabic language employs sounds that do not have exact parallels in English. That is true of some consonants and most vowels. There is no accepted standard for transcribing Libyan place names. Below are various spellings of some of the key towns and cities mentioned in this book. In most cases the reader will be correct in thinking "If it sounds similar, then it probably is the same place".

Bawaba (Bab) Al Arbaeen- During the Italian occupation there were the stations for travelers to get transport from Ajdabiyah to Brega. At 18 km, 40 km, 50 km, and 60 km simple rooms were built and Libyans called them *Dar (a room) Al Tamantash; Dar Al Arbaeen; Dar Al Khamseen; Dar Assateen*. Nowadays, there are only the broken walls of these rooms, but the places are well known by people. During the revolution these places were military front lines for freedom fighters as well as for Gaddafi's forces.

Az Zawiya = Al Zawiya = Zawia – Libyan city 30 km southwest of Tripoli.

Nafusa Mountains – Mountain range running roughly parallel to, and 100 km south of, the Libyan Mediterranean Coast spanning some 200 km between Tunisia and just south of Tripoli.

Misrata = Misurata	Kabaw = Kapau
Ajdabiyah = Ajdabiyeh = Ajdabiya	Wazin = Wazan
Beida =Al Bayda	Sloog = Sloug
Al Qubah =Al Kubba	Sabha = Sebha
Imrir Qabs = Emrir Qabes = Imrir Qabis	Zlieten = Zliten = Zlitan

Recent Libyan and 17 February Revolution Timeline

From the Editors

(For a more complete timeline, please consult http://en.wikipedia.org/wiki/Timeline_of_the_2011_Libyan_civil_war_before_intervention where links to subsequent timelines are available.)

1911 – 1934	Italy wrestles control of most of today's Libya from the Ottoman Empire and pacifies Libyan resistance to Italian colonization.
Sept. 11, 1931	Sheikh Omar Al Mukhtar who led most of the Libyan resistance is captured and executed on September 16, 1931, by the Italians.
1934 – 1951	Libya is governed by Italy until 1943 when Allied successes in World War II drive out the Italians. Libya is a British Mandate until, in accordance with a UN Resolution and after a period of transition overseen by the UN, independence is gained in 1951.
Dec. 24, 1951	King Idris governs independent Libya.
Sept.1, 1969	Colonel Gaddafi seizes power in a coup.
June 29, 1996	In response to Abu Salim prisoners' requests for less restricted family visits and better living conditions, Gaddafi orders the execution of 1,276 Abu Salim inmates.
Feb. 4, 2011	Al Jazeera reports that calls for protests in several Middle East countries are circulating on Twitter. Their list includes a call for protest in Libya on February 17.
Feb. 15	Protests in Benghazi follow the arrest of Fathi Terbil, the lawyer representing the families of the Abu Salim Massacre victims. Protests in Beida and Zintan call for the end of the Gaddafi regime.
Feb. 16-17	Daily protests escalate in Benghazi and in other centers, notably Ajdabiyah, Zintan, Derna, Beida, Tobruk, and even Tripoli. Protests erupt in Zawiya, the western city that controls the coastal route from Tripoli to Tunisia and is the site of the second most important refinery in Libya.
Feb. 18-20	Daily protests continue in many places in Libya. Everywhere they are met by the Gaddafi regime with brute force: automatic weapon and anti-aircraft fire on unarmed protesters. During this time, Gaddafi frees violent criminals, and recruits thugs and sub-Saharan mercenaries who join members of the Peoples' Guards, Revolutionary Committees, and Revolutionary Guards, and sub-Saharan workers in attempting to subdue protests. They are all issued uniforms and yellow helmets so that they blend in with municipal cleaning and utility workers as a deception. They are armed and told to fire randomly to instill fear and confusion.This results not only in unarmed protesters being brutally murdered but also in the entire civilian population suffering losses and intimidations. Defections from Gaddafi's regular forces begin and continue throughout the revolution.
Feb. 20	After three days of burying murdered youths, Mahdi Zew pays the ultimate price as he takes down the gates of the Benghazi katiba, allowing the protesters to overpower the Gaddafi forces who have been firing on them, seize arms and ammunition, and, aided by further defections from Gaddafi's regular forces, gain control of Benghazi. By Feb 20 Benghazi and several other eastern cities are liberated.
Feb. 24-27	Misurata rises up against Gaddafi. Libyan Embassies throughout the world start denouncing Gaddafi's government and joining the struggle for freedom.

Feb. 27	National Transitional Council (NTC) – or Transitional National Council (TNC) depending on the translation – is established in Benghazi.
March 1-5	Freedom fighters (FF) liberate Brega and advance west past Ras Lanuf to Ben Jawad, where they are ambushed during the night of March 5-6.
March 6	Gaddafi's eastern counteroffensive begins. His attempts to retake Misurata start in earnest. Misurata FF set up a trap, capturing several tanks and armor.
March 11	After nearly a month of being under siege, during which time the city experiences random and non-stop artillery and armor shelling, Zawiya falls to Gaddafi forces. Zawiya FF and much of the population flee to the Nafusa Mountains. Gaddafi intensifies his attempts to subdue Misurata.
March 12	Ras Lanuf falls to advancing Gaddafi forces, FF retreat to Brega.
March 13-17	After two days of fighting, Brega falls to Gaddafi and his forces advance on, and capture, Ajdabiyah.
March 17	UNSC approves a no-fly zone in Libya to protect civilians, UNSC Resolution 1973 passes with Russia, China, India, Germany and Brazil abstaining.
March 19	Gaddafi forces advance on Benghazi. The Khamis Brigade artillery shells the city from 20km away, while its armored column penetrates southwestern suburbs and then the city proper. Mo Nabbous is killed covering the events for Alhurra Media. The armored column is bombed by Benghazi FF pilots from the Benina Air Force Base; three of the pilots are martyred saving civilian lives. The French Air Force joins the defense of Benghazi in the afternoon (4:55pm), destroying the elite Khamis Brigade. Gaddafi forces are pushed back to Ajdabiyah in the next days. Gaddafi forces laying siege to Misurata penetrate the city, but their advance is stopped.
March 20	Gaddafi forces advance in the Nafusa Mountains. US (Odyssey Dawn March 19-31) and NATO (Unified Protector March 23-October 31) launch operations with daily missions to protect civilians in support of UNSCR 1973.
March 23	Misurata situation grows more desperate. NATO starts bombing Gaddafi forces shelling and advancing on the city. Misurata situation will continue to deteriorate and civilian casualties will climb until the middle of April. Gaddafi forces advance in the Nafusa Mountains, shelling Zintan with indiscriminate and heavy artillery fire.
March 26	FF liberate Ajdabiyah and continue their advance, freeing Brega. Eman Al-Obeidi runs into Tripoli's Rixos Hotel, tells international press corps about being abducted by Gaddafi forces at their checkpoint and gang-raped and abused repeatedly for several days at a home of one of the Gaddafi high ranking officials. She is wrestled away to prison by security. The Financial Times reporter attempting to help her is deported. Mass appeals and protests to free Eman ignite throughout the world. Attention is drawn to other rapes committed by Gaddafi forces.
March 27	FF liberate Ras Lanuf and advance as far west as the village of Nofaliya.
March 29-31	Gaddafi launches second eastern counteroffensive pushing the FF out of Ras Lanuf and Brega, and then back to Ajdabiyah.
March 31	Moussa Koussa defects.

April 1-20	Gaddafi forces continue indiscriminant shelling in the Nafusa Mountains and Misurata. Situation in the Nafusa Mountains worsens and thousands of civilians flee to neighboring Tunisia for safety. Misuratans are surrounded and have nowhere to flee, but daily ships of hope bring supplies and fighters from Benghazi and evacuate as many severely wounded as possible, as the main Misurata hospital on Tripoli Street is under constant sniper fire. In the east, Gaddafi forces continue to dig-in around Brega, laying mines and fortifying their positions. This will continue into the summer months, causing the international press to declare "stalemate" in Libya.
April 21	Nafusa FF capture Wazin Border Crossing into Tunisia. Misurata FF clear Tripoli Street and city center of Gaddafi snipers.
April 28	Gaddafi forces reclaim Wazin Border Crossing.
May 1	Wazin Crossing again under FF control.
May 11	Misurata FF capture the airport at the Eastern outskirt of the city.
May 15	Misurata FF clear remaining city suburbs, compelling Gaddafi forces to withdraw completely and retreat from the city.
May 29	Representatives from 81 Libyan tribes meet to express and sign support of the NTC.
June 3-5	French Gazelle and British Apache gunship helicopters start massive bombardment of the Gaddafi forces that have dug-in in Brega since late March/early April.
June 6	Nafusa FF liberate Yafran.
June 8	Taking advantage of the NATO break in airstrikes due to bad weather, Gaddafi forces launch a large attack on Misurata and Zintan but fail to make any gains.
June 9	ICC Chief Prosecutor Ocampo announces receiving reliable reports that the Gaddafi administration was buying large quantities of Viagra to encourage soldiers and mercenaries to commit mass rape.
June 11	Misurata FF – now known as the Lions of Misurata in recognition of their gallantry and perseverance in defending their city against Gaddafi's siege – engage Gaddafi forces in Zlieten. FF opposition re-emerges in Zawiya, only 50 km from Tripoli, marking the first significant movements in the city since Gaddafi forces re-captured it in March.
June 27	ICC issues arrest warrants for Muammar Gaddafi, Saif al-Islam Gaddafi and Abdullah Senussi. While yielding little movement on the Eastern Front in Brega, fighting in June had seen FF progress in cleansing the Nafusa Mountains of Gaddafi forces and the Misurata FF edging closer and closer into Zlieten.
July 12	Amazigh FF progress in the Nafusa Mountains allows the opening of an airstrip at Rhebat to provide a direct air link with Benghazi.
July 15	FF engage Gaddafi forces on the outskirts of Brega and suffer heavy causalities.
July 18	FF retake much of Brega and most Gaddafi forces retreat to Ras Lanuf.
July 19-August	Under heavy artillery bombardment and sniper fire, most FF retreat to the residential third of Brega to allow sweepers to disarm the tens of thousands of mines that Gaddafi forces and Russian, Belorussian and Ukrainian mercenaries have planted in and around Brega during the preceding months.

July 28	Nafusa FF liberate Ghazaya.
Aug. 7	Nafusa FF liberate Bir al-Ghanam.
Aug. 15	Nafusa and Zawiya FF once again control portions of Zawiya and completely free Gharyan, one of the last remaining Gaddafi strongholds in the foothills of the Nafusa Mountains.
Aug. 18	FF control Zawiya refinery, the last remaining source of fuel for Gaddafi's Tripoli.
Aug. 19	Misurata and Zlieten FF liberate Zlieten. Zawiya center is under full FF control.
Aug. 20	Brega center is under full FF control. Zawiya city is under full FF control. "Operation Mermaid Dawn" to liberate Tripoli begins. FF reach Aziziya. Tripoli rises up, and Mitga Air Force base is seized by local FF.
Aug. 21	Zawiya FF push eastward, free Janzur, reach Tripoli's Green Square, the heart of Gaddafi's regime, and rename it Martyr Square. The rest of Tripoli is combed and freed of Gaddafi forces in the next 2-3 days. The Rixos, the hotel in which all foreign journalists in Tripoli have been forced to stay throughout most of the uprising and in which they have been held captive for several days, is among the last to be liberated.
Aug. 23	Benghazi FF take control of Ras Lanuf and advance towards Ben Jawad and Sirte.
Aug. 27	Eastern Front advances past Ben Jawad.
Aug. 29	Algeria announces that it is giving shelter to most of the Gaddafi family.
Sept. 11	After two weeks of negotiations between NTC and Bani Walid and Sirte authorities, and an unsuccessful ultimatum, battles in both towns resume.
Sept. 22	Sebha is free.
Oct. 17	Bani Walid is cleared of the Gaddafi forces.
Oct. 20	Sirte is cleared of Gaddafi forces. Muammar Gaddafi is captured and killed trying to flee. Mutassim Gaddafi is captured and killed as well.
Oct. 23	Mustapha Abdel Jalil, Chairman of the NTC, announces a complete liberation of the country at the celebration in Benghazi.
Nov. 19	Saif Al Islam Gaddafi is captured south of Sebha

Yellow Helmets in Benghazi during the days of February 17 – 20, 2011

Map of Libya
Showing Key Locations Indicated in the Book

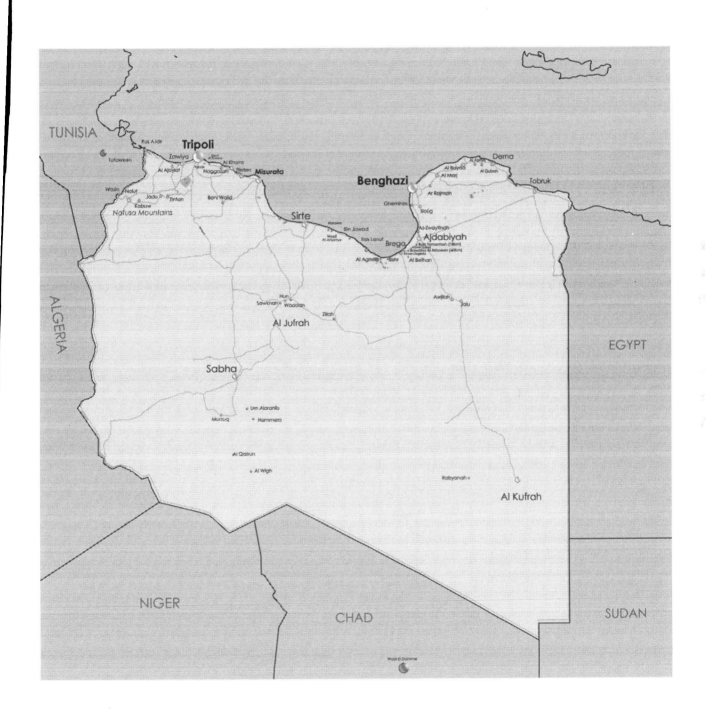

Benghazi Map
Showing Key Locations Indicated in the Book

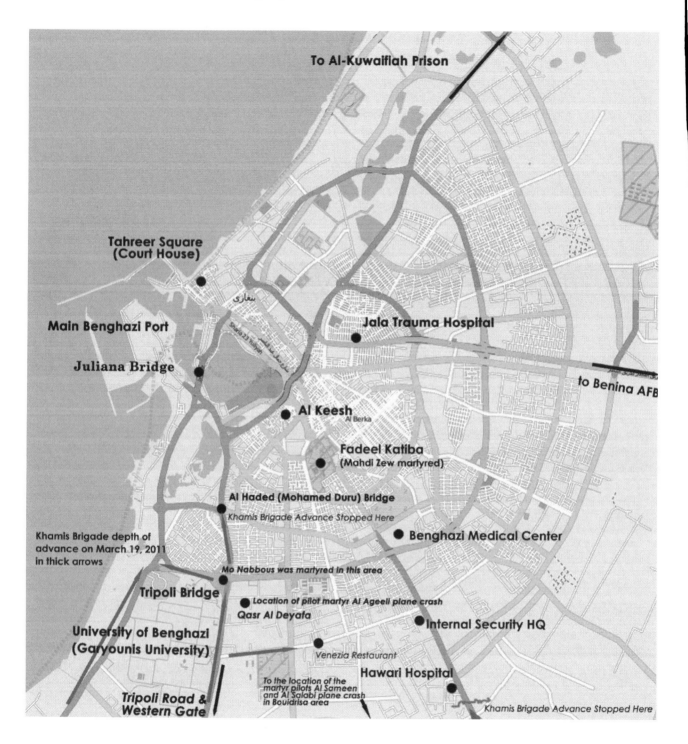

To Al-Kuwaifiah Prison

Tahreer Square
(Court House)

Main Benghazi Port

Juliana Bridge

Jala Trauma Hospital

بنغازي

شارع 23 يوليو

to Benina AFB

Al Keesh
Al Berka

Fadeel Katiba
(Mahdi Zew martyred)

Al Haded (Mohamed Duru) Bridge

Khamis Brigade Advance Stopped Here

Khamis Brigade depth of
advance on March 19, 2011
in thick arrows

Benghazi Medical Center

Mo Nabbous was martyred in this area

Tripoli Bridge

Location of pilot martyr Al Ageeli plane crash
Qasr Al Deyafa

Internal Security HQ

University of Benghazi
(Garyounis University)

Venezia Restaurant

Hawari Hospital

Tripoli Road &
Western Gate

To the location of the
martyr pilots Al Sameen
and Al Salabi plane crash
in Bouidrisa area

Khamis Brigade Advance Stopped Here

14925137R00122

Made in the USA
Lexington, KY
28 April 2012